Teaching in the Community-Junior College

Teaching
in the
Community–
Junior
College

By Win Kelley
Citrus College

and

Leslie Wilbur
University of
Southern California

APPLETON-CENTURY-CROFTS
Educational Division
MEREDITH CORPORATION New York

To Kitty Kelley and Norma Wilbur

Preface

In American education, the twentieth century may be known to history as the "Century of the Community Junior College." A distinctly American phenomenon, the two-year colleges have multiplied rapidly since the first extant public junior college was established at Joliet, Illinois, in 1901. By 1969, nearly one thousand public and private two-year colleges of all types employed an estimated eighty thousand teachers and served close to two million students. And it was expected that the community junior colleges would soon outnumber senior colleges and universities, which in 1968 totaled approximately sixteen hundred institutions. With its relatively fast rate of growth in enrollments and curricula, the two-year college is a popular segment of higher education, a unique school hopefully taking its place as an equal partner in higher learning in the United States.

As the new institution continues to grow and mature, new problems and needs continue to emerge. Many of these needs and problems directly involve the universities, particularly those which train potential junior college teachers. Recognizing the needs, many universities and four-year colleges have installed junior college courses and programs. In the last few years these programs have increased rapidly in numbers.

For those training programs there has been no guide or textbook directed expressly to the new junior college teacher in training. From the beginning, these trainees have had to learn about junior college teaching from books on "college teaching," the implication seeming to be that all college teaching is the same or nearly the same, regardless of the particular type of higher institution. Many of us in higher education do not accept this implication. We believe the evidence that reveals differences in teaching at university, four-year college, and two-year college levels. We believe the differences are significant enough to warrant separate teaching texts for these levels. We believe it is now time for junior college teacher-trainees to have designed for them a textbook-guide that is oriented not toward administration or the junior college as an institution, but rather for the general needs and problems of the new teacher. Although the junior college administrator, the scholar, and the experienced and well-trained teacher may find for themselves something of value in this book, they must remember to whom we address the text. The purpose is fourfold:

1. To foster a realistic perception of employment in the two-year colleges.
2. To assist the new junior college teacher on the job.
3. To serve as a text for the college or university course in junior college teacher training.
4. To supplement the experience of the graduate student whose introduction to teaching is often on the job at a lower division level.

We will attempt to present a realistic picture of junior college employment in spite of the fact that in the general areas of teaching "we are losing over a hundred thousand teachers a year. The teaching profession must be glamorized and must be made truly dramatic. We need the cooperation of television, the motion picture industry, advertising, and indeed all of the agencies of communication to indicate the importance of American schools" (235:135).* The magnitude of the problem seems obvious. Donald A. Eldridge, the 1967–68 president of the American Association of Junior Colleges, wrote "Now the biggest, most urgent, and absolutely fundamental question of all: Where are we going to get the people to staff our colleges, public and private, large and small, all across the country? Certainly not by raiding one another for teaching talent and surely not as primitive tribes once fought each other over hunting and fishing grounds" (100:11). One answer, we feel, is the training of new teachers for the junior college.

In presenting our picture, we have drawn our facts from many sources: our own years of teaching and administration at this level, the study of current published literature, doctoral dissertations, two nationwide surveys (one at the state level and another more limited at the college-faculty level), and from many personal interviews of junior college teachers and teacher-trainees. The new teachers and trainees, in particular, felt a need for a special book that could orient them to junior college teaching. They asked such questions as the following:

What *is* the two-year college in actual practice?

* This indicates a listing in the bibliography at the end of the book.

What are the requirements and opportunities for me?
Once I'm on the job, what general and special roles must I play?
How must I teach?
What kind of supervision will I receive?
What about work conditions, salaries, and the like?
What kind of future security and self-fulfillment can I expect?

In essence, these people felt some anxiety and ignorance about the mundane and more practical side of junior college teaching, even after some of them had spent one or two years on the job. They wanted—and felt some need for—a guide clearly directed toward themselves as teachers. What they really wanted was *adequate preparation*. The need, we feel, is particularly defined in the following quotation from Blocker, Plummer, and Richardson.

> One area in which responsibility must be exercised involves the adequate preparation of teachers. In the past, teaching personnel have been trained specifically for the elementary or secondary schools, and on the Ph.D. level for research and teaching in the four-year institutions. If community colleges are to assume the broad responsibilities . . . it is apparent that there must be certain adaptations in the pre-service and in-service training of teachers for this particular segment of higher education. Instructors in two-year colleges are neither university professors nor secondary school teachers. They require a preparation that is broader than that ordinarily found among university personnel yet deeper than that necessary for secondary school teachers. Both kinds of preparation should be included in upper and graduate divisions for individuals planning to teach in two-year colleges. Ideally, instructors should approach their first two-year college teaching assignment with proficiency in two closely related fields. In addition, they ought to have a real understanding of the functions of the community college (29: 285).

The book's organization follows a divisional pattern that takes the reader on a chronological road corresponding to his growth and development as a teacher: I. *The Setting,* II. *The Assignment,* III. *The Assessment.*

Part I: *The Setting* endeavors to acquaint the novice with the development and scope of the institution and its environment. By thoroughly understanding the two-year college, its teacher benefits and requirements, its opportunities and instructional areas, the reader may more wisely prepare himself for employment. Four chapters give him orientation in (1) Junior College Development in the United States, (2) Benefits for Junior College Teachers, (3) Employment Requirements and Techniques, (4) Selected Instructional Areas.

Part II: *The Assignment* contains four chapters. After the novice becomes familiar with the junior college environment and how he might prepare to secure a teaching position, he must gain an understanding of (5) Academic Duties and Functions, (6) Professional Duties and Functions, (7) the Art of Junior College Instruction: Philosophy, and (8) the Art of Junior College Instruction: Application. These chapters represent his basic assignment in the institution.

Part III: *The Assessment* contains the remaining two chapters. To be a well adjusted teacher, to grow and prosper as a professional person, the junior college teacher must assess and *be* assessed. It is helpful guidance for him to know (9) Faculty Attitudes and Opinions, and (10) Issues, Problems, and Solutions.

Added to the book are three appendixes. Appendix A includes the state exhibits, Appendix B the college-faculty survey information, and Appendix C some questions and projects for study and discussion. Although the professor may use the last in his class, it is added chiefly to aid those who peruse the book on their own. An extensive *Bibliography* reveals the basic research of the authors, provides the reference for footnotes, and lists selections for further reading.

We could never have presented this material without the cooperation of many. Foremost was the publisher, who was willing to present a book designed to meet future as well as present needs. James Roers, college editor of Appleton-Century-Crofts, provided outstanding editorial assistance. We are also indebted to the many state respondents who provided information for our national state survey, to the faculty members who contributed to our college-faculty survey, and to the community colleges where we worked and gained valuable practical experience: Bakersfield, Barstow, Compton, and Citrus.

Several other distinguished persons supplied information, materials, letters, and encouragement for the project. Highly respected in their fields, these include Raymond E. Schultz of Florida State University; Lewis B. Mayhew of Stanford University; Walter E. Sindlinger of Teachers College of Columbia University; Aubrey L. Berry, Executive Secretary, ASCUS, of the University of California at Berkeley; Richard P. Saunders, Associate Executive Secretary, Association for Higher Education; Joel L. Burdin, Associate Secretary, The American Association of Colleges for Teacher Education; Glen Robinson, Director, Research Division of the National Education Association; B. Lamar Johnson, University of California at Los Angeles; Robert W. Miner, Executive Director, National Faculty Association of Community and Junior Colleges; John E. Roueche, Associate Director and Junior College Specialist, Clearing House for Junior College Information, University of California at Los Angeles; C. C. Colvert, Professor and Consultant in Junior College Education, University of Texas; Maurice L. Litton, Florida State University; and Raymond J. Young, professor and junior college consultant, University of Michigan. Finally, Professors Roger R. Kelsey and Roger H. Garrison gave excellent guidance to us at various stages of the manuscript's development; but we, of course, are solely responsible for its final form and content.

Win Kelley

Leslie Wilbur

Contents

lecting a college; Written applications; Interviews; Some adjustments after employment

Part III   The Assessment

Part I The Setting

Chapter 1

Junior College Development
in the United States

Many new junior college instructors know relatively little about the origins and functions of the two-year community college. Most come directly from high school teaching; a few come from business or industry; many arrive from senior institutions where they were teachers or graduate students (355:40). Consequently, a new instructor is likely to perceive the junior college as an extension of his most recent occupation or institution, a glorified high school, or a pale university. The junior college is neither a high school nor a university. It is unique, one of the few American inventions in education insofar as institutional types are concerned. It is because of the growing special needs of new junior college teachers and junior college teachers-in-training that this book was written; the text is directed to them.

We include the words "United States" in the chapter title because recently there has been some extensive development of two-year colleges in other parts of the world; this movement was certainly influenced and stimulated by the American counterpart. Japan's junior college movement is a prime example of this American influence (387).

To understand the sources of unique qualities found in U.S. two-year colleges, you need to be aware of their various definitions, their origins and growth, their purposes and functions, their relationships to other levels, their conditions for establishment, their structures and governance, and their means of accreditation and evaluation. Understanding these elements can help you grasp the important roles played by a junior college instructor.

Definitions

During the past several decades we have seen a series of definitions of the junior college. The frequency of definitions has increased as a growing number of states have had to define the institution in the process of designing enabling legislation for public systems. Although there are many minor variations, several essential patterns emerge as typical. These patterns provide a working definition which will help clarify subsequent chapters.

One can approach the definition from various points of view: by title of the institution, by number of years offered, by programs, by control and/or finance, and by other special means. In the area of titles, we hear of the *junior college, college, community college, teachers college, extension center* (including *division* or *branch*), *seminary,* and *technical institute.* In the area of control and/or finance, there are the *private* (church-related, independent, including proprietary and YMCA), and the *public* (local, district, county, branch, and state). In the area of years offered, we observe junior colleges with one-, two-, three-, and four-year programs. Three- and four-year junior colleges are usually those with one or two years of high school organized with two years of collegiate work. In terms of programs, junior colleges are identified as *comprehensive* or *community* (those offering a general variety) and as special institutions using terms like *business, technical, agricultural* (those offering only special programs in these areas). Even the most reliable sources of information on definition may differ in classifying these schools; i.e., one source lists the types as private, technical institute, branches or extension centers, and public comprehensive community colleges (29:32-44), while another refers to general types—church-related, independent, and public—relating to control and finance (137:4).

Several state definitions of public junior colleges may help to delineate elements common to the rapidly growing public junior colleges. Texas, for instance, says the following:

> A public junior college is an institution of higher learning, controlled by a local board of trustees or regents and operated under statutory provisions. Two years of work in one or more standard collegiate academic curriculum is offered, but one or more years of instruction may be offered which is terminal in nature. A public junior college may confer the associate degree, but it does not grant the baccalaureate degree (19:1).

Kansas defines its junior colleges as two-year institutions, publicly or privately controlled, offering college and university parallel curricula equal to one-half the graduation requirements for a bachelor degree; offering curricula of vocational and terminal education integrated with general education; offering vocational, cultural, or recreational courses either as credit or non-credit programs; and as providing for the needs of out-of-state youth as well as community youth and adults who can profit by such offerings (363:137-148).

Oregon provides a broad definition which is noteworthy for its "open door" philosophy:

> Public community colleges are designated by a variety of names, including junior college, community college, technical institute, extension center, and area vocational school. The public two-year college is an institution of post high school education, publically supported and controlled and usually offering a lower division collegiate course of study, which has been, in the past, the major function of the junior college . . . (349:1).

The Oregon definition continues with the description of the "community" college, a multipurpose institution offering all types of programs for all types of people and dedicated to the principle of lifelong education. The evolution of these types is discussed in the next section.

For our purpose, the typical junior college emerges through definition as a two-year collegiate institution conferring no higher than the associate degree, offering lower division transfer programs and/or terminal-vocational programs of varying length. Because the community junior college is growing quite rapidly in number and size, we will emphasize this type and use "CJC" as a convenient reference; at the same time we must recognize the historical and regional importance of the other types. Primarily, we wish to discuss teachers and teaching in relationship to all types of two-year colleges, but it is difficult to find the proper title to embrace all of these. It seems likely that a definition for this decade and the next must include more characteristics than preparing a student for upper division college or university work. The "new" junior colleges are showing themselves to be multipurpose, "open door" guidance-oriented, geographically convenient, and relatively inexpensive (193:2-4).

Historical Development

The unifying forces contributing to the present status of the CJC are numerous and varied. At least four forces seem to stand out. The first of these was the establishment of the idea itself, proposed by a succession of deans and university presidents: the second force was the economic wherewithal for CJC development in a country that was rapidly becoming the wealthiest in world history. The third force was the practical feasibility of instituting the idea, the ease with which the junior college machinery could be set in motion. The fourth force was the general public's acceptance of the idea of providing an easy access to higher education for all who could desire it and profit by it. The idea, the wealth, the practicability, and the democratic dream—these were major forces which interacted to produce the phenomenon of the American two-year college. While the divisions of this phenomenon vary with the writers on the subject, at least four stages can be clearly identified.

The Initial Two-Year Private College Period (1835?-1900)

The private junior college was the first type to be founded in the United States. The word *initial* is used in our heading because the greatest thrust of growth, as in the case of all other types, came after 1900. Although the earliest date for the first private junior college is open to some question, one investigator reported the first was Monticello College in 1835, and the second was the Missionary Institute of the Evangelical Lutheran Church, later to become Susquehanna University, in Selingsgrove, Pennsylvania, in 1858 (321:13-15). Another writer indicated Lasell Junior College in Auburndale, Massachusetts, as offering two years of college instruction as early as 1852 (34:2). Although it did not start junior college instruction until 1940, Leicester Junior College in Massachusetts could possibly be the oldest continuing educational institution which evolved into a junior college, the school having been founded in 1784 as an academy (137:240). In our national survey, reported in Appendix A, we asked about the oldest junior college in each state. The oldest "reported" college was Packer Collegiate Institute of Brooklyn, New York. The institution was established in 1845 as the Brooklyn Female Academy. The building burned in 1852, and a new building was contributed by Mrs. Harriet L. Packer in 1853, the date mentioned as the beginning of the two-year college program. The school was named after its benefactor in 1854 when the New York State Regents approved the junior college. Today the school remains for women only; it offers a liberal arts education and a major in secretarial science.

Without the most painstaking kind of research, it is rather difficult to name the nation's "first" private junior college or even the oldest continuing institution, chiefly because of the many variables involved in identification, in loss of records, and in inaccurate reporting of facts. In his detailed report of the founding of American colleges and universities, Tewksbury, writing about the one hundred eighty-two permanent senior institutions established before the Civil War, said that "dead" colleges numbered about four times those which had been kept "alive." Among the many factors responsible for the death of colleges were financial disaster, denominational competition, unfavorable location, natural catastrophes, and internal dissensions (360:24-27). Who can say for sure how many and which two-year colleges also opened and closed their doors permanently before 1900? Suffice it to say that of the fifty or more private junior colleges organized in the eighteenth century, only eight such colleges remained in operation by 1900 (138:41).

These first colleges were established as extensions or replacements of private academies offering secondary and sometimes elementary instruction. Generally church-related, the academies saw the two-year college idea as a relatively easy way of broadening their curricula and extending them upward, to keep their students for a longer period of religious instruction, to provide additional financial support through more tuition and aid, to extend the prestige and fame of the college through offering courses in higher education, to become affiliated with higher education goals and purposes, and to become eventually a four-year college by way of the two-year college step instead of the giant leap from secondary to a full-blown liberal arts college. Private control and fiscal independence probably helped these schools develop earlier and more quickly than their public counterparts. Generally small in size and limited in their programs and objectives, these first colleges helped to foster the idea of the public junior college. Other contributions were the use of small classes, individualized guidance programs, intimate dormitory living with stress on social education, homogeneous curricular offerings, and close student-faculty relationships (359). Most of these early junior colleges were founded in New England and other eastern states.

Although no particular educational leader seems to stand out in the development of the first private junior colleges, at least on a national scale, several university leaders were busy during this period in relationship to the general idea of the two-year college. Their idea was not so much to extend academies into junior colleges as it was to discontinue the first two college years at their respective universities. The University of Michigan and the University of Georgia made serious proposals in the 1850's. The chief reason for these proposals was the belief that universities should not engage in secondary work and that the first two years of college were chiefly secondary in nature (42:248).

The idea that stimulated university proposals in Georgia, Michigan, and other states grew from a comparison of the American system with the European system of education, particularly in Germany. "The theory of such a partition was based on a comparison of the American college with the German gymnasium of the time. Men in a position to know, like Tappan at Michigan, Folwell at Minnesota, and White at Cornell, regarded a large part of the work done in the nineteenth century American college as about on a par with the German secondary school" (42:248). It was natural for these and other educational leaders to make this comparison, because many of them had been educated in Germany and other great European universities and felt that high school graduates were inadequately prepared to meet the rigorous demands of college study (29:24). Supported by university presidents and deans presiding during the latter half of the nineteenth century—including such others as James of Illinois, Jesse of Missouri, and Lange of California—the idea persisted that universities should be primarily upper division and graduate education, and lower division should be relegated to the junior college and secondary educational facilities.

Notable is the fact that none of these leaders was able to eliminate the "secondary" years from his institution. The University of Georgia started its plan, but was forced to discontinue it with the coming of the Civil War (79:26-63). Illinois, Michigan, and Stanford talked about dropping the first two years of college altogether. "Both the latter two institutions, however, found the suggestion impractical, Michigan because secondary schools, although improving, were still not advanced enough in the 1880's to send up students prepared to enter junior year and Stanford because it feared the financial consequences of losing students' fees for the first two undergraduate years" (42:248). Many years later, in 1935, the College of the Pacific at Stockton, California, virtually eliminated its lower two years and endeavored to rely upon Stockton Junior College and other "feeder" institutions to provide for the first two college years. A more recent development came in Florida, where in 1967, Florida Atlantic University at Boca Raton was operating as a two-year senior college and where a second upper-division institution, the University of West Florida, opened its doors for the first time. The Florida plan is to make all new universities, as approved by the board of regents, upper-division universities (53:24). Before 1900, however, the idea of the four-year liberal arts college seemed to be too firmly planted to be split into two separately operating divisions.

The Initial Two-Year Public College Period (1901-1920)

The groundwork for the beginning of the two-year public college in the United States was, of course, laid by the results of the private junior colleges and the actions taken by the various educational leaders before 1900. The greatest push toward the eventual public junior college probably came from 1888 to 1900. In 1888, at a meeting of the National Educational Association, President Charles Eliot of Harvard addressed the group on a lively controversy relating to economizing time in education (42:245). He bemoaned the steadily advancing age at which freshmen were entering Harvard. Nineteen, he felt, was too late an age, for the person could be twenty-six before finishing graduate school and starting to support himself. The controversy considered the problem as to where the saving of time could be made. Some thought two years could be saved in the elementary grades, others suggested cutting the secondary school by two years, and still others saw the problem being solved by making adjustments in the college course itself.

William Rainey Harper, president of the University of Chicago at that time, offered a bold solution. Harper's proposal was a radical one. It still is today, in fact. He suggested that the period of secondary education include the last year of elementary school and the first two years of college. This plan would have converted the common eight-four system (eight years of elementary and four years of high school) to a seven-seven system. Harper's plan, studied by a committee in 1903, suggested that the average student should be allowed to accomplish the seven-year high school in six years and the brilliant student in five years (45:22-25). Thus the brilliant students could enter college as early as sixteen years of age. He did not suggest that the four-year college be reduced to two, but that students should be permitted to enter college with advanced standing as juniors. Although President Eliot had advocated the reduction of the four year course to three, Harper felt that those who wanted a full four-year course should be allowed that privilege. Harper wanted to draw the lines between collegiate and university grades between the second and third years of the current four-year college course. Showing faith in his philosophy, Harper, in 1892, separated the University of Chicago into the "Academic College" and the "University College." These terms were, perhaps, the first to be applied to actual institutions (42:248).

Because Harper regarded the first two years of college as essentially secondary education in nature, he urged high schools to expand their programs to include the junior college years in their offerings. He contributed greatly toward this goal by influencing the founding of several public junior colleges, particularly Lewis Institute in Chicago in 1896 and Bradley Polytechnic Institute in Peoria in 1897 (361:47). He was instrumental in 1901 in the establishment of Joliet Junior College, the first of the public junior colleges still in operation. The Joliet Board of Education at first regarded the addition of college courses as an extension of the high school rather than an invasion into the college field. Before long, however, they recognized the extension for what it was—a junior college.

The upward extension developed rapidly in relation to independent junior colleges. After the turn of the century, in addition to Illinois, Michigan and Indiana had developments. An effort at Goshen, Indiana, failed, but Detroit Junior College functioned steadily until it became Wayne State University. California established its first junior college in Fresno in 1910, followed by Missouri and Minnesota in 1915, Kansas and Oklahoma in 1919, Arizona and Iowa in 1920, and Texas in 1921. "These early colleges were true extensions of secondary education: they were housed in high school buildings, had closely articulated curricula, and shared faculty and administrative staffs. They encountered difficulties during their early years because, as a deviation from the trend toward the four-year high school, they were not recognized as an essential part of secondary education" (29:25).

Legislation for the establishment of public two-year colleges started in the 1907 and 1917 California laws and in the 1917 law of Kansas, most of the remaining states enacting legislation after 1920. By this date private junior colleges had multiplied more rapidly than the public segments; there were some 8,000 students enrolled in 52 American junior colleges (42:251). These schools were located in 23 states (237). A marked increase was seen for the 1921–22 year, when there were 207 junior colleges, 70 public and 137 private. At this time total enrollment doubled to approximately 16,000, the public segments surpassing the private segments for the first time, 52 percent to 48 percent. Public junior colleges did not outnumber private types until the late 1940's (138). The highest number for the private segments was 323 in 1947, public segments reaching 327 by 1952.

University extension centers or two-year branches are reported to have been established just prior to the twentieth century; there were 13 universities with centers by 1920, 19 in 1930, 25 in 1940, and 38 in 1950. (262:15) In 1960 there were 73 members of the National University Extension Association (295). These centers and branches developed from a growing need for expanding college and university programs and facilities for various population centers away from main campuses. Many of the earlier centers added upper-division and even graduate instruction on the extension basis.

Institutes, including such types as technical and military, also began their rise before 1920, one example being the New Mexico Military Institute, founded in 1915. At least 144 technical institutes had been developed by 1958 (166:4). Their development as special vocational-technical schools was in contrast to most other types of junior colleges, which concentrated in the beginning on liberal arts and transfer function. Various federal grants in the area of vocational-technical education fostered the growth of institutes as well as specialized programs in the other more general colleges.

Also fostering growth during this period was the starting of an associate in arts degree for junior college graduates who had completed certain required courses and programs. It was in conjunction with its junior college program at the University of Chicago in 1900 that this degree came into being. The degree title stabilized slowly, however, Campbell finding 49 different titles as late as 1934 (48). The degree is now accepted generally across the nation.

The year 1920 could be considered the capstone of the second stage in junior college evolution because the American Association of Junior Colleges was formed in that year (71). During the summer, 34 representatives met in St. Louis in response to a suggestion by the U.S. Commissioner of Education, P. P. Claxton. The decision of that meeting bore results in February 1921 when a constitution and the organizational name were adopted. The general purposes of this association were, and are today, to study junior colleges, to establish standards, and to provide guidance for state and national legislation relating to the interests and establishment of junior colleges. The association's publication, *Junior College Journal,* has been issued monthly since 1930. The association also publishes annually the *Junior College Directory* and compiles the quadrennial editions of *American Junior Colleges,* published by the American Council on Education.

The Period of Expanding Occupational Programs (1921–1947)

It seems natural that junior colleges would emphasize collegiate courses of a transfer nature prior to 1921. Most students demanded these courses. Also, these early colleges were commonly very small—the majority enrolling fewer than 100 students—and they lacked the size and financial backing for the so-called "terminal" programs. However, the idea of occupational programs received perceptibly increasing support from 1921 to 1947. It is interesting to note that junior colleges grew in numbers and enrollments somewhat in proportion to the number of occupational programs installed in both well established and newly founded institutions. The growth of terminal courses was indicated by one writer as moving from 100 courses in 1921, 400 courses in 1925, 1,600 courses in 1930, to over 4,000 courses by 1941 (171). Correspondingly, junior colleges increased from 207 in 1921 to about 560 in 1941, enrollments increasing from 16,000 to approximately 200,000, special and adult students included. One study shows that by 1947, 32 percent of all junior college offerings were terminal courses (67: 246). Undoubtedly, a major reason for the great surge of new junior colleges was the growth of these elaborate occupational or vocational-technical programs. Harris provides an insightful presentation of the recent status of these programs (158).

Once again we find university leaders influencing the development of this period. Alexis F. Lange of the University of California helped to precipitate the idea when he wrote in 1917, "The junior college will function adequately only if its first concern is with those who will go no farther, if it meets local needs efficiently, if it enables thousands and tens of thousands to round out their general education, if it turns an increasing number into vocations for which training has not hitherto been afforded by our school system" (215:472). A few years later, in 1925, the American Association of Junior Colleges began to notice the need for extending occupational programs: "The junior college may, and is likely to, develop a different type of curriculum suited to the larger and ever-changing civic, social, religious, and vocational needs of the entire community in which the college is located. It is understood that in this case, also, the work offered shall be on a level appropriate for high school graduates" (94:3). Fifteen years later, in 1940, AAJC received a grant of money for the purpose of exploring terminal education in junior colleges. Four volumes of books were ultimately published on the subject of exploration (98,99,102, 385).

Occupational programs began to thrive during this period because of other important influences. The Smith-Hughes Act, for instance, set up state agencies for the development of occupational programs. Funds were allocated for the support of curricula, equipment, and instruction, particularly at the junior college level, which was then riding on the coattails of secondary schools. During the 1930's, of course, unemployment was a nationwide problem, and the government realized a need for training younger people as well as unemployed adults for available jobs. Production methods and industrial processes during World War II, in particular, were becoming more mechanized, so workers needed to develop technical skills.

Because liberal arts colleges and universities were inclined toward academic studies and professional preparation, the junior colleges were the most obvious institutions to undertake these terminal programs. Furthermore, the two-year colleges were becoming more responsible to their local communities' needs in the area of vocational-technical courses, many of which were guided and sponsored by local businesses and industries. Thus from 1921 to shortly after the end of World War II, the junior colleges developed a second major program to add to their already established transfer program. Having their own unique identity and purposes, the occupational programs were neither secondary nor higher education, but more accurately a new type of post-high school special education of a terminal nature.

The Period of the Comprehensive Community College (1948—)

Like the other dates mentioned to identify the stages of CJC evolution, 1948 is somewhat arbitrary; and yet this particular year was selected logically. In 1948 at least three significant events fostered the identifying caption, the comprehensive community college.

The first event in that year was the report of the President's Commission on Higher Education for American Democracy. The report declared, "The time has come to make education through the fourteenth grade available in the same way that high school education is available" (379:37). Issued in six volumes, the report was released from December 1947 through February 1948. The Commission proposed that free public education should be extended upward to include two more years of study beyond high school and that every state should establish local community colleges as a part of the public school system so that every person could have easily accessible free education through the sophomore year. The proposed community colleges would offer all types of terminal and general education programs to meet the needs of the local community's work force as well as courses preparing students to continue on to higher levels.

The second event in that year was New York's establishment of "one of the most comprehensive laws ever enacted for the establishment of a state-wide system and was the first state to designate these institutions as community colleges" (33:37). The idea and name, community college, had been discussed and written about several years prior to New York's action, however. By 1939, for example, articles began to appear on the subject (161). The Commission on Terminal Education, in 1940, listed the junior college as essentially a community institution (97). Furthermore, the President's Commission used the term *community college* in its report of 1947–48. New York, however, paved the way through legislation toward the reality of a comprehensive community college system; in subsequent years, other states were to follow the lead.

The third event which had national implications occurred in California, which with New York seems to have set many of the standards in junior college growth and development. Almost from the beginning of its junior college establishment in 1910, California led the nation in the rapid expansion of junior college campuses. As mentioned previously, California had the nation's first junior college state law in 1907. From that year on, the majority of states looked to California with great interest and possibly for guidance in junior college development. The situation was no different in 1948, when the state had 55 junior colleges. Thus the Strayer Report was not only a major event but was also an answer to a state need.

The publication of *A Report of a Survey of the Needs of California in Higher Education* was directed by George Strayer (348). There had been a strong movement to encourage the most able two-year campuses in that state to become four-year colleges. The Strayer Report, as it is commonly known, discouraged the idea by advising each type of college and university to remain within the bounds of its own area of service. The report warned that a trend to expand the junior colleges to senior colleges would eventually destroy the junior college system in the state. The financial burden of supporting a four-year college in each junior college community would be overwhelming in view of the state's additional support of several university and state college campuses, the report said.

If the Strayer Report had not been made and if the state had indeed developed a trend to convert junior colleges into senior colleges, such a trend might have affected and influenced junior college thinking in virtually every state in the union. In essence, the report strengthened the junior college concept and particularly the idea of the community college with its unique contributions to higher education.

In addition to these events, there were other forces contributing to the development of maturity among the junior colleges. When World War II ended in 1945, thousands of ex-servicemen began to crowd the colleges to take advantage of the G.I. Bill of Rights' educational benefits. The junior colleges were especially attractive to the men and women who wanted short-term occupational training. Because of these ever-expanding needs, the junior colleges continued to increase curriculum offerings to meet the demand. Thus these institutions became, more than ever before, truly comprehensive colleges.

The word *community* to identify the junior college did not actually change the institution greatly, for most junior colleges were, in effect, community institutions a few decades before 1948. The name change, however, did create closer community identification and cooperation with each local college. Most persons began to regard their local colleges as personalized institutions of higher education belonging to the people within the college districts.

The growth pattern in the years since 1948 shows the influence of the comprehensive college idea with its multitude of programs and courses for meeting the needs of students and adults. In 1948 there were approximately 500,000 students enrolled in approximately 580 two-year colleges of all types. The 1969 *Junior College Directory* reported October 1968 enrollments as nearly two million students. Faculty members numbered close to 85,000. The total number of institutions had grown from 912 in 1967 to 993 in 1968, an increase of 81. The total included 254 private two-year colleges (a decrease of ten from the previous year) and 739 public junior colleges, 97 of which had enrollments of over 5,000. The state with the largest number of institutions was California with 90. Gleazer (135:7) and others (153:56) had accurately predicted this growth and status by 1970. A survey of status for 1967–68 is reported in Appendix A.

Purposes in Communities

The purposes of the CJC have been defined frequently and variously through the years. In the late 1960's, six major purposes appeared consistently, even though the lists varied in length and categorizations. A model based on current CJC patterns would include (1) transfer function, (2) occupational education, (3) general education, (4) remedial education, (5) guidance and counseling, (6) community service. Although there are many community junior colleges which have not adopted all of these purposes, nevertheless the trend seems to be toward their inclusion.

Transfer education is perhaps the most generally accepted purpose, especially among the more conservative communities and institutions. The provision of the first two years of college at home is well established, even though typically less than half of the entering student body transfers to senior institutions. Transfer education is also the easiest to define and evaluate, because the program is largely determined by the colleges and universities which receive the transfers.

Transfer courses are limited (1) to those required for general education, (2) to major or minor fields of specialization, and (3) to a specified number of electives. While transfer courses may overlap other college programs, the chief emphasis is upon an academically oriented foundation that prepares students in liberal arts and sciences for some form of professional career requiring at least four years of college work. At least 60 units of credit are usually needed for the associate degree and transfer to junior standing at the senior institution. However, students may transfer after only one semester at a two-year college, providing they are otherwise qualified for and are admitted to the senior college.

Occupational programs comprise a second major unit of curriculum, although the term "occupational" is not completely accepted as a label for the programs sometimes known as "terminal." Both "terminal" and "non-transfer" seem to be resisted as being essentially negative in connotation. Nevertheless, the terms are useful to describe programs which are completed at the community college. The expression "two-year" is occasionally used, but it, too, is somewhat inaccurate, because many students take longer than two years to complete an occupational program. "Vocational" is often used, but its use may imply that other programs are not vocational. Thus, "occupational" has become relatively popular as a label for an important purpose of the community college (221:146). That purpose is to train skilled manpower for varied community jobs not requiring a four-year college degree. Business and industry take the greatest numbers of these students.

Occupational education and general education are very nearly opposite, because by definition occupational education describes courses not commonly considered to be of value as part of a liberal education. While general education may enrich a student's life emotionally, socially, or culturally, supposedly it does not increase his vocational competence. Some students take the courses to meet the general education requirements of graduation, either at the community college or a senior institution. But thousands of adults take general education courses without degrees in mind. Often the purpose is simply one of personal development. For example, many adults take junior college courses after their children have left home.

Many junior colleges accept the responsibility of providing programs at sub-college level. Their justification is related to the open-door philosophy, the attitude being that an open door is not truly open unless there are programs appropriate to the student's abilities. Such programs are called by various names—remedial, vestibule, opportunity, and pre-college. Some are essentially basic literacy training. The issue is a provocative one, for some junior colleges are vehemently against the philosophy of offering pre-college level courses. One alternative has been to refer these students to adult or evening high school. Nevertheless, a growing number of colleges, especially those in urban areas and in federally funded programs, have expanded their purposes to include preparation for college.

Community colleges also include guidance and counseling service as one of their major purposes. For many students the CJC is an exploratory institution. They enter not knowing definitely to what their lives are committed. Not only students fresh from high school but older ones sample programs and discover abilities in the process. Upon entry, most students declare themselves for transfer programs. In reality, less than one-fourth of the entering students go on to senior colleges. Consequently, the junior college staff tries to guide a faltering student into a program appropriate to his interests and abilities rather than have him simply fail and leave campus.

In an age of increasingly rapid vocational obsolescence, growing numbers of adults seek second or third careers. Even the vocation of housewife changes profoundly when there are no longer children at home. Often the wife's college career was interrupted by marriage. Starting back to school can be made easier by skillful counseling, which usually includes diagnostic testing and test interpretation as well as program planning.

The sixth major purpose is that of community service. Activities in this category range from virtually nonexistent to extremely elaborate. Budget, of course, plays a major role. Any reasonably ambitious program must combine adequate financial support with board and administrative approval and cooperation. In addition, the successful programs seem almost without exception to have the leadership of a lively, forceful personality and the support of an interested, enthusiastic community. This intricate combination is becoming less rare as the concept of the junior college as a center of community service becomes more familiar. The community college in an urban or a rural setting is often the hub of activities, being used for meetings, offering foreign or historical films, presenting lecture series—generally enriching and serving the community (222).

Junior college purposes and educational programs result from a complex web of influences. Blocker and others provide a rather extensive listing of these influences (29:54). The various levels of influences are local, state, national, and regional. Among the public are community residents, alumni, civic groups, religious organizations, labor, business, political factions, philanthropic agencies, advisory committees, farm organizations, taxpayers' associations, and other special-interest groups. Among the professionals are teachers' and administrators' associations, public and private school teachers and administrators, educational advisory committees, four-year colleges and universities, two-year college associations, athletic associations, accrediting agencies, professional and academic associations, philanthropic foundations, regional two-year college associations, and the

American Association of Junior Colleges. Blocker and his colleagues also point to the influences of (1) basic societal trends such as rapid growth, technological change, and changes in the work force; and (2) educational changes in increased enrollments, finance, curricula, and subsidized research and consultative services (29:46-53).

A specific example of influence, particularly relating to occupational programs, is the Economic Opportunity Act of 1964, which serves as one approach to the war on poverty program (256). Another example of influence is the W. K. Kellogg Foundation's five-year support program to give service and guidance in the development and operation of occupational education programs at junior colleges. The project began in 1967 (334).

Relationships with Other Educational Levels

Commonly called *articulation* and/or *coordination,* relationships with other educational levels move in opposite directions—toward the high schools and toward the senior institutions. Of course, there are other types of relationships, but articulation with schools below and above the CJC is of primary importance if the college is to function properly. Articulation, to put it simply, is coordination between schools or levels of schools, although there are contrasts, as stated by one reliable source: "Articulation and coordination may in fact be contrasted in terms of their differing concerns—articulation centered on the students and their courses of study and coordination on institutional budgets and building programs. Coordinating agencies tend to represent the interests of the state and its citizenry; articulation programs consider the interests of the individual student and his instructors" (208:75).

Purposes and Problems

Articulation activities exist for the purpose of aiding the student as he prepares for entering a higher level of education. At least four major problem areas have been identified (208:75): (1) student-centered problems such as his choice of courses, his degree goals, his attendance as he pursues his goals, his academic and economic resources, and the qualities and requirements of the institution to which he might be accepted; (2) curriculum and instruction problems, such as acceptance of transfer credit, coordination of materials and methods in teaching, course and classroom innovation, grading standards, and quality of teachers and teaching; (3) problems of student personnel services, such as orientation for transfer students, coordination of financial aid programs, counselor's knowledge about institutional programs and characteristics, and facilitation of students' adjustments to the institutions where they enroll; (4) problems of facilities and resources, such as enrollment quotas and priorities, how special courses may differ among institutions, the diversion of students to particular schools like the two-year college, and the coordination of academic calendars (quarter, semester, year-round operations).

A Joint Committee on Junior and Senior Colleges, composed of representatives of three major associations, details issues or problems in the following areas (148): (1) Admissions, (2) Evaluation of Transfer Courses, (3) Curriculum Planning, (4) Advising, Counseling, and Other Student Personnel Services, and (5) Articulation Programs.

The Machinery of Articulation

Area (5) of the committee's guidelines discusses how the other four areas can be implemented into articulation programs. Participants are those most clearly associated with articulation problems. Segments include the various levels of institutions, both public and private, and various state boards, coordinating agencies, and professional associations. Individuals generally include administrators, faculty, admissions officers, counselors, registrars, deans, research workers, students, and various others at local, state, and association levels. Each institution usually has some form of direct representation or at least direct contact with the agency for articulation. Although articulation machinery is voluntary, in many instances involving local cooperation, there are legal provisions for machinery in various states. Oregon is an example (349:108-111).

Articulation procedures involve identifying problems, developing needed studies, proposing solutions, and reaching agreements for ratifying and implementing recommendations. Committees, conferences, interinstitutional visits, publications, and other devices for communication and cooperation are utilized in the machinery. In the areas of communication and orientation, for example, junior college teams are frequently sent to talk to graduating high school seniors, particularly in the years when the local college is trying to introduce an attendance pattern. High school counselors, teachers, and students are also invited to visit the college for an informal tour.

Communication is equally important between the junior college and senior institutions. The success of the CJC is measured critically by subsequent performances of its students.

"If the two-year colleges do not prepare students to achieve their baccalaureate degree goals at some acceptable level of performance, the effectiveness of the entire sub-system will be seriously open to question. Transfer student performance may be thought of as a more critical test of the sub-system than the mere flow of students through junior college into four-year institutions, since transfer is relatively pointless if students have a low probability of succeeding in the upper division" (208:4).

Thus, as far as junior colleges are concerned, articulation is vitally necessary. There are many issues and problems. Articulation machinery includes a variety of local and state efforts to bridge the gap on each side of the junior college level. Students interested in more detailed information should examine the Knoell and Medsker study, which covers ten states (208:78).

Conditions for Establishment

The teachers at a two-year college occasionally participate in its actual establishment. However, such duties typically fall to interested citizens and educational authorities, particularly college boards and chief administrators. Nevertheless, a brief description of college establishment may help you understand how such institutions come into being.

The Need Issue

The biggest issue in the establishment of two-year colleges is *need* (259: 57). How many high school students are available for and interested in attending a local junior college? A potential college must assure itself that a minimum number can be enrolled before embarking upon the long road toward establishing itself. The minimum varies somewhat, depending upon the geographical region and the criteria used by the organizers. In the beginning, high schools added post-high school collegiate courses with only a handful of people enrolled, but today independently organized junior colleges must reach a certain standard of numbers which will guarantee a minimum of costs for operation and facilities. Although many present campuses enroll one hundred or fewer students, a new independent campus usually endeavors to enroll many more than that before opening classes. Optimum size, reports Staerkel, should be from 2,000 to 3,000 students, although a 500-member student body is feasible at higher cost (341:61). Whatever standard is employed, junior colleges cannot be established without a consideration of a sufficient number of available students who need and want at least two years of college education. Colleges are needed only to satisfy student needs, and for no other reason.

Solving the issue of need takes time, but even after a clear need presents itself, many years can elapse before conditions exist to satisfy that need. For instance, "The Oregon 1961 community college law, first enabling legislation in Oregon to withstand the test of application, was forged over a period of about thirty years" (349:7). Lahti reports that agitation for a junior college began in Wyoming in 1930 and that it took fifteen years before the 1945 legislature passed an enabling bill (214:93). But the rising awareness of need seems to have been nationwide. Statements made by a committee endorsed by the Association for Supervision and Curriculum Development are illustrative: "The next half-century will no doubt see the first two years beyond high school become compulsory as awareness increases that the greatly expanded realm of knowledge which most people must possess in order to adequately fulfill their responsibilities of citizenship cannot be attained in 12 years of school" (339:4).

The Benefit Issue

Related to need is the benefit issue. We have suggested that a need exists only if enough students want at least two years of college within their own communities. But why do they want this education? The prime reason may be reflected in the committee's quotation that students are becoming aware that a high school diploma is not enough qualification for participating in today's complex society. A survey report by Moore showed that high school seniors in eight Texas schools indicated the chief benefits to be academic, financial, and social (254). In other words, students gain additional theoretical and practical knowledge of a cultural and vocational nature. They employ this knowledge to gain or improve upon their economic status, and they develop varying social relationships that may not have been possible otherwise. Moore's survey results seem to be typical of most other studies of a comparable nature.

Benefits can be discussed also in relation to the functions of a junior college: occupational education, general education, pre-professional education, community services, and guidance (339:4). The existence of these functions should be evidence that students and communities are being benefited. Specific examples of programs are virtually limitless.

Probably the most important general benefit of a CJC is its tendency to encourage students to continue their education. "There is conclusive evidence that the percentage of high school graduates who continue their education is much larger in communities where community colleges are located than in those where they are not" (117:8). Bashaw (18), Fincher (114), Monroe (253:7) and many others report evidence of this. For example, a Florida report showed that in 33 counties where junior colleges were within commuting distance, 55.5 percent of the June graduates enrolled in college for the following fall, while in 34 counties where junior colleges were not available the percentage was 36.3 (117:1).

The economic value of junior colleges is also a point to consider. Kastner points out savings of junior college costs compared with the costs of the university. While the cost of educating a student varies greatly from one state to another, it is generally accepted that junior colleges do the job considerably cheaper for their students than universities do for their students (197:30).

Medsker considers the junior colleges as serving a great need in the nation's economy and overall progress when he says, ". . . the nation's welfare—indeed, its very security—depends in part upon the upgrading of people and the development of all kinds and levels of talent" (249:42).

Benefits and values of junior colleges are clearly derived from open doors of educational opportunity—doors to vocation, to continuous education, to the community, and to diversity. Gleazer provides a fitting résumé (134:3):

> I believe that the community college is an educational instrument for these times in which we live. It has evolved out of the aspirations of the people of this land, it has responded to the changing and critical needs of the community. It is not an idea superimposed upon the American scene by a national committee, board, or agency. Rather, its form and functions have emerged from the interplay of the values of our democratic society and the facts of economic and social change.
>
> The community college opens doors to occupations and obligations. It is a readily accessible resource for lifelong learning. The community is its vital and dynamic contest for learning. And it comprehends in its programs and services those varieties of personalities and ideas that keep the pools of wisdom constantly refreshed.

The Practicability Issue

Although the need and benefit issues may be satisfactorily solved at the local level, a CJC cannot be established unless there is a workable, legal plan. Indeed, the practicability issue may be the most difficult stumbling block in the process of establishment. Johnson, who has written an informative handbook for those interested in starting a community junior college (193), Harper (153), and many others provide insight into the problems involved. In the following general areas, useful criteria are provided by Morrison and Martorana (257:12-25):

1. Legislation authorizing establishment
2. Petition, election, or action by local board of control
3. State agency approval
4. Adequate assessed valuation for the sound fiscal support of the college
5. Demonstration through a local or state survey of need for college
6. Minimum school age population
7. Minimum total district population
8. Minimum potential college enrollment within a certain period after establishment
9. Educational programs to be offered

10. Available and adequate physical facilities
11. Compliance with state operating policies
12. Proximity of other institutions

A list of procedures for establishment was developed by the American Association of Junior Colleges as follows (154:9):

1. A state legislature authorizes the study of higher education needs.
2. A study commission or survey staff is appointed.
3. The study report is sent to the governor and/or to the legislature.
4. The legislature adopts the state's master plan recommendations.
5. The state passes an enabling law which includes plans for organization, finance, operation, and control.
6. Local surveys are initiated.
7. Local survey recommendations are reported.
8. The local group requests state approval of the local plan.
9. The state approves the local plan.
10. The plan is accepted by vote of the local electorate.
11. The local board of control is elected or appointed.
12. The college is organized (including approval of president, staff, site, curriculum, and receipt of state and local funds).
13. The students are enrolled.

As indicated in both lists, legality is the first consideration in establishing these schools. Most states now have enabling legislation providing the framework, procedures, and minimum requirements. Steps and criteria vary in each case. New Jersey, for example, sets up nine procedural steps for establishing its county colleges (271:11).

In a feasibility study, the question of finance is crucial (341). Generally less expensive than senior institutions, community junior colleges nevertheless represent millions of dollars in operating budgets and capital outlay. Funds come from various sources: the federal government, the state, the community, and students themselves. Grants and gifts of money help. If the college is to be supported by a local property tax, an assessment of the tax potential must be made. State aid, particularly for public segments, is given through a foundation program which assures each college of having a stipulated amount of state money per student. If a college fails to reach the level of the foundation program, the state usually provides equalization money as a supplement. Some states provide financial aid to all their junior colleges, while others aid only their poorer districts.

The feasibility study is a prelude to and part of the formal application for permission to establish a community college. Approval of the application may, in one state pattern, lead to extensive state involvement. However, the more usual pattern is for the approval to lead to a formal public decision through the local district ballot box. The potential district is defined so as to avoid overlapping the boundaries of adjacent college districts, and the voters have the opportunity to approve or disapprove. The voters also decide, sometimes at the same election, upon such matters as the junior college tax rate, the issuance of bonds for building construction, and the establishment of a college board of trustees. The date for the establishment of the new district is invariably placed on the ballot.

Establishment procedures, of course, differ from these steps when a two-year college or branch is formed by universities and controlled by university boards. In the case of public two-year college branches or state-owned independent colleges, a state board makes the recommendation for establishment. The state legislature must approve the new institution, after which the issue is usually placed before all the voters in the state. Private community colleges and two-year university branches are relatively free from state-imposed machinery for establishment. In most cases, these institutions are subject only to decisions of their boards of trustees.

Across the nation there are various approaches to establishing the campus itself (193). The most popular approach has been to use a high school campus in late afternoon and evening during the time when the board and superintendent are selecting a college site, employing an architect, awarding the building contract, and awaiting construction of the campus. Alternatives include (1) renting temporary facilities, such as church, military barracks, or military hospitals, (2) using temporary or prefabricated buildings on the construction site, and (3) holding no classes until the new campus and staff are complete.

The establishment of a new community college can be the outstanding event when the citizens of the community identify themselves with it. If, on the other hand, they perceive it as essentially an alien body, reflecting neither their hopes nor their voices, then their indifference or hostility may weaken or destroy it. The style of establishment has much to do with the community acceptance and subsequent support. When a junior college must ask for additional funds from the voters, a positive vote reflects a composite of attitudes that have to be developed and sustained: confidence, approval, and identification.

Current Governance and Structure

American junior colleges present a variety of patterns in both governance and structure. Governance, a term commonly used in classifying systems of state control, seems to be an expression of many variables. Historical attitudes toward higher education, university receptiveness to potential competition, local willingness to support education beyond high school—these are a few of the determinants of how a junior college system is controlled. Structure, on the other hand, while it is affected by state governance, is much more a reflection of the functions and the size of the institution. Community junior colleges within one state may vary enormously in structure, even though they are under identical conditions of governance. Some familiarity with several basic principles and patterns of governance and structure may help you relate to your own junior college, which functions under controls not always of its choosing and which may be experiencing the strains of growth and related structural change.

Governance is an expression of both state and local relationships to the college. Martorana describes five patterns at state level as governance by (1) a state board of education, (2) a state department of education or superintendent (both (1) and (2) have responsibility for other levels of education), (3) a board of higher education, (4) a board of a four-year state university (both (3) and (4) govern other collegiate institutional types at the same time), and (5) an independent board or commission limited to junior college affairs (228:36). In the past, the dominant type has been the state board of education.

The introduction of local control also determines patterns of governance. There seem to be four major patterns, according to Harper (153:53). The most common is that typified by Texas, which controls its junior colleges through intermediary units, local junior college districts, not necessarily related to county boundaries. Florida illustrates an alternate method, that of establishing county districts of control. Intermediary units are common but not vital to successful governance. Alabama and several other states govern their systems directly from state level. A fourth means of control makes use of the state university as the governing body, which combines state level control with a senior institution.

Blocker, Plummer, and Richardson provide clarification of governance and control from another vantage point (29:84). First, they remind us that the federal government has no direct control over any two-year college. (There is, however, the two-year college for Indians, which is under federal auspices.) They proceed to point out control levels from the state down to the local district: (1) state legislature, (2) state administrative office, (3) state board of control, (4) local board of control, (5) local administrators and faculty.

The typical structure of a local community junior college, whether large or small, begins with a board of trustees, elected by the community voters in the case of public institutions and appointed or elected by officials or alumni in the case of private institutions. The board is the legal body which establishes and approves college or district policy, hires the staff and its administrators, approves the budget, and so on. The board, in essence, runs the college through the leadership and professional training of the district superintendent or college president.

The extent and complexity of college programs and services determine the structure and organization of the college staff. In a few small colleges, one or more teachers are given part-time administrative duties; the more common pattern for all colleges, however, is the selection of a president to "manage" the college on a full-time basis. Assisting and complementing him in the larger colleges are assistant superintendents or vice-presidents, or deans, the titles varying among colleges. The more common plan calls for assistant administrators in the areas of business and instruction. Equal to these or sometimes subordinated to them are other administrators heading student personnel, curriculum, public relations, and the like. If not equal to assistant superintendents or vice-presidents, a third-line administrator is usually designated as dean or director, i.e. a dean of students (for men or women) and a director of public relations. Special programs such as those in technology, industry, and nursing sometimes require a specialist-coordinator. Below most of these officials are the fourth-line administrators, the department or division chairmen. Only in the larger colleges are the chairmen full-time administrators; in most schools they assume teaching duties as well. The faculty and students complete the college structure.

The junior colleges, like business and industry, have had to alter their styles as they have grown. During the "thin thirties" and even the "fatter forties," there were relatively few junior colleges unable to function with a relatively simple structure. However, any institution with an enrollment of more than 5,000 must handle thousands of registrations, tens of thousands of grades, hundreds of texts and courses, and all of the problems that accompany a sincere attempt to do the best possible job for the community. The solutions which the junior colleges have evolved are reflected in structures which seem at first elaborate. A closer analysis reveals an essential structure somewhat similar in all junior colleges.

Development of Accreditation

A picture of CJC development should not be concluded without a brief discussion of the nature of accreditation and its relationship to the junior college movement in the United States. This preliminary discussion should provide you with enough background to approach properly your own role in faculty involvement with accreditation, described in Chapter Six.

Development and Status

The effect of accrediting agencies has been to stabilize the development of community junior colleges and of most other levels of education. Until about the end of the nineteenth century, no significant effort was made to establish such agencies. In 1867, the Federal Department (now Office) of Education was established, and one of its first functions was the collecting and reporting of facts about colleges. Their definition of a college was "any institution granting degrees and having college students in attendance." By 1915, additional criteria included stated standards of admission, at least two years of standard college grade work available, and at least twenty students in regular college status. While the office encouraged the development of criteria for identifying an institution as a college, it is not today an accrediting agency.

Many other groups and organizations tended to point toward the establishment of accrediting agencies. Among them were the National Education Association's Department of Higher Education, started in 1870; the National Association of State Universities, established in 1896; and the Carnegie Foundation for the Advancement of Teaching, founded in 1905. The activities of these three were limited. NEADHE served as an information office for higher education. NASU prepared reports of standards in higher education. CFAT established criteria for college faculty participation in a retirement program.

The lack of organized accrediting groups for over 300 years of our history naturally led to a wide diversity of higher institutions of learning. The quality of teachers and character of instructional programs were particularly diverse. These differences reflected the federal Constitution, which gave to the states the prime responsibility for establishing and directing their own educational systems. In contrast to existing practices in most foreign countries, the United States does not have central governmental control over its educational systems. The Office of Education serves principally as a national information and aid agency. The chief causes of educational uniformity, when it does exist, can be related to various federal aid laws,* to the tendency of most colleges and schools to copy desirable features from each other, and, finally, to the rise of accrediting agencies which carry across state lines and provide standards and criteria for the evaluation and approval of institutions.

Early associations set membership requirements for institutions and personnel. Membership itself was not regarded as accreditation. However, the process eventually expanded into accreditation as we know it today. At the regional level, i.e., grouping of states in a convenient pattern, the first accrediting program was started by the North Central Association of Secondary Schools (1895) in 1909, its first accredited list appearing in 1916. Standards for junior colleges came in 1917 and those for teachers colleges in 1918. The Southern Association of Colleges and Secondary Schools (1895 by a different name) published a list of accredited colleges in 1920. The Middle States Association of Colleges and Secondary Schools (1887 by a different name) developed its first list in 1921. The Northwest Association of Secondary and Higher Schools (1917) also issued its first

---

* Examples are the Morrill Acts of 1862 and 1890, which gave impetus to the land grant college movement and technological education, and the Hatch Act of 1887, which stimulated the growth of agricultural and mechanical colleges.

list in 1921. Western College Association (1924 by a different name) began
its accrediting function in 1948. The New England Association of Colleges
and Secondary Schools (1885), the oldest of these six agencies, did not
adopt accreditation as a function until 1952 (25:10).

State accrediting agencies are usually university boards, state boards,
or departments of education. State universities first began an accreditation
of high schools. The University of Michigan was the first in 1871, although
the University of Nebraska in the same year reportedly began an accreditation of other colleges in order to establish a basis for accepting students'
transfer credits. On a complete state basis, the Board of Regents of the
University of the State of New York (1784) "was the first state agency to
develop machinery for the approval of courses of study in teacher education as well as in liberal arts and many other specialized areas" (24:13-14).
State departments of education, charged with teacher licensing, are concerned usually only with approval of teacher preparing institutions. Most
of the state agencies did not begin accreditation until after 1910.

We can see from these dates that public junior colleges began to develop at the time when accrediting agencies were being formed. At first,
the junior colleges had difficulties in being recognized by these agencies.
"Not only did they encounter delay in inclusion of their representatives on
the boards and commissions of the associations, but for some time they
were expected to meet requirements which were in many cases artificial
adaptations of the standards for four year colleges" (329:39). Today, we
find considerable improvement in the role that junior colleges are playing
in accreditation: they now participate, but perhaps not equally, in regional, state, and professional or specialized accrediting functions.

The many problems and issues in accreditation, as well as the variety
of accrediting groups, led in 1950 to the establishment of the National
Commission on Accrediting, consisting of constituent and institutional
members. The commission endeavors to coordinate and regulate accreditation activities across the nation. The American Association of Junior Colleges, while a constituent member of the commission, does not directly
accredit the junior colleges but publishes instead a list of accredited institutions in its annual *Directory* (154). The list includes pertinent information on each two-year college. A similar list with more detail is found in
American Junior Colleges, published every few years by the American
Council on Education in Washington, D.C. (137). Other groups publish
junior college lists, but these two are the most widely distributed.

Purposes and Values

The general purpose of accreditation is to identify institutions that meet
the standards of the particular accrediting agency or association and, by
such identification, to promote and ensure the highest possible quality in

institutional programs and services. Promotion of quality and an institutional desire to be approved create a great deal of effort and self-study by these institutions, their boards, and their personnel. Accreditation also serves to facilitate the transfer of students between institutions, to inform and aid employing agencies who wish to know the quality of their applicants' education, and to raise educational standards in a profession or specific field. Accrediting agencies serve the students who want to find an appropriate, accredited school suitable to their needs, provide guidance to the general public, and attempt to resolve problems and issues in determining effective standards and criteria for quality education.

Procedures and Criteria

Although each accrediting agency develops its own plan and procedures for approving institutions within its jurisdiction, a common pattern exists for the majority of states and regions. First must be developed the set of standards or criteria each institution is expected to meet. Statements of standards are then provided to each institution. An applying institution asks for an accreditation visit and prepares an institutional status report.

In general, the areas where standards or criteria are most frequently set by accreditation agencies are buildings and facilities, financial structure, philosophy and goals, curricular offerings, instructional effectiveness, faculty, students, and the library. A visiting team of qualified authorities inspects the institution, studies the college report, and ultimately provides the basic information for determining whether or not the school meets the established accreditation standards. Both the institution and the association receive a report of the visiting team, and the approved institution is included among those listed as being accredited. Approval is usually for a set period of time. Subsequent team visitations or periodic reviews determine whether the school will remain on the accredited list.

Accreditation is not without its share of troubles and critics (328), but it seems to be a healthy process. Two-year colleges, as well as other types of schools, have been encouraged by accrediting agencies to develop programs and innovations that sometimes do not fit the conventional pattern: qualitative rather than quantitative criteria have been emphasized in recent years. Fixed standards seem to be less important today. What *is* important is that a junior college's total patterns be clearly and positively related to stated purposes and objectives and to their successful obtainment. Accreditation seems to have fostered the growth and development of the two-year college, and it has apparently enhanced the prestige of these institutions as they endeavor to serve in American society the special needs not always met in other levels of education.

Conclusion

In conclusion, we can see that the junior college institution has developed through approximately four growth stages until today it is a substantial and distinct segment of higher education. It is generally identified as a comprehensive community college (although other types are recognized) offering education for transfer, occupational training, remedial instruction, general orientation, guidance and counseling, and community service. It attempts to relate its programs and services to the general community as well as to high schools and senior institutions. Its establishment by law provides a direct line of communication between the institution and the people; it is a democratic institution designed to provide post high school higher education at low cost and with easy accessibility to all citizens of the nation who need and can profit from the experience. It functions under various forms of organization and governance, depending largely upon its basic form of control and finance. Finally, through the process of accreditation by special and regional groups, its courses and students are accepted by the majority of senior institutions and by the general public; and the accreditation process assures some concentrated effort toward its continual improvement and expansion.

Even though this unique institution has apparently reached its maturity and has established direction and adult status, there are those today who feel that the junior college is still searching for an identity (274). Some even change identity by converting to a four-year college. Pueblo College, for instance, was once the largest community junior college in Colorado; it became Southern Colorado State College in the fall of 1963. No doubt there are new developments ahead which may drastically create new alternatives. Even now there are some stirrings of an "experimental junior college," a movement toward innovations in programs and services described by B. Lamar Johnson, among others (190,191). Diverse as the states are, it is likely that we will continue to see a 20-year span of evolution among the 50 different state community college systems.

Chapter 2

Benefits for
Junior College Teachers

Undoubtedly many states work diligently to improve benefits for their junior college teachers, but our national survey (summarized in Appendix A) revealed very little attention to these benefits. Printed or mimeographed in soft covers, the state studies mailed to us did not often mention the word *benefit* when referring to teachers. Almost all of the studies dealt with such areas as organization, finance, articulation, new growth and enrollments, trends, and needs. States with the largest number of junior colleges placed emphasis upon the growth of and need for instructors, but omitted any discussion of ways and means to attract them.

It is the purpose of this chapter to examine the benefits and advantages of junior college teaching. The following areas are discussed: Significant Causes and Effects; Salaries; Retirement; Certification, Employment, and Tenure; Leaves from Duty; Insurances; Professional Memberships; Miscellaneous Benefits; and finally, the Status of Benefits.

Significant Causes and Effects

Appreciation of teacher benefits requires some understanding of how or why they develop. What really causes junior college teacher benefits apart from those natural to the profession? At least five primary points are evident: (1) demand for new teachers to meet the educational requirements of an expanding, highly complex society, (2) rising teacher qualifications as set by institutions, agencies, and members of the profession, (3) increasing prestige of the teaching profession which draws more and more talented, intelligent, and professional people within the ranks, (4) competition among various schools in geographical proximities in seeking the best qualified applicants, (5) the new faculty power in influencing decisions of administrative governance and control.

The first point is merely a matter of increasing enrollments and creating new colleges. The first chapter showed how these institutions are growing and expanding in numbers. The greater the growth, the greater the demand for new teachers. The greater the demand, the greater the chance for better benefits.

The second point relates to the preparation and requirements for employment, discussed extensively in the next chapter. The profession is setting "tougher" standards for all its members. Higher standards in teacher qualifications tend to mean greater benefits.

The third point follows naturally. When a profession improves its status, prestige increases. Increased prestige attracts better qualified members to the profession, and top talent not only helps the professional prestige but causes concern among citizens to improve faculty status and benefits.

The fourth point is a matter of one college district trying to stay equal to if not ahead of its neighboring districts. Competition has always helped to improve any business or profession for, in the scramble for the best quality, benefits become a vital lure. A keen competition speaks well for benefits, of career motivation and satisfaction of junior college teachers (92).

The fifth point covers the negotiations that are conducted between faculty and administration and boards. A few years ago faculty lacked power to direct and control their benefits and other matters, but today in many states faculty power groups can virtually share equally in controlling decisions that affect them. Among other goals, faculty naturally influence the establishment of better benefits for themselves.

Teaching benefits may develop rapidly when they are undergirded by state law. Rather than evolving slowly and haphazardly, district by district, minimums in salary or maximums in teaching load may be spelled out specifically through state recommendations, such as those of the Department of Education in Maryland (225:2) or the Texas Higher Education Coordination Act. Texas, for example, spells out carefully a number of recommended faculty benefits in Section 14 of its 1965 Act (167).

We have suggested that competition for teachers is produced by the increasingly complex needs of an advancing civilization and by its demands for society's more capable people for the task of teaching. The effects of this competition are many; benefits attract top intellectual talent to the profession, serve to give teachers greater security and happiness, and produce a finer educational program to enhance the growth and development for all citizens in all walks of life. In the following pages, we shall examine some of the effects of these benefits.

Salaries

Perhaps the most significant benefit in any profession is the pay for one's service, although this should never be the only consideration. Teaching salaries have risen steadily throughout the nation for a considerable number of years. Early in our country's history, teachers worked for hardly more than room and board. In the 1940's, starting salaries averaged from $2,000 to $3,000 a year. In the 1960's, starting salaries were double those of the earlier period.

As teachers gain on-the-job experience today, their salaries continue to increase each year through a regular system of increments which extend to about 12 or 14 years. The result is that teachers can presently earn as much as $15,000 to $20,000 a year, depending upon the type and wealth of a district. A 1966 report by the NEA Research Department indicated that Alaska, California, New York, and Connecticut, in that order, led the nation in average salaries of classroom teachers, the high annual average being close to $10,000. In 1969 this average crept close to $12,000. On the other hand, administrators, especially superintendents or college presidents, usually earn twice or three times as much as the average teacher. In the largest institutions, the top officials may earn more than $40,000 annually. Clearly, education has made tremendous advancements in salaries as compared to those of a generation ago.

What about junior college teaching salaries? There is, of course, a great deal of variation among the states. Almost every salary study, including our own survey, indicates that prestige universities lead the way in the establishment of high salaries. Universities are followed in order by the various types of colleges, high schools, and elementary schools. Although not based on a complete sample, our 1967–68 survey revealed that junior college salaries ranged from $5,000 to $15,000, the average being about $9,000. Teachers in private colleges averaged about $1,500 less than those in public institutions, although exceptions existed. States which had the largest numbers of junior colleges tended to have higher salaries than those with the least numbers. Geographically, colleges in the South tended to fare less well than those in other regions. However, one must remember that the cost of living is slightly less in that section of our nation. Those wanting rather complete and current reports on salaries might turn to the National Education Association and such publications as *Faculty Salary Schedules in Public Community-Junior Colleges* (108).

Teachers have certain other benefits which are closely related to salaries. Some of the following criteria are standard; others are not yet universal among the states.

1. There is no differentiation between men and women in salary schedules.

2. Employees proved to be wrongfully discharged are paid all salaries withheld from them during any dispute.

3. Teachers ordered to military duty are paid at least a full month's salary at the termination of employment; these teachers' positions are guaranteed to them upon their return from service for at least one year if non-tenured teachers and for permanent status if they are tenured teachers.

4. Salary deductions are permitted for such items as retirement, organizational dues, insurance premiums, and community fund donations.

5. Salary payments may be extended to twelve months for ten months of employment; in these cases, the district withholds a percentage of each monthly salary for two equal installments for August and September.

6. Those who begin their teaching at the beginning of the second semester are paid no less than one-half the annual compensation for that position.

7. Each salary payment for any calendar month shall be paid no later than the fifth day of the succeeding calendar month.

8. Part-time contract teachers for the regular day program are paid the appropriate, corresponding percentage of the annual salary for that position; i.e., if an instructor is on a 50 percent schedule of work, he is paid one-half the annual salary he would have received had he been working full-time.

9. There is no differentiation in rate of compensation between night teaching and day teaching when night classes constitute part of the full-time load for a teacher.

10. Instructors are paid for school holidays, sick leaves, sabbaticals and other such absences as may be excusable under prevailing laws. (See *Leaves From Duty*, p. 40)

While each junior college district has the freedom to establish its own salary schedule within the restrictions found in certain state laws, schedules are basically similar. Typical is the following sample schedule in use by one college during the 1969–70 school year:

A Sample Junior College Salary Schedule for the Year 1969–70

Step	I. B.A. or Equiv.	II. M.A. or Equiv.	III. M.A. plus 30 hours	IV. M.A. plus 50 hours	V. Earned Doctorate
1.	$ 7,700	$ 8,220	$ 8,740	$ 9,260	$ 9,780
2.	8,170	8,690	9,210	9,730	10,250
3.	8,640	9,160	9,680	10,200	10,720
4.	9,110	9,630	10,150	10,670	11,190
5.	9,580	10,100	10,620	11,140	11,660
6.	10,050	10,570	11,090	11,610	12,130
7.	10,520	11,040	11,560	12,080	12,600
8.	10,990	11,510	12,030	12,550	13,070
9.	11,460	11,980	12,500	13,020	13,540
10.	11,930	12,450	12,970	13,490	14,010
11.	——	12,920	13,440	13,960	14,480
12.	——	——	13,910	14,430	14,950
13.	——	——	——	14,900	15,420

Our sample is a *single salary schedule,* that which is based on education and experience rather than on merit or a professional ranking system. Almost all schools except senior colleges and universities use this kind of schedule. The steps represent the number of years of teaching, and the columns represent the amount of educational training. In virtually every state, people with industrial, technical, and vocational field work experience are placed in the columns which most nearly equal their experience, whether or not they have the academic degrees. The word *equivalent,* applied sometimes to all columns of the schedule, means the amount of field experience which would equal the degrees. In a few states, these instructors are issued vocational-technical credentials (certificates) which automatically equate experience with training and degrees.

The sample shows that a teacher with at least a master's degree can reach maximum salary in his column in twelve years; furthermore, the schedule provides him with an incentive to take further training and course work. For the new teacher, most schools and junior colleges will grant credit for three to five years of previous teaching experience in another district; military experience is also often counted in this computation. With five years of acceptable previous experience, the new teacher in a district would start on the sixth step of the schedule and in the column or class paralleling his course work and degrees.

Class V, the earned doctorate,* provides an attraction for teachers with this degree to elect the junior college (with its unique advantages) over the senior college and university (with many pressures for publication and research). If the teacher with a doctorate wants to be rewarded solely for his teaching, he usually goes to the CJC, where he receives his automatic increments to maximum salary. There he does not have to face the frustrating, often political game of waiting years for the chance of salary promotions under an academic ranking system of payment.

According to Freiberger and Crawford (122), academic rank was introduced by Tacoma Park Junior College and Los Angeles City College. While it is used by a growing number of junior colleges, according to Harrington (155), it is often used apart from the regular schedule. In other words, merit pay (the academic rank system) may be an additional reward above and beyond the basic single salary schedule. In some cases (chiefly the independent junior colleges), the ranking system has no relationship to salary but only to years of service. For instance, a teacher may be classified as an instructor until he gains tenure, and then he becomes an assistant professor; after the seventh year (the usual sabbatical year), he becomes an associate professor. Full professors may then be named through a merit system which may or may not be associated with salary. This system appears to be a workable compromise between the prevailing CJC system and the ranking system of the senior colleges and universities. In their own eyes, CJC teachers deserve the title of "professor" as much as their counterparts in lower-division instruction in the other colleges and universities. Tillery provides a discussion of the perils and promises of academic rank for junior college instructors (366).

As a final note on this section, we suggest that salaries will continue to rise for a number of years in an expanding economy. There is little reason to doubt that many CJC teachers in the 1970's will earn more than $20,000 a year. Considering the purchasing power of the dollar during the 1960's and the salaries being earned by others with comparable training and experience, this figure should already prevail. Regardless of dollar values and progress made in other professions, however, CJC salaries will probably always remain a couple of steps behind the maximums at the wealthier universities.

Retirement

Along with salary is a second important benefit, teacher retirement, because one must think of the future as well as the present. Our survey

* Many schedules place the doctorate allowance in a footnote rather than among the schedules' columns.

showed that virtually all states protect CJC teachers through state retirement systems or private equivalent programs. Some of these states, such as Maryland and Minnesota, supplement teacher retirement programs with federal social security.

The method of retirement participation calls for monthly contributions by the employee (deducted from salary warrants) and similar contributions by the local district or the state. The amount of retirement pay is determined largely by the number of years the teacher has credited to him in the retirement system, the amount of contributions he has made, and a consideration of the salary earned during his teaching career. Each state is different in the way its retirement system operates. Several sample plans were received in our survey, but many of these outdate themselves rapidly. As a measure in comparing various state plans, however, one might expect to retire at approximately half the salary made in the highest salary years. Fifty percent retirement pay, of course, would demand a career of roughly thirty years of teaching service. If we project to the time when top salaries reach $20,000 per year, it is not unpleasant to think of half of this as retirement pay for each year of remaining life.

Certification, Employment, and Tenure

Specific requirements related to this section are discussed in the next chapter pertaining to the securing of employment. Here, we are concerned only with your rights and privileges as guaranteed by state laws. Collectively, legal provisions concerning certification, employment, and tenure furnish excellent protection for the teacher. However, the truth is that all states have such laws affecting elementary and secondary staffs, but very few of these laws are extended to protect teachers in higher education. Our survey showed that only a few states—Oregon, Washington, Arizona, Kansas, Florida, Missouri, California, and possibly several others—have laws which affect the welfare of junior college teachers. In most states policies relating to this section are left to the individual employing institutions in higher education. While most states lack certification laws affecting junior college teachers, some of these same states do have laws pertaining to CJC employment and tenure rights. In this section, then, we shall discuss standards and criteria in general terms without specific reference to individual states.

Certification requirements in a state include certain rights. If a teacher qualifies for a teaching certificate or credentials, he is issued one by the appropriate state agency. The chief step is the proper application to the agency's office. If the teacher is refused a certificate or if he is dissatisfied with any action taken by the agency, he ordinarily has the right of appeal. With proper evidence an appeal could reverse the decision of the agency. In the case of revocation or suspension of a certificate, the teacher normally has the right of a hearing for the presentation of his side of the case. The hearing is held before a county or state board in most cases. If he has been further denied his petition, the teacher may institute court proceedings. Another protection may be that certificates which expire while the holder is engaged in military and other service during war continue in force for a period of time (six months or so) after the holder honorably leaves such service or has been placed on inactive duty.

While teachers enjoy certain rights when certified by a state, let us not forget the underlying purpose of state certification: It is designed essentially for the protection of students. The prevailing educational philosophy, promoted and adopted by educators and the public alike, is that children from kindergarten through high school should not be exposed to incompetent, unqualified, and possibly harmful teachers. By licensing teachers for the public schools, the states help to maintain a higher quality of teachers and public instruction. The same philosophy and actions have not been extended to most institutions in higher education, probably because of the strong feeling that college students, being more mature and adult, can cope more easily with occasionally inadequate instruction. A further reason is linked with the traditional academic freedom enjoyed by higher institutions of learning. Even in the few states which certify junior college teachers, there are many proponents of the abolition of junior college teacher certification.

To understand your employment and tenure rights, you must understand the difference between the terms *probationary* and *permanent*. A probationary teacher is one who has taught in a school district for two or three years, depending upon the state involved. If he is hired for the next year beyond this probationary period, usually the fourth year, he is considered a permanent teacher, one who has "tenure." Tenure usually cannot be transferred to another school, unless the other school is part of the same district or administrative organization of colleges. In a new district, the teacher would return to probationary status and work his way once more into tenure status. The chief difference between probation and tenure is that the latter assures the teacher of more protection against dismissal.

In most states you have the right to be employed as early as January first for the ensuing school year. You have a right to expect a written rather than an oral contract, for the signed document affords equal protection to you and the hiring district. The district cannot discharge you during the contract year except for cause, and you cannot resign during this period without the consent of the district. The contract should include certain details, such as the amount of annual salary, the number of months of service, and the general area of your duties. During the contract year, the district may re-assign you to other duties or subjects, your chief protection being that you must not be assigned to duties which you are not legally qualified to handle. Remember, moreover, it is not in the district's best interest to have a teacher function in an area for which he is unqualified. In the case of contracts to administrators, the district can legally re-assign an administrator to teaching duties. If the administrator is a permanent employee, he has tenure only as a teacher.

Probationary teachers are notified of their re-employment at least by May 15 in most states. Within a set period of time after this notice of election, the teacher must signify his acceptance or rejection of the offer. The teacher accepts his re-election by signing the new contract and rejects it by returning it unsigned. An accompanying letter of resignation is optional on the teacher's part. The only time he would *need* to resign is during a contract year or when he has permanent status. After accepting and signing a permanent contract, the teacher is automatically re-employed each year. Up to July 1, in most cases, he can resign this position without board approval; after July 1, approval is necessary.

Only a few states have statutory tenure laws protecting junior college teachers; tenure policies are left to the individual institutions in most states. Under the circumstances, it is difficult to determine standards in the computation of service credited toward tenure. In general, a probationary year of service should consist of at least 75 percent of the number of days the regular schools of the district are maintained. An interruption of teaching for military service should not change one's status in a district if and when the teacher returns to it.

Statutory laws pertaining to the dismissal of teachers do not cover junior college teachers in many states. Even without this kind of protection, permanent teachers, in particular, normally cannot be dismissed without the most exact kind of evidence. A college board has the burden of proof, and the teacher may fight his case through the courts. His cause, if valid, may be championed by various state or national teachers' associations. The American Association of University Professors, which junior college teachers may join, is one such national group.

The grounds for dismissal of a permanent teacher may include such charges as immoral or unprofessional conduct, aiding or advocating the commission of criminal acts, dishonesty, incompetence, unfitness for service, physical or mental conditions unfitting a teacher to associate with students, persistent violation or refusal to obey college laws, conviction of a felony or crime involving moral turpitude, violation of certain sections of state codes, and membership or activities in subversive groups.

Various permanent teacher dismissal cases on record show that the odds of winning are in favor of the accused instructor. In cases of dismissal for incompetence, a board must prove that it has warned the teacher of the incompetence and has furnished him with an opportunity to correct his faults and overcome his problem. In cases of dismissal for mental disability, a board cannot or should not act until the subject has been examined by a recognized psychiatrist. Although the teacher must submit to the examination, he may have his own psychiatrist or physician present at the examination. These and other difficulties surrounding the dismissal of permanent teachers undoubtedly prompt many school boards to take occasionally an easier route: that of keeping the teacher but making life so miserable for him that he may ultimately resign.

As stated previously, probationary teachers lack certain dismissal rights enjoyed by tenured teachers. While probationary teachers can be dismissed rather easily at the end of a school year, normally they cannot be dismissed *during* the school year except for cause, in which case they have the same kind of protection given to tenured teachers. When dismissed at the end of a school year, probationary teachers may request and receive a written statement of the reasons for dismissal. The stated reasons should relate solely to the welfare of the schools and students thereof. Sometimes the board may grant the teacher a hearing. In very large districts, a hearing officer (a qualified neutral) may preside over the meeting.

In almost all cases, probationary teachers lack the right of judicial review on the question of the sufficiency of reasons for dismissal. Actually, a dismissal of a probationary employee at the end of his contract year is not so much a dismissal as a refusal to rehire or recontract. It is probably true that most teachers accept the opportunity to resign before the end of the contract rather than be disgraced by dismissal or open board hearings concerning dismissal. Occasionally, this acceptance may be unfortunate, because if he knows that his case is just, the teacher should face up to his professional responsibility to help rid a district of injustices against himself and other teachers. Although distressing, sometimes a public hearing is worthwhile and even advantageous to the profession.

Leaves from Duty

You should already be familiar with school holidays and periodic time off in the school year, to be enjoyed by students and teachers alike. Perhaps no other profession can boast of as many holiday leave benefits as does teaching. However, tradition alone is not a sufficient reason for the continuation of holiday leaves. The chief reason stems from an understanding of the nature of teaching and learning. Both activities involve a rigorous taxing of the mind, and research of these activities has shown that both teachers and students function more proficiently with intermittent relief from their mental activities. Mental vigor can be renewed and strengthened more easily, not from constant strain but by these frequent breaks in continuity. Another way to regard holiday leaves is that they are appropriate compensating factors for teachers, receiving as they do salaries somewhat less than is normal for other professions requiring similar preparation.

Community and junior colleges operate generally on the same schedules as do the elementary and secondary schools. The normal opening time is the day or week after Labor Day in the fall, and the normal closing time is the end of May or the first or second week of June. Senior colleges and universities, on the other hand, usually open a week later in the fall and close a week earlier in the spring. Only a few two-year colleges, chiefly branches of senior colleges and universities, follow the same schedules of these higher institutions.

Teaching contracts are normally for ten months duration (September 1 to July 1), although actual employment time is closer to nine and a half months. The nine-month or ten-month contract gives the teacher a long summer when he can earn further credits in a university, accept other employment as a diversion, travel, engage in independent study or writing, or simply loaf. Most junior colleges operate their own summer schools for six weeks or more, in which case the teacher may wish to earn extra income through summer teaching at his own school. Even with summer school, most institutions close down instruction for part or all of August. Becoming more prevalent is the quarter system or year round operation in which teachers are given one quarter for their vacation period, not necessarily the summer quarter.

Official holiday leaves are set by the various state education codes or by local mandates. Two weeks usually are allowed for Christmas vacation and one week for Easter vacation. In many cases, a district allows its teachers one or two days (of no classes) between fall and spring semesters or between quarters. Colleges may (mandatory under some state laws) allow affected teachers to be absent for certain religious holidays not included in the official holiday calendar.

Teachers are granted short leaves of absence if a member of the immediate family should become critically ill or die. Immediate family members include mother, father, husband, wife, son, daughter, brother, or sister. Sometimes the leave is granted for other near relatives living within the immediate household. Short leaves for bereavement or critical illness may be granted with pay; an extension of the leave normally results in loss of pay.

Our survey showed that the majority of states have no uniform statutory laws affecting junior college sick leaves, such policies in most states being left to local districts. At least ten states had sick leave laws affecting CJC teachers during 1967. These laws included the grant of so many sick leave days per year, accumulative indefinitely in some states. At least one allowed the teacher to transfer his sick leave to another district within the state.

When a teacher is absent from his school duties because of illness, he is paid full salary for each day of earned sick leave he has coming to him.

If his illness extends beyond his accumulated sick leave days, he may, in some cases, be paid the difference between full salary and what is paid to his substitute; such a benefit may not exceed a certain period of time in these cases. Many districts require that illnesses be verified by a doctor.

A sabbatical leave is that which is granted normally after six or seven years of employment in one college. The leave may be for one-half year at full salary or one full year at half salary in most cases. A board sometimes may provide that the leave be taken in separate six-month periods when a year's leave is requested; in this case a divided one-year leave is completed generally within a three-year period. Salary payments for the most part are provided on the same monthly basis as for the remainder of the college staff. A sabbatical leave policy may require the teacher to furnish the college district with a suitable bond indemnifying the board against loss in the event the teacher fails to render at least two years' service in the district following the return of the teacher from his leave. Sabbaticals may be granted more than once to the same teacher as long as he has completed the required years of service between such sabbaticals.

In the United States, approximately one-third of the two-year colleges have sabbatical leave plans in operation, according to Litton's survey (219). His study revealed that nearly half of the public junior colleges granted sabbatical leave; of the non-public junior colleges responding, less than one-fifth had sabbatical leaves in operation. Six states—Michigan, New York, Pennsylvania, Illinois, Washington, and California—accounted for 65 percent of the colleges reporting sabbaticals (273). Our survey indicated that these leaves were largely a matter of local policy rather than state mandates.

Sabbaticals are allowed for such purposes as self-improvement through study, research, or approved travel. Of prime importance is that sabbatical leaves should result in increased benefit to the college students who are to be taught by the teacher when he returns. It is not intended that sabbaticals be used for personal purposes nor for mere pleasure or vacations but to increase the proficiency and competency of the instructor and to bring more excellent instruction to the college program.

A leave of absence for one or two semesters may be taken by permanent and probationary teachers by making application in writing to the college board and receiving its approval. While such leaves normally are granted without pay, a particular college could decide to pay the teacher the difference between his regular pay and that of his substitute. Some acceptable reasons for the ordinary leave of absence are (1) improvement of impaired health, (2) graduate study or research, (3) exchange teaching or teaching in an overseas institution, (4) military service when the teacher is drafted or called to duty, and sometimes (5) extensive travel for educational purposes, (6) pregnancy, (7) jury duty, and other reasons.

Insurance

Some states provide insurance programs for CJC teachers. Perhaps the most common state program is industrial accident and illness insurance. Monies deposited in a state compensation insurance fund cover teachers free of charge. If the teacher suffers any kind of personal injury while in the performance of his school duties, his expenses are paid by this kind of policy. A state's labor code may require that the teacher be provided with disability indemnity for expenses connected with the injury and for any resulting accident or illness leave.

All public and private CJC teachers should have access to some form of group hospital insurance, which is much cheaper than an individual policy. Group insurance plans are sponsored by a local or state faculty association, by a national organization such as the National Education Association, or by an association of teachers in one subject area. Such group programs usually require that a certain percentage of a college faculty become members before the group plan is put into effect. District contributions stabilize health insurance plans and often result in lower premiums. Other group programs, besides health and hospital insurance, are available usually for those interested in income protection, life insurance, home insurance, all-coverage insurance for personal effects, and automobile insurance.

Related closely to insurance protection are the many local and state federal credit unions for teachers. As a member of a teachers' credit union, you can secure various types of loans, often with automatic insurance which pays off the loans in case of the member's death. Most of these unions include savings accounts that earn favorable interest rates. Other services of a credit union may include a mutual fund for teacher investments, a special services program which offers discounts in the purchase of goods and services, and perhaps an automatic professional liability policy which protects teachers from law suits arising from responsibilities in teaching.

Professional Memberships

Aside from a membership in the National Education Association, the teacher's strongest professional membership may be in his own state teachers association, normally affiliated with NEA. Belonging to these two associations is more of an obligation than a requirement, although some colleges may exert pressure upon a teacher to obtain these memberships. Professional membership in general and subject-oriented associations sometimes includes many special benefits not necessarily given to nonmembers. All teachers, however, have an ethical responsibility to support their national and state teachers' associations, and the greatest support can be given through membership.

In lieu of or along with membership in state and national NEA groups, the teacher has the right to join the somewhat contrasting American Federation of Teachers, AFL–CIO. Both the AFT and the NEA work continuously toward the betterment of teachers and education but differ strongly in some of the methods used in reaching their goals. The AFT generally is more inclined to be amenable to teacher pickets and strikes than is the NEA. The latter's position is that teachers should continue working, whatever the problem, while professional negotiations are carried on with local and state authorities for teacher, student, and school improvements. In the 1968 national convention of NEA, delegates passed a resolution which softened the policy on teacher strikes. You, the teacher, must decide where your loyalties lie and which of the two groups you should join if only one membership is desired.

Some memberships at the state and national levels are limited to college teachers. At the national level is the American Association of University Professors, 1785 Massachusetts Avenue, N.W., Washington, D.C. The association's name is somewhat misleading, for membership is open to college as well as university faculties and to instructors as well as professors. The organization was formed in 1915 with a charter membership of 1,362 full professors. Membership in 1969 included over 90,000 college and university teachers of all ranks and 1,143 local chapters on various campuses. A constituent member of the American Council of Education, the association's aims are to defend academic freedom and tenure rights, to improve faculty salaries and fringe benefits, to maintain academic and professional standards, and to promote faculty roles in college and university government. Its main publication is a quarterly magazine, the *AAUP Bulletin*. The first president of the association was the distinguished educator John Dewey.

Another national association, although not designed strictly for individual faculty membership, is the American Association of Junior Colleges, with headquarters at 1315 16th Street, N.W., Washington, D.C. The association is organized primarily for institutional membership, but it serves a valuable purpose for junior college faculties as well. Along with publication of research and related information pertaining to the two-year college in the United States, the association produces a monthly *Junior College Journal* to which faculty may subscribe.

A recently organized association is the National Faculty Association of Community and Junior Colleges. Affiliated with the National Education Association, this organization restricts its membership to teaching faculty. Its purpose is to advance faculty interests, and it invites membership from both public and private institutions. It has headquarters at 1201 16th St., N.W., Washington, D.C.

The American Association for Higher Education is a national organization open both to teaching and administrative faculty. It has members from every type of higher education institution, not only in the United States but in many foreign countries as well. The AAHE is also an affiliate of the National Education Association. Its mailing address is the same as that of NFACJC.

At the state level there are many associations for two-year college personnel. These state associations tend to do locally what the AAUP and the AAJC do nationally. As indicated in our national survey results, only three states reportedly had associations of junior college faculties in 1968: California, Minnesota, and Texas. Seventeen states reported state institutional associations. Thirty-three states did not indicate any existing junior college associations. In general, faculty associations are more inclined to work toward improving the lot of junior college teachers than are the more general associations.

State organizations are understandably most effective at state level, because they commonly maintain liaison with members of the state legislature and often act as communication channels, voicing the attitudes and opinions of their members. State organizations tend to be less effective nationally, because they represent but one voice in fifty. Consequently, the national organizations frequently serve as reservoirs of fact and opinion related to national legislation. At both state and national levels the concentrated voices of higher education are greater than that afforded to one individual.

Along with considering membership in these associations, you should belong to the professional group organized around your special area of teaching. The combination of all of your professional memberships should bring you personal stimulation, advancement, and enlightenment as well as many more impersonal benefits which generally improve your profession.

Miscellaneous Benefits

The benefits discussed so far are of major importance to most teachers, but there are many other miscellaneous benefits worth mentioning. One of these is the opportunity to teach, a factor considered greater in the CJC than in any other level of higher education. Marsee says, "It is generally understood that junior colleges are teaching institutions—not research centers. It is true that faculties of junior colleges are not 'research oriented,' compared to faculties of four-year colleges and universities. One of the attractive features of the junior colleges is that instructors are not confronted with the frustrations of progression through the system of 'publish or perish'" (227:25).

Another concern of teachers is academic freedom. It is important to note that there is no clause in the Constitution which guarantees a teacher the right of academic freedom, although the 'reserved to the states' doctrine of the Tenth Amendment may imply this right. College boards have the power and obligation to determine the nature and extent of academic freedom in their institutions. Most colleges have protected this freedom for teachers. McKenney establishes the fact that "there is evidence to assume that academic freedom on the college level is becoming broader and more respected" (245:6).

Of course, there are limitations upon academic freedom. The AAUP 1940 statement of principles indicates that teachers must relate their use of controversy to their subjects and, in effect, must instruct rather than persuade. The teacher is also warned that when he is speaking in the community, he must make it clear that he is acting as a citizen rather than an institutional spokesman, as the public may judge his profession and his institution by his utterances. The point is also made that "limitations of academic freedom because of religious or other aims of the institution should be clearly stated in writing at the time of the appointment." Academic freedom varies with the region or state. Branch colleges and extension centers may have the same freedom as their parent institutions. Urban area colleges are more permissive than rural area colleges. Church colleges tend to restrict freedom in relationship to aims. Public community colleges, if locally controlled, have conservative tendencies.

Clark reports advantages or benefits of CJC teaching in his study of San Jose (California) Junior College teachers (60:125). He cites the following: (1) age level of students, greater maturity, (2) voluntary enrollments, (3) relative academic freedom, (4) greater depth of subject matter usage, (5) opportunities to help students who are undirected, (6) more interest from students, (7) more business-like students, and (8) absence of discipline problems, compared to high schools.

Blocker and his colleagues list somewhat different advantages and benefits (29:156): (1) part of a dynamic movement, (2) opportunities for experimental teaching, (3) no doctorates required, (4) status in the community, (5) less supervision and control than elementary and secondary teachers have, (6) opportunities for promotion, (7) stimulating teacher-student relationships, (8) good pay, (9) opportunities to enter university teaching, (10) opportunities to work on doctorates while teaching, and (11) participation in shaping a new image of an expanding community college.

Sometimes considered a benefit is the faculty teaching load, which is almost always smaller than loads at lower levels of instruction. In the area of faculty load, Maryland standards say, "The size of the classes and the teaching load of the individual instructor must be such as to promote both effective teaching and effective learning. Effective teaching requires that the instructor have ample time for preparation (including both general reading and specialized study), correction of papers, conferences with individual students, participation in non-classroom responsibilities both at the institution and in the community and recreation" (230:2). The Maryland State Department of Education considers the standard teaching load to be about 15 hours, with lab or shop teachers not assigned ordinarily beyond 20 to 22 standard class periods per week.

Our college-faculty survey revealed an overall average load of credit hours per week as exactly 14, with averages starting at 13.2 for composition and literature teachers to 14.9 for mathematics and social science teachers. The overall contact hours per week were 15.4, with averages starting at 14 for health education teachers to 17 for music teachers. As for numbers of students assigned to teachers, the overall average was 145 per term. Music and engineering teachers averaged 103 students as the lowest figures, while social science teachers had the highest average at 232 students per teacher per term. Although the samples were small, these figures are in line with prevailing standards found in most states.

Discussed frequently in junior college literature is the benefit to part-time junior college teaching by full-time employees in such business and professional jobs as research science, merchandising management, operation analysis, construction and management engineering, social work, research chemistry, aerospace technology, internal revenue, biological oceanography, commercial art, naval astronomy, and personnel management (213). Kennedy reports a study of 935 part-time staff members in Illinois and Maryland junior colleges and indicates that the extent of this opportunity is very wide (202).

The regular staff can also find in the junior college extra remuneration from night and summer school teaching, from voluntary research and publication projects, and from consulting services.

The Status of Benefits

The most complete and recent studies of benefits were two doctoral dissertations completed at Florida State University in 1967. These companion studies were written by Findley (115) and Roberts (315). Findley studied fringe benefits in private junior colleges, while Roberts covered the same ground in public junior colleges. The researchers covered all the colleges listed in the 1966 Directory with replies from most of the schools. The studies dealt with individual schools rather than with states as a whole. Twenty different fringe benefits were covered in the survey with each one being found in at least a few junior colleges. Although the studies were not available at the time of our compilation of facts, the authors, through Dr. Maurice L. Litton of Florida State University, provided us with summary data. The major benefits are listed here with the percentage of two-year colleges offering them: health insurance (94.0), faculty travel (93.2), retirement (91.3), sick leaves (83.2), major medical insurance (81.3), social security (65.8), life insurance (60.2), leaves without pay (56.1), leaves with pay (48.3), faculty club (33.9), on-campus health services (31.2).

The private and public junior colleges differed considerably in these areas. A greater percentage of public junior colleges offered these services in every case except on-campus health services. The greatest difference was in sick leaves: public, 92.3 percent; private, 58.9 percent.

In conclusion, we can find numerous benefits for junior college teachers, but the Findley and Roberts studies show us they are not all standard among the junior colleges. Nevertheless, every CJC will have *some* form of major and fringe benefits to offer us. They can be yours shortly after you sign a contract to teach in one of the nation's two-year colleges.

Chapter 3

Employment Requirements
and Techniques

Proper counseling of CJC teacher trainees demands orientation into the college setting. Included should be developmental history and teacher benefits and opportunities as well as a thorough investigation into employment requirements and techniques. Paramount, of course, is being enrolled in a junior college teacher training program and matriculating toward the necessary degree for employment. If you happen to be already employed in some technical or vocational field, you may still find it necessary to take some preparatory courses in some college or university.

Those persons aspiring for administrative positions must accumulate several years of successful teaching experience. Subsequently they can enroll in junior college leadership programs, such as those offered by Teachers College of Columbia University, University of Florida, Florida State University, University of Texas, University of California, Stanford University, and the University of Southern California. Typical programs lead to an Ed.D. or Ph.D. with a major in higher education allowing full-time or part-time study while professionally employed.

Junior college teacher training programs did not appear until after 1950. In that year, not a single college or university offered a preparation program for junior college teachers (398). By 1955, at least 23 institutions were reportedly offering such programs (70). In 1969, at least 100 extensive programs were offered in various institutions. In that year, for instance, on a half-million dollar grant by the Ford Foundation, the St. Louis Junior College District and Southern Illinois University were cooperating on an internship for teachers. The University of Southern California had cooperating programs with many junior colleges in the Los Angeles area.

An examination of the college catalog for an institution should reveal the depth and scope of the curricula in junior college education.

Employment requirements and techniques to be discussed in this chapter include the following: state certification requirements, training, experience, personal qualities and attitudes, placement offices, selecting a college, written applications, interviews, and adjustments after employment.

State Certification Requirements

A state teaching *certificate*, sometimes called *credential*, is a license which asserts that a state has examined a teacher's qualifications and has found him eligible to teach at a specified level and in a specified subject area within the public, parochial, or private schools of the state. All states require public elementary and secondary staffs to be certified by the appropriate agency within each state. Some others also require certification for teachers in public junior colleges, public kindergartens and nursery schools, and parochial and private schools.

In states requiring junior college teaching certificates, teachers generally follow similar certification requirements. These requirements may include United States citizenship, oath of allegiance or loyalty, securement of employment, recommendation by a college or employing officer, a specific age requirement (usually eighteen years), a fee requirement, a general health certificate, a chest X ray, and a special course requirement. An example of the latter requirement is a successful course credit or an examination on the Constitution of the United States. Professional education courses and directed teaching are also frequently required. The lowest degree requirement normally is the bachelor's degree, although a master's degree often is an employment prerequisite. Additional conditions for the credential may include identification cards with physical description and fingerprints; evidence of good moral character, such as a letter from a church leader; and, of course, college and university transcripts of courses taken and degrees earned or an official letter from the higher institution (acceptable to the state) verifying the amount of work and degrees taken.

In 1968, at least six states required the oath of allegiance or loyalty, although this requirement has lately been questioned in the courts. Typical is the California oath required of teachers:

> I solemnly swear (or affirm) that I will support the Constitution of the United States of America, the Constitution of the State of California, and the laws of the United States and the State of California, and will by precept and example, promote respect for the Flag and the statutes of the United States and of the State of California, reverence for law and order, and undivided allegiance to the Government of the United States of America (Section 61, California School Code).

This oath may be taken before any person authorized to administer oaths or before a member of the governing board of a school district or county district. Citizens from other countries must vow to support the institutions and policies of the United States during their period of employment within the state. The State Board of Education suspends or revokes a certificate upon the violation of any part of the oath.

Schools usually discharge teachers and states usually deny, revoke, or suspend teaching certificates on such grounds as lack of general qualification, physical disability, addiction to intoxicating beverages, addiction to narcotics or habit-forming drugs, moral turpitude, certification document previously revoked, practice of deception or fraud in the application, failure to show good moral character, conviction of certain offenses as defined in a penal code, and evidence of being a sex offender or a sexual psychopath.

Teaching certificates are classified usually as *regular* (standard) or *special*. A regular certificate is that one normally required for teachers of academic subjects. The special certificate is that one normally issued in trade and industrial education. The former emphasizes degrees and academic training, while the latter emphasizes successful experience in the trades or industry as the usual prerequisite. The special certificate may be called a technical or vocational credential, although some states also issue special certificates to librarians, guidance counselors, teachers of special subjects, teachers of handicapped children, school psychologists, and so on. In those states requiring certification, junior college administrators normally must have an administrative credential. Both teaching and administrative credentials are issued for definite periods of time, up to five years in some cases and for life where life diplomas are granted.

Teachers who do not qualify for the regular or special certificate sometimes are issued temporary credentials to teach in a state. Emergency certificates may be issued at times when an employing officer or superintendent-president cannot find a qualified teacher and recommends to the state that a particular candidate be granted the temporary certificate for the current year only. While the teacher may receive his certificate when there is a need for his services, he must agree to qualify for his regular certificate within a specified period of time.

Because certification requirements vary among the states, you should become familiar with your prospective state before proceeding too far into your educational preparation for CJC teaching. Counseling may be lacking in this area, and you may consult such references as *A Manual on Certification Requirements for School Personnel in the United States* (12) and *Requirements for Certification of Teachers, Counselors, Librarians, Administrators for Elementary Schools, Secondary Schools and Junior Colleges* (397). Both of these books are revised periodically.

Training

Perhaps the most significant philosophy in this text is that junior college teaching differs appreciably from teaching at other levels (185:216). The major differences involve not only the age and type of students and particular institutional functions but also the degree and amount of teacher preparation needed. The typical junior college teacher needs greater depth of subject matter than the typical high school teacher needs. And he requires greater breadth in a field of knowledge than does the typical college-university teacher. He is like the medical surgeon who has greater knowledge than the general practitioner but does not specialize in any one type of surgical operation. In short, his level of training must be different from and approximately midway between that required of high school and college-university teachers.

In 1949 the American Council on Education reported that either knowledge or experience in the following areas were needed in the preservice preparation of junior college teachers: (1) philosophy and background of junior colleges, (2) growth and development and special problems of junior college students, (3) curriculum construction and the art and science of effective instruction, (4) supervised teaching in the junior college, (5) understanding of the occupational and general education services in the junior college, (6) occupational competence for occupational instructors, and (7) training in a special and broad teaching field for academic or general education teachers (384:11-13).

These needs remain virtually unchanged today. On the subject of preparation of junior college teachers, the Garrison study noted that faculty themselves expressed needs in virtually all seven areas; the study was released in 1967 (126:70-74). Many states express similar needs. Arizona, for example, currently has requirements covering the seven areas. Among other things, the state required for the junior college certificate certain professional education courses, special junior college courses, and practice teaching that would enhance the teacher's proficiency at the junior college level (10). Charles and Summerer (57), Maul (232), Blocker (26), among several others, provide insight into the needed training of junior college teachers.

Findings seem to indicate little change in the necessary training programs in the last twenty years, but another view is expressed by one private college dean who wrote in a letter to us, "In general, we do not want special training for junior college teachers. Good liberal arts training, the necessary degrees, and the enthusiasm, ability and motivation for teaching in a four-year or a two-year liberal arts institution remain our criterion for teachers" (336).

Virtually all junior colleges in the nation are free to require teacher training above the minimum requirements set by accrediting agencies and state certification laws. One may be allowed to teach with only a baccalaureate degree in most states, but the master's degree for teaching academic subjects is today's standard for CJC employment. Post-graduate work beyond the master's degree is favorably acknowledged, but the majority of junior colleges are not searching strenuously for people with the doctorate. The feeling is strong that doctors of philosophy or education, because their programs have been organized traditionally, are too narrowly specialized to offer much or to find satisfaction in teaching courses at the freshman and sophomore levels (126:70). Junior college teachers secure doctoral degrees more for personal satisfaction and professional growth and advancement than for any practical need for CJC teaching.*

In preparing for his college degrees, the teacher majors and minors in academic subject areas, professional fields, or vocational-technical programs in which he wishes to teach. Academic subject areas include the natural sciences, social sciences (usually other than education and educational methodology), humanities, mathematics, fine arts, or other subject areas equivalent to those of an academic subject. Preparation is completed usually in graduate schools of arts and sciences. Professional schools are the sources of teachers in nursing, library, business, social work, agriculture, engineering, and education.

A third type of junior college teacher, found more frequently in larger community colleges with diversified offerings, is the one who gains most of his knowledge from experience rather than from university courses and degree programs. He teaches the vocational-technical subjects in such areas as auto mechanics, building construction, cosmetology, and drafting. He may or may not have earned a degree from technical-vocational schools in colleges and universities.

In addition to becoming a scholar who has mastered a subject area or a craftsman who has mastered a skill, the junior college teacher also needs specific preparation and training in the art and sciences of teaching his subject (126:70-71). If superior teaching is indeed a prime CJC objective, then the trainee must take certain methodology courses to enhance this goal. He must study the philosophy and methods of teaching and learning, the psychology of junior college age groups, the instructional aids, and testing and measurement. He must cap these practical courses with the most practical of them all—supervised teaching at the junior college level. This on-the-job internship allows him to practice his methodology and theory upon actual students in a two-year college. While some education course requirements for teachers may be virtually useless, as so many have

* As this book went to press, we noted rumblings for a new kind of teaching doctorate for CJC teachers. An example of a doctor of arts degree in teaching was written by Mary Wortham in the December 1967 issue of the *AAUP Bulletin*. Within a few years the new doctorate may be a reality in many university training programs.

claimed, those described here are very significant to success. Common sense should tell us that mastery of a subject does not guarantee a built-in ability to teach it. Some of our greatest scholars have poor reputations as teachers, and some of our greatest teachers have poor reputations as scholars. Our aim is to gain proficiency in *both* scholarship and teaching ability. Chapters Seven and Eight provide discussion of the problems in teaching proficiency.

A third major area of preparation for CJC teaching is the study of the institution itself. In higher education, one should know something of the environment in which he works. We are talking about the history, philosophy, and purpose of higher education, and particularly about the CJC as an institution. The previous chapters have discussed the general development and status of this institution; remaining chapters add additional comment.

Experience

After a trainee completes his educational program, what are his chances of going directly into CJC teaching? The Research Division of the National Education Association reported that in 1959 about 20 percent of the new junior college teachers came directly from graduate schools. Maul's 1965 study shows the percentage to be 23.7 for all junior colleges—23.0 for public and 27.2 for private (232:8). A 1963 study reported that the majority of 2,783 new faculty members in 429 public and private two-year colleges in fifty states and territories had been hired without any previous teaching experience (26). Excellent credentials and recommendations help tremendously. One or more faculty members or administrators may know a recent graduate and recommend him. Perhaps the new graduate attended the junior college for his lower-division work and made a vivid impression upon those who influence or have a hand in hiring. There are many variables which may be advantageous to the new teacher securing a CJC position as his first job.

On the other hand, teaching experience should count heavily in employment, especially if the teacher is equal in training and degrees to other candidates for a position. Most studies show that the largest group of new CJC teachers come directly from high school teaching. For example, new research division studies reported in 1965 that, through eight years of investigation from 1957 through 1965, three of every ten new junior college teachers came from high school positions; the percentage was 32.2 for public and 22.3 for private junior colleges; 17.1 percent came from staffs of colleges and universities, while 11.3 percent came from business and industrial occupational fields. These three groups were the largest as far as experience categories are concerned (23.8). Our own college faculty survey found nearly 50 percent of the respondents had worked previously in high schools.

The use of so many former high school teachers at the junior college level is understandable. College employing officers tend to regard high school teaching as a proving ground for CJC teaching. Both institutions tend to emphasize teaching rather than research and publication. Also, upper classmen in a high school are not far removed from CJC students insofar as their basic characteristics are concerned. Furthermore, high school teachers tend to be more available, more interested in moving into higher enducation where they can often obtain increased professional prestige and teaching benefits. We conclude, however, that those who have taught successfully in a CJC usually get the highest consideration for employment, with senior college and university teachers, high school teachers, and elementary teachers following in order. The most important previous experience, then, is that which employers relate most closely to CJC needs.

Other important employment criteria are the stability of previous teaching experience and the number of years devoted to teaching service. A person who has taught eight years in one school could be considered more stable and qualified than one who has taught a total of twenty years in many different schools. The number of times one has been offered tenure in different schools could be an important criterion to some hiring officials. Teaching experience supplemented by professional or technical-vocation field experience is better than either of these alone, according to many college officials. For instance, a drama teacher with five years of professional theater experience and five years of teaching may have a better chance for a new teaching job than one with ten years of experience in either of these areas alone, other considerations being equal.

Personal Qualities and Attitudes

To secure and hold a CJC position, you need to have certain personal qualities, attitudes, and abilities that are not necessarily guaranteed by training and experience. A study by Endicott shows that personal qualities may be the most important criterion for job securement; of secondary but necessary importance are courses in a major or teaching field, followed by grades in these courses (101:19). Think of yourself as you read the following items, which could be considered as one selected list of "Ten Commandments" for successful junior college teaching.

1. *You must desire and enjoy teaching.* There are hundreds if not thousands of different occupations and professions in our society. Are you positive that teaching is what you want to do through most of your life? Practice teaching should help to provide an answer. If you use teaching merely as a fill-in or stepping stone to *some other* profession, the chances are that you will not be the most effective teacher—or a happy one.

2. *You must prefer teaching a variety of adults, young and old.* Students at these levels are distinctly different. If you teach at the collegiate level

when your interests and aptitudes lie in another level, you may be an unhappy and ineffective teacher.

3. *You must be sold on the values and contributions of junior college education to society.* If you teach in a CJC without being convinced that it is serving a worthwhile purpose in education and that it should have as much respect and value as any other type of college, you may be discontented and ineffective.

4. *You must like a community college atmosphere of academic work and life.* Local junior colleges have very close identification with specific communities and therefore generally create a different atmosphere from one surrounding senior colleges and universities. Local two-year colleges are as much a part of communities as are local elementary and secondary schools. Within the academic work and life in the CJC, you should find a suitable academic climate.

5. *You must be reasonably satisfied with the maximum salaries and benefits you can obtain at the two-year college level.* As you discovered in Chapter Two, some teaching benefits are shared by teachers at all levels of education, but some others relate only to the junior college. You cannot make your maximum contribution without being reasonably satisfied with what the CJC can offer to you personally.

6. *You must be dedicated to your task.* You are dedicated if you utilize all of your energies and enthusiasm in the job that must be done. Fulfilling the five previous commandments does not automatically imply that you have this dedication. Here we are talking about total commitment and vital drive and motivation. We are talking about inspiration and eagerness, resourcefulness and industry.

7. *You must be vitally concerned about the growth and development of your students.* Your task is to take your students down the educational path toward certain goals. Your aim must be to help these people obtain some measure of success as they traverse this path and to enhance their growth and development by fostering in them the pride of self-accomplishment. No other aim in teaching can be as significant.

8. *You must strive to become an excellent teacher, one who knows and uses effective methods and techniques.* Fostering positive growth and development depends, in part, upon desirable teaching procedures. Classroom procedures and policies will vary even among excellent teachers, but there is a general standard conducive to the best climate for learning. Your methods must relate to two realities of community junior college teaching: its transfer courses are restricted to the lower division; its student body may include many who are neither highly motivated nor academically strong.

9. *You must know your subject matter and students and express positive attitudes toward both.* If methods and techniques are half of teaching skill, then subject matter mastery and knowledge of students are the other half.

Mastery of subject matter should develop with teaching experience, and the teacher must continually learn from this experience in order to improve his mastery. Your ultimate success also depends upon the degree of enthusiastic, optimistic feelings you have toward both your discipline and your students.

10. *You must have other personal attributes that make you a genuine, empathetic human being.* You may not be the kind of person who is denied a teaching certificate on grounds listed in various state education codes, but you might be a rather unhappy person. According to Pullias, you can be no better as a teacher than you are as a person (298:41). Though needed personal traits may be extensive, generally you must be a well-adjusted, socially acceptable person, and with your students you need to be *fair, friendly,* and *firm.*

Other writers might list slightly different commandments, but this checklist is valid. It embraces general recommendations in areas of personal qualities, attitudes, and abilities necessary for effective and happy teaching.

Placement Offices

A national association of placement chiefs and bureaus is the Association for School, College, and University Staffing (ASCUS). The association grew out of a 1923 meeting of college department bureau secretaries and was known for nearly thirty years as the National Institutional Teacher Placement Association. It changed its name in 1962 to ASCUS. The purposes of the association relate to standards, cooperation, information, promotion, enhancement of the concept of staffing, and research (356:168). The ASCUS *Annual* is free to teacher candidates registered with the placement bureaus in an institution holding membership in ASCUS. It includes a list of all member bureaus along with numerous advertisements for teaching positions in all parts of the nation. The annual should be of valuable assistance to you in finding a CJC position.

Shortly before or after your graduation from a college or university, you should establish a personal file with a placement office. The two principal types of documents kept in a personnel file are (1) transcripts of college and university credits and degrees and (2) various letters of recommendation testifying as to your experience and qualifications for teaching. It is your responsibility to request these documents and other necessary materials for your file. The placement office usually furnishes you with its own blank forms for letters of recommendation. You must send these to people who know your work and will offer the highest type of recommendation to prospective employers. These letters are returned to the office and kept in your confidential file until they are sent to prospective employers.

In general, a placement office will not include in your file a letter which is, in essence, more of a denunciation than a recommendation. In fact, it is unethical for a person to write a recommendation if he cannot, in good conscience, write an effective one. According to one Indiana study, letters of recommendation may fall short in predicting the success of new teachers (377:35). Copies of your transcripts of credits and degrees, of course, are requested from the transcript office of the institutions. Once your file is established, it is extremely important that you keep it active and up-to-date. For a rather complete discussion of the duties and responsibilities of both placement agencies and clients, see Fawcett (109).

College or University Placement Office. In selecting the placement office most likely to be of life-long service, consider first the office of the institution from which you have received your highest degree or graduate instruction. Concerned about filling teacher vacancies at all levels of education, this office often knows of vacancies and makes recommendations for employment. Often this service is free, but some offices charge a nominal fee. Although it is unlikely that your institution does not have a placement office, you may learn of other institutional placement services in the Directory of Membership of the Association for School, College, and University Staffing, 130 Sixth Street, N.W., Atlanta, Georgia.

State Education Associations. In 1969, CJC teachers could turn to at least twenty-four state education associations for assistance in obtaining teaching positions. In most cases, these offices were maintained by state teachers associations which had listing services or active placement bureaus for teachers at all levels. Some are exclusive junior college teacher groups. In some states an association placement service is free, usually to members only. In other states an initial fee is charged for registration and maintenance of your confidential file, with perhaps a small percentage of the first year's salary if the teacher is placed directly by the office.

State Department of Education. Like teacher associations in many states, various departments of education also maintain position listing or placement offices which are free, or charge fees or percentages of the first year's salary. These services in 1969 were in at least 18 states. If office addresses are missing among the state entries in Appendix A, you can write directly to the respondents named with these entries; if they do not forward your letter to the right office, at least they will furnish you with the proper address.

State and National Public Employment Service. The United States Employment Service coordinates about 1,900 local offices of state employment services which serve teachers, supervisors, and administrators at all levels of education. By filing your papers in any of the local employment service offices, you may have your application referred to one or more other states through the Professional Office Network. In 1969 the network had 122 offices that had been designated as nationwide professional placement offices. Supporting and supplementing the network were centralized teacher placement offices in 17 states and the District of Columbia. The addresses in these states were as follows:

Arizona: 207 East McDowell Road, Phoenix 85004
Colorado: 251 East 12th Avenue, Denver 80203
Connecticut: 500 Capitol Avenue, Hartford 06106
District of Columbia: 1000 16th Street, N.W. 20036
Idaho: 305 Main Street, Boise 83702
Indiana: 10 North Senate Avenue, Indianapolis 46204
Kentucky: Capitol Office Building, Frankfort 40601
Massachusetts: 6 Somerset Street, Boston 02108
Montana: P.O. Box 367, Mitchell Building, Helena 59601
New Jersey: 601 Broad Street, Newark 07102
New York: 444 Madison Avenue, New York City 10021
North Dakota: 119 Second Street, Bismarck 58501
Oklahoma: 107 North Robinson Street, Oklahoma City 73102
Pennsylvania: Seventh and Forster Streets, Harrisburg 17102
South Dakota: 310 South Lincoln Street, Box 730, Aberdeen 57501
Texas: TEC Building, Teacher Placement Division, Austin
Washington: Old Capitol Building, Olympia 98501
Wisconsin: 105 South Blair Street, Madison 53703

Professional Associations. We suggest here and elsewhere in this book that you should belong to one or more professional associations, for they can provide you with a stimulus for professional growth, opportunities for identification as an expert in your field, and acquaint you with specialists at other institutions. As a member, you can use placement services in many of these subject-area or general associations. Placement services offered by 112 associations are found in *Placement Services for Personnel in Higher Education* (217). These associations frequently list job opportunities for college teaching in their journals and other publications. The American Association of University Professors, for example, lists vacancies and "teachers available" in their AAUP *Bulletin.* For a small fee you can advertise your credentials for a particular job. Many CJC teachers have secured placement in this manner.

Commercial Placement Agencies. Private employment offices provide placement services for teachers. Generally, they charge a registration fee and, upon placement, a percentage of the first year's salary. The National Association of Teachers' Agencies, 620 Case Building, 82 St. Paul Street, Rochester, N.Y., can provide you with a list of member agencies (58 in all) which have met certain standards and have subscribed to the association's Code of Ethics. Not a member of NATA but used frequently by independent school employing officers is the Cooperative Bureau for Teachers, 22 East 42nd Street, New York, N.Y. Most of the reliable independent placement agencies advertise their services in the various journals of state teachers associations.

Selecting a College

There are various criteria in determining whether a particular college is where you should work. McKenna lists criteria to be considered (244:25). Selecting a teaching position, he says, is a more complex process than identifying the top minimum salary. A new teacher must investigate the total salary structure, including fringe benefits. Security is more than tenure; it is when a college recognizes competency that superior teachers are most satisfied and secure. The colleges in demand are those with well defined policies in both remuneration and security. Opportunity is equally important, McKenna writes. Greater consideration should be given to those colleges which assume responsibilities for the advancing and upgrading of their teachers. Along with your own plans for personal improvement, these conditions—desirable remuneration, adequate security, and the college's desire to maintain its staff members—imply job satisfaction.

Investigating these and other conditions may require you to visit a college, to talk with faculty members, to "feel out" the atmosphere of the campus, and to seek evidence of the college's character and status, aims and functions, policies and procedures. Many of your findings can be made simultaneously with your actual application for a position, although prior evaluation, if possible, would save you time and energy in trying for a job you cannot fully appreciate. As you know, the two chief means of communication with a prospective employer are writing and talking, i.e., letters of application and interviews. The next two sections discuss these important aspects of securing employment.

Written Applications

In most cases a letter of inquiry is the first communication a teacher may have with a prospective employer. He can telephone or visit the college if he is near enough, but this first contact is chiefly to determine if there is a vacancy. Rarely will he receive an interview until he has made application on the college's official application form and until the college decides that he is worthy of an interview. Even if the teacher lives nearby, the letter is considered the most desirable method of *initial* contact. When something is put into writing, it becomes a record. It gives the college officials a chance to evaluate the teacher's ability at written communication, a necessary skill for all good teachers. It is more official than a phone call or visit, and it can be filed for reference. Start your junior college career, if there is to be one, by putting your first communication in writing, and *make that letter one that creates a favorable impression of you and, above all, one that is likely to bring positive results.*

How *can* the teacher create this favorable impression and bring positive results? A college director of a placement bureau provides some answers (344:33). Use standard writing paper, use a standard business letter style of writing, spell words correctly, type (or write legibly in dark ink if you must) on white paper, be brief, and use about three or four paragraphs. Do not send a carbon copy or a printed form letter. The first paragraph should state the position you desire and why you are interested in the school. The second paragraph should refer to your background and to highlights of an attached résumé. The last paragraph should request an application and state your availability for an interview.

Perhaps these rules for paragraph content are standard. If so, there is still room for originality of organization and particularly language style. By all means, don't treat your letter as if it were a fanciful creative writing project. Keep it brief and business-like, but not *too* brief; a letter that says, "Dear Sir—I'm looking for a junior college position in the field of English and would like an application from you if there is to be a vacancy this fall —Yours truly" certainly fails to stimulate much interest. Although the writer *might* receive the application form with such brevity, he will not make a very good first impression.

Your letter should not be too long. If you wish to go into detail in the first inquiry, you should include the information in a résumé that accompanies the letter. A *résumé* is an inventory of your background and qualifications—a personal outline. Like the letter of inquiry, its main purpose is to get you an interview, to interest an official in your potential contributions to his college. It is an excellent kind of job-hunting tool. If the résumé is included, the letter itself can be rather brief. The letter and résumé should not duplicate information. Keep in mind that the résumé includes approximately the same information that is requested on an official college application form. Generally the facts are organized in outline form such as this:

I. HEADING: Name, address, telephone number.

II. PERSONAL DATA: Age, marital status, height and weight, perhaps a small photograph of yourself.

III. POSITION DESIRED: Include appropriate description.

IV. EDUCATION: List high schools and colleges and special school attended. Include majors and minors, degrees, and dates.

V. TEACHING EXPERIENCE: List in chronological order the teaching positions held, beginning with the last position. Include places, dates, and responsibilities assumed. Be complete. Don't omit any positions.

VI. MILITARY AND OTHER WORK EXPERIENCE: Give full description with dates and places.

VII. MISCELLANEOUS INFORMATION: List special skills and abilities, professional contributions and achievements (publications, organizational memberships, honors and awards, etc.), interests and hobbies.

You should avoid a lengthy résumé in prose style. Be positive. A résumé is a kind of advertisement for yourself. Don't mention problems you have had at other schools or what you would like in your "ideal" college situation. This advice is not as ridiculous as it sounds. Some people do include verbiage and suffer unwittingly. In one case, for example, a competent teacher mailed at least 30 application letters and résumés to colleges in the state. Only three responded and one of these finally granted an interview without hiring him. The reasons for the poor response? His résumé was a 40-page essay about every single job he had held. He included all the negative arguments from various unappreciative employers and his own complete rebuttals. The picture of his "ideal" situation was so unrealistic it could not be appreciated by prospective employers. Obviously, the résumé writer must know what to say and how much to say if the résumé is to bring him success.

The idea of multiple submissions of letters and résumés seems acceptable these days. If you were to wait for a reply from one source before sending to another, your job attempts could take considerable time and cause loss of desirable positions. Remember the law of percentages: send out enough feelers to guarantee an adequate number of responses. By weighing a variety of offers you can be more certain of getting the best available job.

The following checklist for writing letters and résumés may be helpful to you:

1. Select 20 or more junior colleges in the area where you would teach.

2. Address your letters to the head of instruction by name, if possible.

3. Write each letter separately; *never* mimeograph or have letters printed.

4. Keep the letter brief, preferably one page in length.

5. Type the letter and keep it clean and neat.

6. Use good English and sentence structure, and be careful that all words are spelled correctly.

7. Have a business-like approach in your style. Do not try to be aggressive, humorous, familiar, or overbearing.

8. Try to capture the attention of the reader in the first paragraph. The best way to this is to be brief and to the point.

9. State immediately the purpose of your letter.

10. Briefly include information about yourself, such as area of experience and competency and position desired.

11. Discuss briefly your qualifications for the job.

12. Request an official college teacher application form.

13. Show a desire for an interview and the means for accomplishing it. (Don't expect the official to travel to your state.)

14. Indicate the placement office where your confidential file is kept.

15. Offer to send additional informaton and ask for an early reply.

16. Do not duplicate information if you include a résumé with your cover letter. It is suggested that you do include a résumé. Prospective employers prefer them because they are easy to read.

17. Keep the letter with a résumé more brief than the letter without a résumé.

18. Use a mimeographed résumé for convenience; unlike the letter, the résumé is an outline of your qualifications credits which can be legitimately duplicated.*

19. Make your résumé in outline form rather than in essay form.

20. Keep the résumé as short as possible, no more than two or three pages—preferably one.

21. Don't mention negative or unpleasant aspects of your work experience.

22. Include *few* rather than *many* divisions in the résumé, such as (I) Identifying information, (II) Position Desire, (III) Personal Data, (IV) Educational Training, (V) Teaching Experience, (VI) Military and Work Experience, and (VII) Miscellaneous Information (memberships, honors, etc.).

23. Edit and revise your material before mailing it out.

Interviews

Regardless of how good an instructor you are or how many qualifications and fine recommendations you possess, an interview usually makes the big difference in being hired for a teaching position. For any kind of teaching job, what happens in the interview situation is crucial to success. Let's look

* We admit there is disagreement on this point. Stevens, for instance, says "a carbon, dittoed, or mimeographed copy should NEVER be used" (344:32). We know of *no* evidence of duplicated résumés causing failure to obtain a position.

at some significant factors and some reasons why interviews frequently result in failure for the prospective teacher.

Dress. That a teacher should be dressed properly and wear his clothes well is elementary, and yet some interviewees are utterly careless. In one case, a qualified applicant lost a junior college position because the seams of her nylons were twisted about her legs. It may seem ridiculous, but it happened. In another case, a man's clothes were shabby and unpressed. The interviewer concluded that what the applicant wore to the interview was an expression of personality, and the official's decision was influenced accordingly. The employer usually offers no criticism unless he offers employment, and the applicant rarely knows that improper clothes may be a reason for his losing a job. In general, clothes should be conservative in style, be of current design, fit well, and be clean and pressed. Men should have shined shoes and stockings that don't droop. Women? Among other things, it seems, they should have straight stocking seams.

Physical Appearance. Unfortunately, many good teachers are passed over because of physical appearance that cannot be helped very much. Don't despair, though, these extreme types obtain jobs every year. Sometimes a warning is given. A friend was hired with this admonition: "You're really too fat. You should lose at least twenty pounds. I'll give you one year to do it." Sometimes an interviewer objects to such physical things as long hair, beards, and moustaches.* Dirty teeth, messy hair, and gaudy makeup on the face are inexcusable and should be corrected before the interview. Most administrators will react with kindness and understanding to physical conditions over which the applicant has little or no control.

Personal Mannerisms. One administrator was once reported to have said he had not hired a male teacher because he did not like the way the man carried his briefcase. Such criticism seems ridiculous, but some may be valid. A man may exhibit strong feminine actions or a woman exhibit strong masculine actions. An applicant may make continuous nervous movements denoting insecurity and lack of confidence or the applicant may be tensely sober and show absolutely no sense of humor. The applicant may smoke obtrusively, have an unpleasant or irritating vocal quality, employ a distracting idiosyncracy of gesture, stance, or sitting position. An applicant should try to cultivate physical mannerisms that are polite, graceful, and unobtrusive during interviews and other official social encounters.

Educational Goals and Philosophy. A study of education job-seeking clients at New York University Placement Services found that those students and alumni who had certain goals and purposeful behavior obtained

---

* Although the clean shaven face is still in the majority there is a strong trend today toward beards and moustaches. A few recent court cases have upheld the teacher's right to have them in spite of occasional disapproval by administration or members of the community.

the desired jobs they were seeking, while those with vague, confused goals and passive behavior did not obtain education posts, despite a teaching shortage (343).

Undoubtedly many applicants express philosophic viewpoints contrary to a college's basic beliefs. To say that you're against the open-door policy or that only the intellectually gifted should be taught in college is not to gain approval of the typical CJC interviewer. Make no mistake about it, the interviewer will explore your education or teaching philosophy to determine whether your beliefs coincide with the college's goals and purposes. The important thing is to *have* a philosophy; the next important thing is to have the ability to articulate this philosophy in a logical and clear manner.

Interview Organization. Many applicants fail because of poor interview preparation. Before meeting your interviewer, you should plan your important questions. Make a list of these and check them against valid criteria. Have only a few questions. Ask those requiring more than a yes or no answer. Use single, straightforward questions. Use pertinent questions. Use questions that follow propriety. Check your questions for clarity. Have available all the facts needed for answering those questions from the interviewer. When you actually face him, consider and remember the following criteria for the best impression: (199)

1. Be business-like, but show a sense of humor.
2. Don't rush yourself or the interviewer.
3. Use tact in the discussion.
4. Be a good listener.
5. Let the interviewer direct the discussion.
6. Be flexible enough to adapt to changes in the line of questioning.
7. Do not digress, but stay on the topic at hand.
8. Speak directly to the person or persons interviewing you.
9. Listen carefully to what is said and answer questions honestly.
10. Volunteer such information as you know can further your candidacy, if questions are slow in coming.
11. Do not, however, interrupt the speaker.
12. Be enthusiastic, but not beyond the point of sincerity.
13. Be confident of your ability.
14. Do not stumble along as you answer and question, but use a smooth rate of speech.
15. Do not go overboard in trying to be funny, but be cheerful and smile.
16. Be careful of posture; let the interviewer invite you to sit down and let him terminate the discussion.

17. Be careful not to show your nervousness by playing with hat, pencil, and the like.

18. Ask intelligent questions, and then only when the occasion presents itself.

19. Avoid flowery or stilted language; be natural; choose the appropriate words in your mind before saying them aloud.

20. Let your statements be specific and exact.

21. Do not brag and boast of your great ability and experience, but state your qualifications as a matter of fact.

22. Take a few brief notes if necessary and provide some time for verification of these with the interviewer.

23. Show a keen interest in the college and a desire to be one of the faculty members.

24. Make sure the interview has resulted in a clear understanding of the position you seek and a reasonable evaluation of your qualifications.

25. Express pleasure at having met the interviewer, at least by the end of the interview. Do not press for a decision.

An experienced placement director says: "There is no substitute for the impression that a neat, conservatively dressed, well-groomed person with a firm hand-shake and a courteous manner makes on the prospective employer the first time he meets you. If in addition, you give evidence that you know who you are, and where you are going, the chances are that you are going to get there. You have developed interview readiness" (344:33).

Some Adjustments after Employment

Oftentimes we wonder why a teacher is released from a contract or is refused renewal of a contract when he is considered to be good enough to secure one in the first place. It is easy for us to blame the hiring officer for this condition, for it shows that he made a mistake in his initial judgment of the teacher's worth. But let's be clear on one point: what looks attractive on paper may look rather inadequate in actual performance of duty. Naturally, administrators make mistakes in hiring certain teachers, for the *real* test is how well the teacher fits into the college pattern with all its complex roles to be played. Yes, some teachers are unjustly dismissed, and these cases are deplorable; on the other hand, aside from many other reasons, a teacher is justly dismissed if he makes no attempt to adjust to the varying conditions of his employment. Obviously, to secure a job is not to hold a job; these are two different functions. If you do not fit naturally into your new teaching position, the alternatives are adjust, get out, or work toward change.

There are six major areas where junior college instructors frequently encounter friction in their professional adjustments. Fortunately there is a considerable latitude in the instructor's response to the style of (1) the institution, (2) its policies, (3) his colleagues, (4) his community, (5) his discipline, and (6) his administrators. The choices range from obdurate refusal to compromise on any issue to spineless willingness to accept outrageous demands.

Institutions can and sometimes need to be changed, but they change slowly and reluctantly. Their stability is also an advantage, one which you should recognize. Policies are also established in order to provide guidelines which can be applied without prejudice. The district without policies is vulnerable to pressure and prejudice. Colleagues are never ideal. Every faculty has a number of persons to whom you must adjust.

Like it or not, being a junior college teacher places you in a special status in your community. You will need to adjust to past, present, and future students as well as their friends and parents. Equally demanding is the field of one's subject matter, which requires a lifetime of study and growth. Adjustment ranges from stagnation to unending renewal.

Your relationship with the college administrators should allow for bilateral adjustment. Their support can prove invaluable, especially in doubtful or controversial situations. While it may represent an adjustment for you, briefing them on your actions also makes them share the responsibility.

Blocker and Wolfe (28) presented a study supporting adjustments when they listed criteria, in rank order, used in the retention and promotion of faculty members in two-year colleges: (1) professional growth, (2) teaching performance and effectiveness, (3) experience and length of service, (4) contributions to the development of the college, (5) scholarly research and publication, (6) community service, (7) attitudes toward the profession, and (8) rapport with students, faculty, and administration. Specific studies in each of these areas can also be cited. Rainey, for example, revealed that 41.4 percent of 58 junior college presidents and deans used professional writing as a criterion for hiring, retaining, and promoting teachers, while 20.7 percent said that writing had a positive effect on salary (303). Obviously, these eight criteria represent attitudes, goals, and adjustments that need to be considered.

If you can qualify for and secure a CJC position and if you make the necessary adjustments on the job, you should have a long and happy tenure in your institution. In the next and final chapter of Part One, we shall complete the generalized picture of the junior college setting by indicating selected if not major instructional areas, the content of which was provided by specialists in various geographical areas of the United States.

Chapter 4

Selected Instructional Areas

This chapter is largely the work of 118 specialists from twenty-two colleges representing major geographical portions of the United States (see Appendix B). The samplings of programs include the major portions of general education, transfer education, and terminal education. The report included here is suggestive rather than definitive; it complements the setting of the community junior college. It provides an insight into the most common instructional areas and a prelude to assignment duties and assessments. Discussed briefly are thirteen areas, followed by a general summary.

Art (9 specialists)

Courses and titles vary. Samples include design, drawing, composition, painting, lettering, ceramics, art history, art appreciation, sculpture, arts and crafts, commercial art, graphic arts, printmaking, anatomy and life, water color, studio art. Most of these fall into required and elective subjects for majors, but some, like art appreciation, are considered general education. Most colleges offer the basic courses, while larger schools have diversified offerings.

Students also vary. In the open-door college, there is a large block of average students, a small percentage of excellent students, and many who are below average. Art majors tend to be of good quality. Counseling and motivation are needed for better student performance.

Rated high by the respondents were these teaching methods: laboratory, discussion, audio-visual aids, independent study, student perform-ance, lecture, field trips, and observation of student work. Rated less effec-tive were textbooks, conferences, written exams, and objective exams. Not used very often and considered ineffective by most were team teaching, programmed learning, television, and oral exams.

Mentioned most often as a value or advantage to teaching art was the belief that art is a creative and satisfying field for a student's personal development. Some felt that, since art is an elective, students tend to be self-motivating. Teachers can gain personal rapport with students and can see readily improvement in student work.

Mentioned as some disadvantages were these: teacher loads, com-puted as labs in many cases, are too great; there is high subjectivity in evaluating most art classes except for art appreciation and some commer-cial art areas; communicating the abstract is difficult; sometimes there is a negative administrative attitude toward art; budgets are sometimes too small for the quantity of supplies needed.

Most respondents indicated that opportunities for art teaching were good in their geographical regions. While there was a good supply of ap-plicants, in most cases, the demand for qualified teachers was strong.

In general, art teachers need to be versatile in several areas of art, such as ceramics, sculpture, and art appreciation. Three respondents felt that the bachelor's degree was adequate preparation, while four indicated the master's degree was needed. Two thought that professional art experi-ence was more important than degrees. Most wanted new teachers with previous experience in teaching, professional art work, and with special preparation for understanding the nature of the CJC.

Common new teacher weaknesses included lack of outstanding train-ing in studio areas, little awareness of the character of the community junior college, lack of good preparation in more than one art area, lack of knowledge of techniques and approaches of professional artists, and lack of specific awareness of the nature of students' prior training.

Respondents suggested that new teachers should keep standards on the level of students' capabilities; have a strong background in art history and survey courses, with a major-minor in studio art courses; know Eastern as well as Western art; be aware of community college functions and char-acter; know how students learn and apply these methods; maintain per-sonal and emotional equilibrium.

Business Education (9 specialists)

Sample courses taught are typing, shorthand, business correspondence, office machines, accounting, marketing, management, corporation finances, office and personnel management, secretarial-stenographic skills, business administration supervisory techniques, data processing, and bookkeeping.

Respondents tended to agree that business education students are low to average in ability, with a few who are superior. They exhibit all levels of skills, wide ranges of ability, and experiences limited to little or no high school business courses.

The specialists felt that laboratory work in business courses was the best or most-needed method of teaching. Also ranking high were textbooks, objective exams, lectures, discussions, conferences, student performances, and audio-visual aids. Rated average in need and use were written exams, observation, field trips, and programmed learning. Used very little were team teaching, independent study, television, and oral exams.

These teachers mentioned such advantages in business teaching as freedom and variety in class, close relations with students, helping students find a career, satisfaction of seeing end results of instruction, helping students gain confidence, perhaps fewer disciplinary problems, constant change of programs due to new business developments, and close association with the community and business world.

Listed as disadvantages were lack of electronic data equipment, expense of equipment, high cost per student for instruction, wide variety of classes requiring multiple preparations, inordinate number of failures and dropouts, loading teachers on the lab-hour formula, difficulty in keeping up with new business developments.

Teaching opportunities seem to be excellent for the well-trained and experienced. Most respondents felt that the supply exceeds the demand for new and inexperienced teachers.

The best qualified business teacher applicants have a master's degree, business field experience, and previous teaching experience. Other important qualifications are proper attitudes, dedication to helping all students, research in teaching and education, teaching ability, interest, and desire.

Respondents felt that new teachers lacked adequate business field experience, intellectual curiosity, and willingness to participate in counseling and advisory activities. They suggested that trainees should use business experience to supplement theory, train carefully in electronic data equipment, try high school teaching first, dedicate themselves to the idea of service to the student.

Composition and Literature (13 specialists)

Most community junior colleges provide two areas in this field: the remedial reading and writing, non-transfer courses and the regular academic, college-credit courses. Basic credit courses include English composition, English literature, American literature, world literature, modern literature, and business and technical English. One may find courses in special areas of creative writing and a particular type of literature such as drama, poetry, and the like.

High school grades and placement examination scores determine whether students are placed in the terminal or the regular college courses. Most respondents felt that students were about average, with some tendency toward below average. There are few students comparable to the better ones in the university. Some teachers reported a high student dropout rate during the first year; many of these students were members of minority groups. One estimate was that about 50 percent of new students enrolled in remedial or developmental courses.

Six English teaching methods rated consistently high were discussion, written exams, textbooks, lecture, student performance, and conference. Average ratings fell to audio-visual aids, observation, objective exams, independent study, lab work, oral exams, and team teaching. Used very little and rated low were programmed learning, field trips, and television teaching.

Advantages in the teaching of English courses included variety of subject, the living language, development of human relationships, lighter teaching loads, and the fact that literature covers virtually everything.

Listed disadvantages were the burdens of reading and marking papers, disagreement on what should be taught, lack of time to do a good job, difficulty in relating the subject field to vocational needs, and problems in motivation.

The general feeling was that teaching opportunities in English were extensive "because every student takes one or two basic courses." The demand was considered greater in composition than in literature. Although many applications were reported, the consensus reported a shortage of highly qualified people, particularly in the high skill areas.

Almost all contended that the master's degree was a necessity, and most wanted experienced applicants. Other qualifications mentioned were integrity and respect for students, realization of differences between the community-junior college and other levels of higher education, less specialization in literature and more attention to communication skills, serious attitude and purpose, more orientation toward student needs, experimentation and creativity in teaching.

According to the specialists, common weaknesses of new teachers included treating students as if they were enrolled in universities, lack of inventiveness and originality in conveying subject matter, insufficient experience, lack of broad knowledge, and lack of sympathy for and understanding of students.

Chief suggestions for new teachers or trainees were those related to these common weaknesses. Emphasis was placed upon learning to teach the poorly prepared students at the CJC level, having a greater familiarity with grammar and composition, having broad training and knowledge, and being enthusiastic and creative in teaching.

Engineering (4 respondents)

Courses cover such subjects as engineering drawing, descriptive geometry, engineering statics, engineering physics, math through calculus, and so on. Engineering majors get most of their special course work in the upper-division level, while the junior college offers the foundation courses.

The consensus was that most students are average or better. Careful screening helps to eliminate many from the pre-engineering programs. Said one specialist, "We get high school graduates with S.A.T. scores of 800 plus; many graduates attain executive rank."

The specialists gave a perfect rating (A) for lectures as a method of teaching. They also agreed that team teaching was the poorest method. Other high ratings went to textbooks, lab, discussion, student performance, and written exams. Average ratings were given to independent study, field trips, audio-visual aids, and objective exams. Low ratings went to observations, conferences, programmed learning, television, and oral exams. In their general teaching approach, the teachers attempt to assimilate industrial situations in every subject area possible.

Advantages or values in engineering teaching included the chance to engage in private consulting work, the fact that class loads were less than those in the high school, and that research requirements were not as highly emphasized as in the four-year colleges and universities.

Two people saw no disadvantages, while the other two mentioned the high cost of equipment for engineering-related subjects and the lack of students enrolled.

All four specialists ranked teaching opportunities "good to excellent." They said that the supply of qualified personnel was inadequate. "Much of the staff is recruited from industry; they have the basic experience and knowledge, but must acquire teaching abilities."

One person mentioned the need for a master's degree, while the other three thought a bachelor's degree was sufficient. "The degree should be in civil engineering with five to ten years of varied work experience," said one respondent.

Reported weaknesses of new teachers included inappropriate personality to deal with students, lack of industrial experience, and poor teaching techniques.

Two suggestions offered were: "Get an engineering degree, become a licensed professional engineer and land surveyor, get all practical experience possible" and "Use some of your summer vacation time to work in industry to further academic prowess in your profession."

Foreign Language (10 specialists)

Most of the colleges sampled offered two years of Spanish, French, and German. A few offered Russian. The courses were usually divided into beginning, intermediate, and advanced levels. Placement of the students depended upon their high school background in the languages.

In general, the abilities of foreign language students varied about as much as the abilities of all CJC student bodies, although some teachers mentioned the special student interest and quality whenever the language course is not required for graduation. Others felt the languages were difficult for students due to the neglect of this area in the high schools.

The specialists favored the use of language laboratories and textbooks most often. Other high ratings were given to performance (recitations in the language), and audio-visual aids. Medium values were given to objective, essay, and oral exams; independent study; discussion; lecture; observation; conference; and programmed learning. Of least value to these teachers were team teaching, field trips, and television.

Some chief advantages in foreign language teaching were listed as fewer students per class, personal enrichment in learning the language and culture of another people, opportunities for outside employment where the language is needed (such as foreign service), chances to study abroad (an income tax advantage, also), immediate usefulness of a language, better understanding of one's own language, and relationships with other of the humanities, and current affairs.

Some disadvantages included problems of convincing the administration of the values of foreign languages and of scheduling adequate classes, the problem of mastering the language rather than using a common method of keeping a day ahead of the students, the lack of contacts with ethnic groups (in small communities), and the infinite opportunities for making errors.

Most teachers seemed to agree that the demand for teachers was limited because of the smallness of the foreign language programs compared to regular required courses. However, it was felt that the supply of well-qualified teachers in this area was small enough to foster good opportunities.

A master's degree is needed for teaching the language, most respondents said. Previous junior college teachers have the edge for employment. Also considered important qualifications were travel or study in the country of the language, previous work experience requiring use of the language, knowledge of A-V equipment, receptivity to new ideas, and an ability to teach students at the CJC level.

Teacher weaknesses included lack of oral competency in the language, no travel or study in the foreign country, poor teaching experience, and ineffective teaching methods and techniques.

Respondents suggested that new teachers or trainees should develop oral proficiency, strengthen ability to present grammar in an interesting and imaginative way, get some practical experience, train in at least two languages, understand the total program of foreign language study, and travel or study abroad to learn everything possible in the native country.

Health, P.E., and Athletics (4 specialists)

Sample courses mentioned in this area were personal health, administration of athletics, intramural athletics, fundamentals of sports, first aid, service P.E. programs, professional P.E. programs, co-ed P.E. programs (archery, modern dance, fencing, bowling).

Students in the basic or required courses include virtually the entire student body with its variety of abilities and intelligences. The more talented athletes are attracted to the sports activities, especially the competitive or intercollegiate programs. Many of the athletes seem to have no other interest, reported some respondents. Many lack good study habits and self-motivation. Occasionally a community junior college will enroll a superior scholar or athlete in this area, but the consensus was that this was infrequent.

On the question of teaching methods, the highest average ratings went to student performance, discussion, objective and essay exams, lab, lecture, conference, and audio-visual aids. Rating less well were textbooks, independent study, programmed learning, field trips, television, team teaching, oral exams, and observation.

Advantages in teaching physical education courses seemed to be the greater interest among students (as compared to student interest in other fields of study), with less need for teacher motivation; providing opportunities for students to release their energies in a physical rather than an emotional manner; the relative ease in seeing growth and progress; and the opportunities to know students better than in more academic situations.

Problems and disadvantages included insufficient time for accurate evaluation (as most time is spent on physical activities), insufficient facilities and equipment for athletics, some academic snobbery against teachers in this area, lack of student talent in coaching for winning teams.

All specialists felt that a master's degree was needed by teachers in this area. Previous teaching experience, training or course work in junior college education, and a positive attitude for teaching all were considered important. High recommendations were considered important for coaching athletics.

It was felt that many new teachers had improper attitudes toward medical problems (not stressing harmful effects of tobacco, alcohol, drugs), that new P.E. teachers were not well qualified to teach health education, and that teacher personalities were sometimes unstable and unpredictable.

Sample suggestions to new teachers included these: P.E. teachers should have a good background in recreation, intramurals, and health education; special emphasis is needed for teaching methods, evaluation techniques, and public relations; teachers should not expect junior college students and programs to be university level; teachers should be dedicated and prepared to encounter many frustrating problems in this area.

Mathematics (10 specialists)

Depending upon the size of the college, courses may be divided into remedial, beginning college, and advanced programs. Example courses are general mathematics, algebra, plane trigonometry, math for teachers, analytic geometry, calculus, technical math, and statistics.

According to the consensus, students ranged widely in abilities and experiences in math. Some respondents ranked their students "average or below" and others found many "above average." Most comments dealt with the general inadequacies among the students.

The math instructors disagreed on several ratings given to methods of teaching. Scoring highest on the average were objective exams, lecture, discussion, textbooks, and independent study, in that order. Lower value was given to audio-visual aids, observations, written exams, conferences, lab, and student performance. Rated at the bottom were team teaching, programmed learning, field trips, television, and oral exams. Writing out math problems and answers by students was a dominant method of teaching.

Mentioned as special advantages in this teaching area were the following: well-defined sequential curricula which clearly labels prerequisites and responsibilities, less research and more conference time, a possible respect for math and mathematicians, opportunities to know and work closely with students.

Disadvantages included: difficulty in teaching math, particularly to poorly prepared or lazy students; some widespread misunderstanding of math and mathematicians in general.

Opportunities for math teaching were considered "good to excellent" by most respondents. The typical reply was that the supply of good teachers was small and the demand was "average to great." Large colleges or multiple colleges within a region had the more favorable opportunities because of greater needs.

Nine respondents indicated that a master's degree was minimal, and five of these mentioned graduate work beyond the master's. Other frequently mentioned qualifications were ability to teach, previous teaching experience, constructive attitudes toward CJC students, loyalty and devotion to teaching, commitment to the CJC philosophy, and an experimentalist attitude in constructing learning exercises.

The most common weaknesses among new teachers were related to training, experience, and attitudes. New teachers were criticized for being too tradition-bound, for lacking desire or ability to work with CJC students, for doing little "beyond the call of duty," and for negativism and lack of understanding.

Suggestions included these: take all the math available, know your subject, be prepared to motivate a diversified student body, use experimental approaches, be satisfied with and dedicated to the task.

Music (7 specialists)

The usual courses include band, choir, music theory, music appreciation, special ensembles, applied music, music history, and basic humanities. Basic classes in instrumental techniques cover bass, woodwind, percussion, and strings. Ensemble participation includes such courses as band, choir, and chorus.

The general feeling was that music students range from poor to superior in intelligence, achievement, and talent. Most music students were considered to have insufficient backgrounds for effective college training. Typical students are liberal arts transfers or adults from the community.

Respondents agreed that student performance should be rated an "A" as an effective method of music teaching. Other high ratings were given to discussion, conference, audio-visual aids, independent study, lab, lecture, field trips, textbooks, and written exams. Average ratings were given to objective exams, team teaching, oral exams, observation, television, and programmed learning. No method was rated below a "C" grade, on the average. Methods differed with the course. For example, lab methods were used for instrumental classes, independent study meant music lessons to some, field trips included attendance at concerts, and oral exams meant private music exams in such subjects as voice and instrumentals.

Advantages in music teaching included these: close personal contact with students, opportunities to really *see* student progress, helping students find purpose and beauty in their lives, the chance to transfer ideals and enthusiasm to those who would someday be music teachers, concrete application of what is learned in music and, in music organizations, opportunity to work with students on a performance or concert tour (allowing for social and counseling roles).

Time, teaching loads, and kinds of students were mentioned most often as disadvantages or problems in teaching music. Music teachers tend to spend many hours on rehearsals and performances, their teaching loads are frequently too heavy, and quality students for public performances are too few in number. Budgets, administrative attitudes, and community support were each mentioned as problem areas by at least one specialist.

Only two of the seven respondents found that opportunities were good and that the supply of teachers was limited. The consensus was that applicants generally were inexperienced, were "unknown quantities," and that high-qualified music teachers were not abundant.

Qualifications needed included a master's degree (although professionals are used for applied music), teaching experience, attitudes and ideals compatible with those of the CJC, excellence in teaching, training in theory courses as well as performance areas, and a strong humanities background.

The music teachers mentioned these weaknesses among new teachers: lack of academic training, poor teaching and performing abilities, little experience in the profession, poor interest in helping students, and improper attitudes. Said one, "They must teach well in several areas; too often they lack broad training; some tend to be prima donnas."

Sample suggestions for new teachers were these: begin training very early—piano instruction is most important for any music major; remember that junior college students seldom have great talent, but they will learn well with a clever, talented, understanding, and enthusiastic teacher; learn theory as well as band or chorus; become a versatile musician.

Natural Sciences (10 specialists)

In this area are such courses as biology, botany, zoology, genetics, microbiology, anatomy, conservation, physiology, lab techniques, and embryology. The first two generally are required of all students; the others are for majors or those needing the courses for various vocational-technical fields.

All specialists noted the generally average level of students compared to those in senior institutions. They said: students have to work harder to achieve; many have a tendency to postpone studying; many have unrealistic ambitions beyond their actual abilities. Some teachers felt that their students were more purposeful than the student body as a whole but did not know how to apply themselves very well.

Specialists differed widely in their views of some of the common teaching methods. Top value, according to an average, went to lecture, textbooks, lab, objective exams, discussion, and audio-visual aids. Considered less valuable were independent study, written and oral exams, performances, observations, conferences, and field trips. Rated poorly were team teaching, programmed learning, and television.

Mentioned as advantages in this teaching area were such items as the natural, innate curiosity and interest of students in at least some aspects of natural science (which helps reduce barriers and defensive attitudes among students), direct contacts, satisfactions in presenting quite complicated abstractions, many new developments in the field, scientific and objective content where personal opinion is minimal and where there is little room for propaganda, opportunities for varied learning methods which help to meet individual differences in the classrooms.

Disadvantages or problems dealt with the great time needed for lab preparation and the lack of time for individual investigations, lack of lab space, conformity to lab methods because of scheduling and other complications, lack of credit for lab work compared to lecture courses, and lack of choice in textbooks meeting four-year college requirements.

Five of the 10 found that opportunities were most favorable, the demand being equal to or greater than the supply of teachers. Some felt the supply was short in most areas except the basic subjects like biology. The other five respondents found few problems in securing good applicants for vacancies or new positions.

According to the consensus, new teachers should have a master's degree, perhaps some teaching or industrial experience, methodology in teaching, broad background or outlook with respect to the entire academic discipline, positive attitudes toward education and particularly the CJC, the ability to communicate well and make practical applications of the subject.

New teachers were considered weak in training, experience, abilities, and attitudes. Lacking was the broad, inclusive outlook; appreciation of relationships between natural science and other fields; knowledge of how to handle a class; ability to understand young people; enthusiasm and dedication.

The specialists gave a few suggestions to the new teachers: be prepared to learn how to use teaching machines, visual aids, and other new methods as our economy continues to require greater training in science; have a solid background and gain a general knowledge of related fields; have a balanced major in botany and zoology; take professional courses in education to understand better the nature of students and methods of teaching and evaluations.

Physical Sciences (6 specialists)

Physical science courses may be survey, general, or introductory courses in the first year and advanced courses for majors in the second year. Generally taught are chemistry, geology, physics, astronomy, and special courses for pre-engineering, nursing, elementary education, and other fields. Larger colleges offer more variety than smaller schools.

Typical comments about the types of students are these: we get all kinds; most are well-motivated but intellectually "dull to average"; they are above average in general chemistry and average in physical science; many are low high school achievers (about one-half).

In methods of teaching this area, the following ranked high: lab, performance, discussion, lecture, textbooks, written exams, and audio-visual aids. Less important were independent study, objective exams, field trips, conferences, observation, and oral exams. Poorly rated were team teaching, programmed learning, and television. Study guides and demonstrations rated high. In some schools, the attempt was to implement the "systems" approach to education.

Interesting advantages in physical science teaching included these: we have more interesting "toys" in our lab; the sciences tend to draw inquisitive, active students who are more fun to work with; in this area a teacher can broaden enormously his students' awareness of the world; we get smaller classes and a larger proportion of better students.

Disadvantages included lack of equipment, frustrations in getting adequate supplies, student frustrations with the subject matter, the need to cover more subject matter in a short time, and the lab loading formula.

Five of the six specialists felt that teaching opportunities in this area were "good to excellent" in their colleges and geographical regions. The demand seemed to exceed supply, a situation requiring the use of part-time or inadequately prepared teachers.

Most said that a master's degree is required. Other points of qualifications included a major in science education plus heavy concentration on educational technology, a modern rather than traditional attitude (perhaps more important than experience), willingness to experiment and change the course to meet student needs, ability to communicate fundamentals to students, and the need for previous work experience in science.

Respondents said that new teachers tended to be weak in experience, human warmth, and willingness to listen to students, broad knowledge of the general area, positive attitudes, and adaptability to the CJC.

These suggestions were given to the new teachers: take additional courses in general physical science and in physics; take professional education courses to improve your teaching; train in the use of A-V equipment; get some high school experience if possible; study the primary problem of the evaluation of learning.

Social Sciences (8 specialists)

Example courses mentioned by respondents were economics, United States history, Western civilization, sociology, government (federal, state, and local), American issues and problems, general psychology, social problems, current affairs, geography, world history, marriage and family, criminology, anthropology and student government.

It was agreed that social science students represent a cross-section, the quality of these students being lower than those found in senior institutions. Majors in this area tended to be of better quality than the non-majors. A typical comment was "We get a wide range of ability; 30 percent are adults, 80 percent select transfer programs on entry, but less than 30 percent *do* transfer."

Six methods of teaching social science rated high: lecture, textbooks, objective exams, written exams, discussion, and audio-visual aids. Receiving smaller support were independent study, student performance, field trips, conference, oral exams, observation, and television. Rated below a "C" grade in value were team teaching, programmed learning, and laboratory. Book reports, term papers, and outside speakers were mentioned as valuable methods.

Six of eight thought there were distinct advantages to social science teaching, such as no lab as in some science and business courses, no excessive paper work as in English, and no "busy work" to fill time; there is enough concrete material to be taught. Four thought the area itself had inherent advantages in helping students adjust, "since we understand human behavior somewhat more than do other teachers." Social science opens new avenues of thought and broader cultural horizons, creates self-understanding and understanding of the races and related problems, and stimulates and challenges through the history of man, his past, present, and future.

Disadvantages included lack of time for scholarship, inadequacies of library materials, the need to teach many different courses, lack of support or respect from some administrators and colleagues, and lack of government funds for social science. A sensitivity to low academic esteem dominated many of the critical comments.

The consensus was that there is a great demand for classes but that the supply of teachers seems to be plentiful for the demand for new teachers. The more common areas (history, geography, political science) had a surplus of applicants, while more specialized areas (anthropology, economics, psychology, and sociology) lacked good applicants. In the general field most said opportunities were "good to excellent."

Mentioned as common new-teacher weaknesses were lack of imagination, enthusiasm, personality, dedication, experience, and training. Said one respondent, "Any genuine student will emerge from grad school armed with a mountain of factual notes to which he can add his own research; but, unless he breaks precedent in his use of them, he lapses into mediocrity." Another said, "A brilliant mind is a liability rather than an asset if the teacher cannot communicate his thoughts to the level of the learners." Courses in methodology and theories of learning were considered helpful by some.

Suggestions for new teachers were generous. In summary, new teachers should complement history teaching with an appreciation and knowledge of the humanities, prepare lectures well in advance, be enthusiastic in teaching, avoid the dry and dull facts and dates in teaching and examining, get as much life experience as possible in order to supplement textbook knowledge, stay abreast of current developments in the field, read constantly, and communicate meaningfully to students.

Speech and Drama (10 specialists)

Speech courses may include the practical public speaking units (under a variety of names) and such special courses as discussion, debate, argumentation, forensics, and oral interpretation. Sometimes offered are speech therapy, semantics, and voice and diction. In the drama field the usual courses are drama literature, theater history, acting, play production, and stagecraft. Other courses are found in larger colleges, while smaller schools are limited to the basic courses in speaking and acting.

Students in speech and drama tend to represent a wide range of socio-economic backgrounds and to display a wide range of abilities, said most specialists. Drama students tend to be more confident and varied in emotional behavior than those in speech courses. Stage fright and fear of audiences tend to be a common trait for both. The majority declare for transfer.

As expected, student performance was the highest average rating among the teachers. Speech and drama are essentially performance subjects. Also scoring high were discussion and observation. Rating in the "C" grade bracket were lecture, oral exam, lab, audio-visual aids, objective exams, field trips, and independent study, in that order. Scoring poorly were team teaching, programmed learning, and television.

Advantages in teaching speech and drama included these: lighter loads for play directors, closer contact with students in performance areas, opportunities for public performance and therefore public relations, seeing students develop personality and confidence as well as skills, constant new content (in speeches and plays), less paperwork than in some classes, opportunity to learn new content through speech subjects covering virtually all areas of the curricula.

Chief disadvantages were these: because of the highly subjective and creative area, there are fewer facts to deal with, making evaluation difficult; constant public exposure (public performances) could be a handicap for some; classes are too crowded for much individual help; heavy extra-curricular demands rarely pay extra money, insufficient budgets (for plays and forensics) can be problems; some students are uncooperative in play production; many students lack talent for acting; securing cooperation and support for speech and drama activities is difficult.

Teaching opportunities seemed to be less plentiful in drama than in speech, chiefly because the average college tends to use only one of two instructors in drama and several in speech. The imbalance is caused by the fact that speech may be required and drama may be considered more specialized, attracting fewer students. The shortest supply was found in debate and forensics. In general, more speech and drama teachers exist than there are available positions.

Most indicated the need for a master's degree, impressive professional and prior teaching experience, and special interests, knowledge, and abilities relating to CJC needs. One of the special needs is for teachers to work in the extra-curricular areas of forensics coaching and play directing.

Respondents said that new teachers tended to be weak in most of the qualifications needed. New teachers lacked sufficient minimum training, professional experience, proper attitudes for CJC teaching, flexibility, and humility. Shared by most was the point that many could not teach in *both* speech and drama but were too severely limited to one of these.

New teachers were urged to learn as much as possible about the technical side of stage productions, to learn research techniques and proper methods of communicating to students, to get experience in the field rather than go for more degrees, to prepare generally in the area rather than to specialize, and to have a diversified and broad training, for "the better your general background, the better speech and drama teacher you'll be."

Technical-Vocational Education (19 specialists) *

Programs and courses in this broad area are many. For example, they may relate to nursing, architecture, mechanics, electronics, medical technology, cosmetology, industry, textiles, data processing, agriculture, home economics, and forestry technology. The extent of a sample program can be found in medical office practice and procedures: government medical care programs, insurance forms, medical law, mail, privileged communications, telephone techniques, medical histories, fees and collections, record keeping, office conduct, dress, typing of reports, case histories, and insurance forms.

Specialists in this vast CJC program agreed that students represent a wide spectrum, with some courses having better types of students than others. A technical institute respondent, for instance, claimed that his students came from the top 50 percent of their high school graduating classes (in such areas as math, trigonometry, chemistry, and physics). Other examples of higher quality students were mentioned in bio-medical sciences and those in X-ray and laboratory technology. Much depends upon the size of school, the prestige of a program, and the entrance requirements. Most of the students, it was reported, are vocationally ori-

* There are so many technical-vocational areas that they had to be generalized together here.

ented; "they want to *do* things rather than *reflect* on things and ideas." Motivation to prepare for work is generally high, but many are poorly conditioned for rigorous training programs.

Laboratory work and textbooks were given the highest rating by the specialists. Following closely were lecture, student performance, discussion, and objective and written exams. Of less value and next in order came audio-visual aids, field trips, conference, observation, independent study, team teaching, oral exams, and programmed learning. Television averaged last. Some felt that all methods and study arrangements should be useful in meeting the needs of so many varied individuals, i.e. no particular practice was more important than another.

A few saw no advantage or special value in teaching this area, but most found some special benefits: "This general field is neither pseudo nor static; this is an advantage, for it makes a man grow." "There is self-satisfaction in preparing people for work; this is not so true in liberal arts fields." "Generally, we have closer identification with communities, fewer discipline problems, larger numbers of job opportunities, higher salaries."

Some disadvantages were mentioned also: "The image in which he is held by liberal arts academic minds never appears to be as respectable because he does things with his hands; yet who would build the buildings, design the equipment and facilities used by the academic mind if not technicians and tradesmen." "We have more student contact hours than most teachers." "There is time-consuming travel to and from the participating agencies for pre-assignments and laboratory experiences." "We sometimes lack modern equipment; costs are high, and other subject areas frequently have greater priority in the budgets."

Seventeen specialists thought that opportunities for teachers in this area were most favorable. The consensus was that there is a continually strong demand for the really capable teachers, and supply is inadequate. Most administrators must recruit from industry and other places outside the normal source of teacher education colleges. Many prefer to remain in the field where salaries tend to be better, and many come to teach only on a part-time basis, particularly at night. Mentioned as areas having increasing opportunities were electrical technology or electronics, mechanical technology, architectural engineering, nursing, medical lab technology, and bio-medical sciences.

Fifteen people felt that the bachelor's degree was needed by new teachers, while six mentioned the need for a master's degree. "A few years of work experience related to the subject field" was mentioned by 16 respondents, while 14 talked about needed training and teaching abilities. Sample comments are these: "Experience is vital if the program is to be practical; teacher attitudes are the most important factor next to subject matter competence, but you can't really separate the two." "Courses in methods of teaching and course construction seem important and valuable; teachers in trades such as welding acquire 90 percent of their knowledge on the job as welders; most excellent trade teachers have no formal college training." "Selection of these teachers should be left to a well-qualified vocational director and not to an academically oriented administrator." "Most mechanical faculty should be graduate mechanical engineers, preferably with some industrial experience." "An artistic aptitude is important and an engineering background useful in the field of architectural engineering technology." "Keen interest in the junior college and knowledge of its philosophy are needed."

Weaknesses of new teachers were noted: universal lack in all fields—communication, experience, and motivation; lack of degrees and training; teachers not at all sure they want to associate with technical-vocational education; inability to keep up with scientific and technological advancements; weakness of many college graduates on applications in this area; lack of desire to teach in the CJC; inability to teach at the level of the students; no knowledge of CJC philosophy.

It was suggested that new teachers should get much practical training in the field, know the aims and objectives of the two-year program, remember the students are preparing to become productive citizens in just two years, have enthusiasm for the subject and gain some knowledge of proper teaching techniques, know how theory works in practice, don't assume that technical textbooks are always right, teach in the area only when happy doing so and when other attitudes are positive. One specialist said that, after 30 years of work in technical-vocational education, he could not really recommend any young man's entering this area of teaching. His reasoning stemmed from his "battles, trials, tribulations, and frustrations" in striving for status, recognition, and stability.

General Summary

To the teaching specialists supplying these instructional areas reports, teaching methods or procedures varied extensively. We asked them to rate various common methods by the A-B-C-D-system, insofar as their respective fields were concerned. These grades translate to 4,3,2,1, as averages were determined. While the means of effecting methods and techniques are discussed in the chapter on the application of the art of teaching, our purpose here is to report the status of these approaches. While the samples are small, results show what at least one group of specialists feels.

The 118 specialists provided the following averages for the selected methods: Lecture, discussion, and textbooks (3.3), lab and student performance (3.2), audio-visual and objective exams (3.0), essay exams (2.9), independent study and conference (2.7), observation (2.5), field trip (2.4), oral exam (2.1), programmed learning (1.8), team teaching (1.7), and television teaching (1.6).

The entire group of 16 methods and procedures rated on the average by specialists in each field: Music (3.2), technical-vocational, health and P.E. (2.9), art, business education, and natural sciences (2.7), composition-literature, physical sciences, and social sciences (2.6), engineering, foreign language, and math (2.5), and speech-drama (2.4). The average for all fields and instructional areas was 2.7.

To determine how the specialists differed in their evaluation of the methods of teaching, we indicate *one* as perfect agreement, *two* as a spread of two grades, and so on. Again, results are shown from two standpoints.

From the standpoint of methods, the greatest spread of grade responses on the average was for independent study (3.5). Other differences in rank order were programmed learning and conferences (3.3), essay exams and observations (3.2), lab, A-V aids, and oral exams (2.9), lecture, team teaching, performance, and field trip (2.8), television and objective exams (2.6), and discussion and textbooks (2.5).

From the standpoint of disciplines, the largest spread of grade responses on the average was in the field of technical-vocational programs (3.4), followed by composition-literature and math (3.3), foreign language (3.2), music and speech-drama (3.1). Tending toward greater agreement were teachers in natural sciences, physical sciences, and social sciences (2.8), art and business education (2.7), health, P.E., and athletics (2.6), and engineering (2.4).

Only four perfect agreements were found: engineering people agreed on lecture (A) and team teaching (D), health and P.E. people agreed on oral exams (C), and music people agreed on student performance (A). The overall average of grade differences for all specialists in all fields was 2.9.

Conclusions and other summary findings follow in the order of questions asked:

1. COURSES: These varied greatly within a college but were similar from one college to another, depending upon the type of college; the variety is desirable because it meets the needs of more students.

2. STUDENTS: Most respondents reported a wide variety of students from poor to superior, the majority being average. The community colleges attract many unqualified for senior institutions or even for the CJC, and thus many dropouts or failures occur. Nevertheless, the colleges consistently provide at least one or two years of higher education to vast numbers not otherwise reached.

3. METHODS: Teachers, even within one field, widely disagreed on the values of various methods of teaching. The traditional lecture and textbook generally got high use compared to newer forms like programmed learning, team teaching, and television teaching. All forms of teaching have value. Each teacher must decide on his methods after a

proper analysis of himself, his subject, and his students. He should not be afraid to experiment and to learn new and possibly better approaches.

4. ADVANTAGES: Most specialists found advantages of teaching in their respective fields. Advantage and value seem to be necessities for one entering a field and expecting to be happily adjusted. Some fields do seem to have clear advantages over other fields, but much depends upon the person himself and particularly upon colleges and administrators seeking to equalize such factors as teacher loads and responsibilities.

5. DISADVANTAGES: More comments were given in this area than in the preceding one, for unhappiness stimulates comment. Some disadvantages may be difficult to overcome, but most problems can be resolved through cooperation and respect.

6. OPPORTUNITIES: Several respondents in each area indicated favorable opportunities for employment within the areas, but most said these opportunities were greatest for the best qualified people. In many fields, competition is keen with many applicants, while a few fields have minor difficulties in filling positions.

7. QUALIFICATIONS: Mentioned time and again by most specialists were the need for graduate degrees, more training and experience, and a special need for understanding the entire framework of the CJC. Attitudes and abilities are crucial.

8. WEAKNESSES: New teachers were found to be weak in several areas in all of the instructional fields. For the most part these weaknesses fell in areas mentioned in the preceding item. Experienced teachers usually find new colleagues lacking various qualifications needed for successful teaching; improvement takes time.

9. SUGGESTIONS: Answers in this area were varied and sometimes prolific in nature. Most suggestions dealt with teacher qualifications and weaknesses. Taken together, they provide provocative guidance from those who are confronted with the issue of what is needed in teaching within these instructional areas.

Also asked of the respondents, but not reported previously in this chapter, was a statement of comparison or contrast between CJC teaching and teaching at other levels. More than 100 of the respondents agreed with literature which indicates that differences stem largely from the nature of the CJC level compared to other levels. Most felt that CJC teachers should have special training apart from that given to secondary and university trainees.

Part II follows with a discussion of the various assignments given to CJC teachers.

Part II The Assignment

Chapter 5

Academic Duties and Functions

At every educational level, from kindergarten through graduate school, successful teaching depends largely upon the teacher's knowledge of and his preparation for his required academic duties and functions. Despite a general overlapping of duties and functions between each level, the junior college pattern is somewhat different from others. Although patterns among junior colleges also differ to some extent, nevertheless a standard core of duties and functions can be expected in the CJC where you teach.

The major question raised in this chapter is "What *are* these duties and functions?" Some practical answers to this question can help you anticipate the specific requirements in your own selected institution. The areas we cover are Profile of Duties, Curriculum Determinants, the Course Outline, Textbook Selection, Instructional Equipment and Supplies, Attendance Accounting, Grade Accounting and Counseling, the Class Policy and Orientation, and a general listing of miscellaneous responsibilities.

Profile of Duties

Academic duties and responsibilities are usually outlined in college faculty handbooks. (205). Such handbooks list the teacher's obligations to the district and his profession. The folowing are typical examples of responsibility areas: the course outline, textbook selection, audio-visual use, teaching policy, attendance accounting, grade accounting, student counseling, office hours, supply budget, room inventory, room comfort, fire safety, bulletins and announcements, the teaching of values, academic freedom, and maintaining one's teaching schedule.

To determine the status of these sixteen academic responsibilities, we asked our specialists in the college-faculty survey to rate the responsibilities in one of three ways: (1) as an individual or independent duty or responsibility, (2) as a joint or group effort involving persons other than the individual teacher, and (3) as an activity which is not done in the college or for which no teacher is responsible. Responsibilities with majority percentages of ratings used for classification purposes were as follows:

I. Individual Duties:

Grade accounting 92%
Attendance accounting 90%
Office hours 85%
Audio-Visual aids 80%
Academic freedom 77%
Teaching of values 68%
Teaching policy 65%
Course outline 64%
Student counseling 63%
Maintaining schedules 60%

II. Group Duties:

Textbook selection 65%
Supply budget 55%

III. No Duty:

Fire safety 58%

IV. Receiving No Majority:

Room inventory
Room comfort
Bulletins and announcements

Using the majority of responses in each college as the status of the duty at that college, we found the following duties as independent in these numbers of colleges: Grade Accounting 22, Attendance Accounting 21, Audio-Visual Use 19, Student Counseling 19, Academic Freedom 17, Maintaining Schedules 17, Office Hours 16, Teaching of Values 15, Course Outline 14, Textbook Selection 14, Teaching Policy 13. The other five duties (Supply Budget, Room Inventory, Room Comfort, Fire Safety, Bulletins and Announcements) were not used in the majority of colleges as either independent, group, or "no duty" areas, although Fire Safety was classified as no duty of instructors in exactly half of the colleges.

All of these duty areas exist in two-year colleges of various types in all parts of the nation. Some are chiefly individual responsibilities, some involve teachers and administrators working together, and some involve no teachers whatever. Colleges are inconsistent in their involvement of teachers in these activities.

Curriculum Determinants

Curriculum in its broad definition can be a label for every planned learning activity on campus. However, customary usage embraces only the subject matter. Curriculum is a major bond between the student and the instructor, and the instructor plays more than one key role. At the same time, the instructor is far from being the sole determinant of what he teaches.

There are at least six major curriculum determinants other than the individual instructor. Blocker and others provide a sociological analysis (29:202-205). Other institutions, the community, the institution, the faculty, the department, the students—all help select and shape what is taught at the CJC. Understanding their roles will help you to perceive your own special responsibilities and boundary lines.

Any CJC which sends its students to a senior institution must provide for the transferability of its lower division courses. The courses which transfer most easily are those which most nearly parallel the course descriptions of the senior institutions. While the instructor has considerable discretion within the boundaries of the course description, nevertheless he must work within its boundaries if his students are to be as well prepared as the students who spend their first two years at a senior institution.

Another institutional determinant is the high school responsible for the curriculum precedent to the freshman's arrival. What is studied at the CJC should not duplicate high school work unnecessarily; at the same time the CJC cannot leave too great a gap between its starting point and the end of high school preparation. A knowledge of high school courses and materials is invaluable when giving shape and substance to CJC courses.

There is, in addition, the guidance furnished by other junior colleges. Innovation can be stimulating, both for the instructor and the student. However, work which is non-comparable can cause difficulties for the student who must transfer to another junior college. Creativity in curriculum has to be tempered by an awareness of other institutions.

Communities may help shape the curriculum in three general ways: vocationally, emotionally, and economically.

1. Vocational needs of a community are typically reflected in vocational courses, especially at the tax-supported community college. The non-transfer or terminal programs depend particularly on feedback from local employers. Advisory committees are used commonly to design job-oriented curriculum. Many new courses are suggested by community employers. Frequently the employer furnishes the job requirements, while the faculty design the appropriate curriculum.

2. Emotional attitudes in a community vary greatly; the majority

usually prevail in determining curriculum. Emotion may create or destroy curriculum. On every campus are boundaries, usually invisible, as to what curriculum may be added or kept. Most instructors sense these boundaries rather than perceive them explicitly. Especially sensitive areas are sex, religion, and politics. Thus, care must be taken to understand the community when topics, examples, texts, courses, and other instructional devices are selected. Stimulating instruction sometimes risks community reaction. The knack is to perceive the limit so that you can gauge the safety of the distance beyond.

3. Economic support from a community usually requires that the CJC reflect substantially the taxpayers' aspirations for higher education. Two years of transferable education at home is the most common expectation. With taxpayers' support come suggestions for the curriculum. The motivation is not vocational or emotional at all times; often it is simply the pride of part-ownership in a local college. Programs, facilities, and staffs are expensive, and local residents have a voice in curriculum through their elected trustees and a strong independent voice if they are tax-paying supporters.

Your most direct involvement in determination of curriculum will take place at several levels. The immediate one will be in your own subject matter field. As a specialist, you will be responsible for the development of curriculum in your field of competence. The process is described in greater detail elsewhere in this chapter. Bloom provides many useful techniques in defining educational objectives for the development of curriculum. He poses four useful major questions:

1. What objectives should the school or course seek to attain?
2. What learning experiences can bring about goal attainment?
3. What organization of the learning experiences would provide continuity and sequence and help the learner integrate what might be isolated learning experiences?
4. How can the effectiveness of the learning experiences be evaluated? (31:25)

Some departmental programs require development by several staff members. Frequently departmental committees are used to analyze and design freshman courses, because these may require numerous sections. The essential task is that of reaching a consensus on course objective and standards, then designing guidelines broad enough to allow the individual instructors to apply their own unique talents.

Faculty members are also becoming involved in the general determination of curriculum. The earlier pattern of the administration, and in particular that of the dean of instruction assuming the role of curriculum arbiter and coordinator, is changing. The "curriculum committee," composed of department chairmen as well as faculty association or senate members, is assuming an increasing role in curriculum determination.

Making newspaper and television news headlines across the nation in recent times has been the sixth curriculum determinant: the students. Although students always have had opportunities to influence curriculum change, lately an impatient and sometimes militant minority of students have created public controversy over multiple demands. The students are finding success in their methods. Black study programs, rather elaborately initiated at several community colleges, are only one example of student effectiveness in curriculum matters.

What shall be taught remains a major question in each generation. The issues are many and the answers intricate. The six basic forces just described make curriculum determination a dynamic activity that never really achieves its final goal, for the goals continually change.

The Course Outline

After curriculum has been determined, it is translated into a course outline. As a new teacher, one of your first acts should be to examine the course outline for each course you are to teach. The need for this examination should be clear. You never should face a class for the first time with the intention of following only your own plan of course organization, for the college has already developed, through individual instructors and committee action, a plan that has met approval and which is expected to be followed by the individual teacher.

You need not be a slave to the outline, however; if you find that the outline can be revised satisfactorily to parallel your own subject-matter approach, you usually can alter the plan with official approval. The key figures whose approval is required are the head of instruction, the department chairman, and other instructors who must teach the same course. The rule then is to study and revise, if necessary, the course outline.

What, essentially, *is* the course outline? It is your organizational plan and the instructional details for the teaching of the course. The content of the outline differs somewhat from one CJC to another. Some plans list only the subject-matter content covered in the course; others are more elaborate. The more complete plans might include the following divisions: Title and Description, Required Background, Course Objectives, Textbooks and Bibliography, Minimum Student Materials, School Facilities Available, Course Content Plan, Methods of Instruction, and Methods of Evaluating Outcomes.

Perhaps central among these are the aims, procedures, and outcomes; *aims* are what we seek to do, *procedures* are how we propose to do it, and *outcomes* are the evaluative results. Delmer Goode discusses these aspects (141). In determining aims, we ask such questions as, "Can students reach them or are they possible and desirable?" We find procedures through the criteria of suitability, simplicity, student involvement, flexibility, and variety. Through various kinds of tests and observations we determine outcomes. Although there are many kinds of outcomes, most if not all are reduced to student behavior. For a clearer understanding of the needs in these areas, study through the following sample course outline.

A Sample Cover Page

COURSE OUTLINE FOR
INTERPRETATIVE SPEECH 10

Catalog Description: "This course is for those who need training and experience in the selection, preparation, practice, and delivery of various types of literature for oral interpretation. The aim is to develop interpretative speech skills needed for certain professions and occupations and useful for creative outlets in recreation and entertainment." Three Hours.

The Sample Outline

I. TITLE AND DESCRIPTION: Interpretative Speech 10, a three hour course in the speech arts curriculum, two hours of lecture and one hour of lab practice. The course will be offered for one semester as an introduction to reading and interpretative speech skills needed for various professions and occupations as well as for recreation and entertainment. The course is in the lower division and can be transferred as a requirement or as an elective to most senior colleges and universities. Those needing the course most are speech and drama majors and also English majors who expect to teach. Anyone who must read and interpret printed material on his job will find the course helpful, perhaps required.

II. REQUIRED BACKGROUND: None. Those, however, who have had a course in literature and/or in public speaking are more apt to feel at home in the subject.

III. COURSE OBJECTIVES: (Serving both general and special education goals)
   A. To become acquainted with the type of literary material most suited to the needs of the oral interpreter.
   B. To analyze effectively and select authors and their writings as a basis for excellent interpretation.
   C. To understand and use correct procedures in the preparation, practice, and delivery of interpretative speech.
   D. To improve the role of the listener in the evaluation process of interpretative speech activity.
   E. To learn about and appreciate the values of oral interpretation as an aesthetic representation of mankind's creativity.
   F. To provide a foundation of necessary training for additional education and work in the field of speech arts.
   G. To provide, where possible, opportunities for public performances.

IV. TEXTBOOKS AND BIBLIOGRAPHY:
 A. Basic Text: Charlotte Lee. *Oral Interpretation.* Houghton Mifflin, 1965.
 B. Supplementary: Charles Woolbert and Severina Nelson. *The Art of In-terpretative Speech.* Appleton-Century-Crofts, 1956. Joseph Smith and James Linn. *Skill in Reading Aloud.* Harper and Brothers, 1960. Chloe Armstrong and Paul Grandes. *The Oral Interpretation of Litera-ture.* McGraw-Hill, 1963. Gladys Lynch and Harold Crain. *Projects in Oral Interpretation.* Henry Holt, 1959.

V. MINIMUM STUDENT MATERIALS: Basic Text and notebook.

VI. SCHOOL FACILITIES AND EQUIPMENT AVAILABLE: Speech classroom, tape recorder, microphone, phonograph, projectors, records, and films.

VII. COURSE CONTENT PLAN:
 PART ONE: Nine weeks. Background content and choral practice and performance for project activities in oral interpretation.
 A. FIRST WEEK: Historical development of oral interpretation.
 B. SECOND WEEK: Definition and values.
 C. THIRD-FOURTH WEEK: Methods of selection and evaluation of material for oral interpretation.
  1. Sources of material
  2. Selection of material; extrinsic factors
  3. Analysis: intrinsic factors
 D. FIFTH WEEK: Preparation and presentation: Voice and body skills.
 E. SIXTH WEEK: Performance and evaluation
 F. SEVENTH-EIGHTH WEEK: Choral group interpretation
 G. NINTH WEEK: Review and examination

 PART TWO: Nine weeks. Specific types of interpretative content and indi-vidual practice and performance.
 A. TENTH-TWELFTH WEEK: Intepretation of prose.
  1. Exposition
  2. Description
  3. Narration
  4. Performance
 B. THIRTEENTH-FIFTEENTH WEEK: Interpretation of drama.
  1. Acting and interpretation
  2. Setting and properties
  3. Plot
  4. Character
  5. Technique
  6. Performance
 C. SIXTEENTH-SEVENTEENTH WEEK: Interpretation of poetry.
  1. Language: content, attitude, stanzas, wording, imagery, allusions, tone color
  2. Structure: regular, blank verse, free verse

3. Types: narrative, lyrical, dramatic, humorous
4. Performance
D. EIGHTEENTH WEEK: Final review and examination

VIII. METHODS OF INSTRUCTION. (Objectives met by the following)
A. Lectures by the instructor
B. Exercises in interpretation: individual and choral
C. Recording and playback by use of tape recorder
D. Use of evaluation forms in interpretation
E. Oral discussions and evaluations by students and instructor
F. Papers and reports in the analysis of authors and literature
G. Coaching of students for contests involving interpretation
H. Listening to famous interpreters on records and tapes
I. Use of motion pictures or video tape
J. Lab exercises in vocal and physical control of material
K. Performances, where possible, for college and community

IX. METHODS OF EVALUATING OUTCOMES:
A. Use of point system for better detail of measurement
B. Use of a ranking system of total cumulative point scores and the division of these scores into alphabetical grades
C. Use of stated and printed criteria for effective intepretation
D. Use of paper and pencil tests based upon reading, discussions, and lectures (theory, principles, and facts included)
E. Use of specific criteria for projects and reports
F. Use of individual conferences with students to determine needs, problems, and possible solutions
G. Use of subjective judgments in areas where objectivity is inapplicable

The chief responsibility for starting a course on its way through administrative machinery rests with the instructor most clearly involved with the new course. A petition for a new course (or changes and dropping of courses) usually proceeds from the instructor to the department chairman, the head of instruction, the curriculum committee, the college president and/or administrative council, and finally the board of college trustees. The course outline should accompany the petition. Petition information, following a form developed by the college, may indicate fulfillment of criteria by saying that the new course should

Avoid duplication of existing courses,
Be needed by a sufficient number of students to fill one or more classes,
Have an available, qualified instructor,
Take equipment and facilities into account,
Demonstrate compatibility with the college's philosophies and objectives,
Meet budget approval,
Fall within the lower division offerings,
Contribute to the enrichment of general education.

Curriculum development is usually the responsibility of a joint faculty-administrative committee. Details of this committee and other professional duties and functions are included in the next chapter.

Textbook Selection

When you begin to teach in a CJC, you may have whatever textbook has been selected previously by your departmental colleagues. If you dislike the text or any of the other printed aids currently in use, make the best of it until such time as new adoptions are in order. Normally, a textbook is adopted for a three to five year period for greater efficiency and economy, especially for the bookstore. Stabilizing a text has economic benefits also for the students, who thus have a chance to sell and buy used texts.

If you are the only one teaching a particular course, you will probably choose the text. If two or more teach a course section, book selection is usually decided by consensus or majority. Most colleges have a policy that the same basic instructional materials should be used by all who teach the same course. This means the same edition, copyright date, etc. Such coordination can be of extreme importance to the student who has to transfer sections mid-semester. Quite often different supplementary texts are allowed, but such texts are usually not "required to purchase."

Unless one teacher handles a course alone, textbook selection is usually determined in a departmental meeting presided over by the chairman. Several textbooks are recommended for examination and possible adoption. All members should have an opportunity to examine all the books, a job that may require several weeks during the school year. Finally, a vote is taken and the selection is made. The chairman then reports these adoptions to the head of instruction, who ordinarily approves them. The bookstore is given the list of adoptions, new and old, by April or May; the bookstore head is responsible for ordering these books for the summer and/or fall terms.

Although college instructors are generally free to select whatever books they want, they have the obligation to select books and materials wisely. Points to consider are the following:

1. Recency of publication, thoroughness of revision
2. Clarity and adaptability of the organization and content to satisfy your needs and the course you teach
3. Language appropriate to the level of junior college students
4. Author's qualifications and the validity of his research and reports
5. Sufficient amount of teaching aids, such as pictures, projects, and questions for study and discussion
6. Comprehensiveness, depth, and objectivity of subject matter treatment

Item six, dealing with objectivity, is apt to cause the most trouble. Because junior colleges are closely identified with specific communities, many local citizens may be concerned about slanted presentation of subject matter. By *slanted*, we mean views which favor one side of a controversy. For instance, the selection of a history textbook which espouses a political cause (like communism for America) would be foolhardy. Remember that your students will take the book home, and share it with their parents and friends, who may complain to the college president and board.

In many cases, colleges have procedures whereby community citizens can challenge any book or instructional material used in their particular college. Be prepared to justify any book selection if it falls into the critical category. If you are unsure, discuss the question with the department head or person in charge of instruction. Of course, many public complaints may be based upon misunderstanding and unjustifiable fears; but, if a teacher uses his lectern to preach and persuade instead of to teach and inform about all sides of issues, then he violates the special status of his position. He should strike a delicate balance between vague neutrality and propagandizing; he should train the students to think and decide for themselves.

Instructional Equipment and Supplies

Proper use of instructional equipment is necessary to good instruction. In the course outline, you'll remember, is a section regarding facilities and equipment available for teaching the course. If you know your teaching area as well as you should, you will have no difficulty in planning the use of instructional equipment. At this time, we offer no instruction on the selection of equipment and supplies: we only point out the necessity of using them. Undoubtedly you will have several areas within your college, often the library, where equipment and materials are stored. Frequently you will find a director of instructional technology or a co-ordinator of instructional aids to assist you in planning and using all available resources.

We can itemize your duties as follows:
1. Determine what material aids are available.
2. Conduct an extensive study on the values of these various aids.
3. Select specific aids which would help you teach your course.
4. Order these aids by buying them through the departmental budget or requesting them through the library's AV aids office.
5. Place your order well in advance of the time you will need to use the materials.
6. Properly prepare your students prior to the actual employment of the materials.

7. Exercise proper techniques when the materials are in use.
8. Follow-up the use with class discussion and student testing.
9. Return all equipment and materials to their sources unless these aids are checked out to you permanently.
10. Evaluate the use of the aids in your class to determine if you should use them again or make some change in your procedures.

Although techniques are discussed in Chapter eight, it may be helpful at this point to look again at our sample course outline to see how a few examples of instructional technology can be applied to it. By examining some aids for the oral interpretation course, you may think of certain applications within your own subject area.

Technical Aids	*Non-Technical Aids*
Listening to radio, tape, and records of famous interpreters of literature	Attending a live performance by an oral interpreter (field trip)
Observing still and motion pictures of interpreters and key geographical areas where the literature developed or where interpretation first became an art	Participation in the preparation, practice, and delivery of individual interpretations of various types of literature
Inspecting a map showing key cities where theatrical interpretation thrives	Physical practice in learning how to use a manuscript before an audience
Learning how to use a microphone and recording device as aids to clarity and projection of voice	Exercises in voice control—rate, duration, volume, pitch, quality, rhythm, etc.
Using an overhead or opaque projector to illustrate the proper structure, cutting, and editing of literary material	Physical activities in cutting and editing printed material
Recording classroom performances with a TV or motion picture camera	Oral reading exercises
Using a teaching machine for programmed study of theory, facts, and principles in interpretation	Observing classroom performances
	Group participation in choral reading and interpretation

It is your duty to secure training in the use of instructional materials and to apply this training in class whenever the subject lends itself to the use of these materials. Not only does instructional technology add an element of entertainment to the serious business of learning, but it also aids immeasurably in helping the students to grasp essential information and to retain it for longer periods of time. As new technical devices continue to be invented for classroom use, it is important that you keep up with them and apply them profitably in your teaching.

Attendance Accounting

In states where junior colleges are supported by state funds on the basis of attendance reports, it is your duty to keep accurate records of student attendance. In other states or in private junior colleges that receive no state financial support, attendance accounting is still considered important as a means of contributing to the student's grade. Such is not the case in many four-year colleges and universities, where attendance sometimes is not required.

Attendance accounting procedures are apt to vary in details from one CJC to another, even though the state may require a uniform overall procedure. In some public junior colleges, for example, attendance in each class is registered by the teacher twice each semester, each time accounting for the number of hours each student was in a class for a one-week period. In many larger colleges, each teacher is provided with electronic-data-processing attendance cards for each student registered in his courses. Some states pay a considerable sum to support the public CJC through attendance figures and there is, therefore, great pressure for clerical accuracy. Whatever system is used, indicate it in front of your roll book so that attendance accountants and others such as substitutes who must refer to it know how to read your symbols or those adopted by college policy.

Important to attendance accounting is your system of roll taking. A standard method is to prepare a seating chart and use it to check the absences immediately. As you find empty seats, you might call out the names of those who occupy them just in case someone is in the wrong seat. Perhaps it's best to wait until the second week to establish definite seating, because in a CJC there may be shifting around from one course to another; this is particularly true in the public junior colleges. Some students may decide on the first day the course is not for them; others may enter your course for the first time on the third or fourth class day. It is wise, regardless of when you prepare the seating chart, to call the roll at the first few meetings just to learn the names and to become acquainted with the current pronunciation. Roll taking, particularly in very large classes, may be done by some assistant or trusted student.

Regarding withdrawals and additions to the class roll, the college will probably inform you of these students by placing a form notice inside your school mailbox. For accuracy and for keeping your roll book up to date, you should make these changes on the day that you receive them. For withdrawals be sure to cross out the names of the affected students on the seating chart; in the roll book indicate the date and a W for withdrawal. New students are added to chart and book with an entering date. Comments about the grades of students who withdraw are in the next section.

Grade Accounting and Counseling

In addition to attendance reporting, the keeping and reporting of student grades is probably your most important required academic duty. At the middle of the semester or quarter, a large number of community colleges require that students be notified of their progress. In these schools the teacher must provide a mid-term warning to those students who are not measuring up to the satisfactory or C grade level. It is a fair requirement for several reasons: (1) Students themselves need to know at this time how well they are succeeding insofar as class averages and class goals are concerned. (2) The counseling office needs to know which students are in trouble so that counselors as well as teachers themselves can help these students improve their achievement. (3) The admissions or related office must know whether probationary students are in danger of being eliminated from the college or of being denied the privilege of graduation. (4) The professional staff as a whole should be informed about these students and the percentage of the student body they constitute. (5) Finally, and not necessarily last in importance, are parents, who frequently are kept officially informed.

Mid-term grade reports indicate college interest in individual and overall student progress. The object is not to ridicule or scold the student in trouble but to inform him, while there is still time left in the courses, that he is at the danger level and can raise his standing in certain specific ways.

Five of the most common criticisms are (1) absent too often from class; (2) does not turn in all assignments; (3) does his work carelessly; (4) scores too low on quizzes and examinations; (5) seems to have emotional problems that interfere with class achievement.

Mid-term grade accounting may consist of completing warning notices showing current grades and reasons for them. When electronic-data-processing cards are used, the college provides one for each student with his name and other identifying information printed across the top. If grades are not required for any but those students doing unsatisfactory work, you simply throw away the extra cards. On the cards used, mark the bubble indicating the grade, whether it be *unsatisfactory* or the specific grades of D and F.

Even though you may not be required to report mid-term grades to your college office, it is wise to make such a report to your students, because most may wish to strive for a better class standing before the final grades are calculated. You could announce these grades orally in class, but it may be less embarrassing if a listing is placed on the class bulletin board. Each student can be given a code number, possibly one which corresponds with the student's number in the roll book. At his convenience, the student can check his class standing in relation to the total group. When the grades are posted, you can announce that you are available for individual conference appointments relating to these grades. In some cases you may request that a particular student in trouble see you about his grade; make the request privately if you can.

At the end of the term after the final examinations have been graded and recorded, you must once again complete a grade sheet or electronic-data-processing card for each student. Junior colleges normally use the familiar alphabetical grades, A, B, C, D, and F, although this traditional system is frequently attacked (63). At this time you must also account for those students who did not complete the course. Though systems will vary in minor details, the following system is typical: Students who have withdrawn from your classes within a specified time set by the college are given a W. Those who have withdrawn after this date are sometimes given a W/P (Withdrawal, Passing) or a W/F (Withdrawal, Failing). Those students present at the end of the course but not completing essential work are given an I, standing for Incomplete. Increasing in popularity as a substitute for specific grades are the so-called "credit-non credit" courses. The most important step is to familiarize yourself with the specific procedures at your college.

Essential to grade accounting is the establishment of a plan of grade distribution. No one can dictate to you how to assign your grades, because this function is the strict domain of the professional teacher. Nevertheless, you should know the grading philosophy of your institution. Some helpful information about junior colleges, moreover, may change your ideas about grading. Unlike elementary and secondary education, college education is not mandatory. Children in the lower grades represent heterogeneous groupings, characterized by wide dissimilarities found in any cross section of people. Because higher education is freely elected by students, they tend to fall into homogeneous groupings insofar as their innate intelligences and abilities are concerned. In this respect, students in the senior institutions of higher education are expected to be intellectually more homogeneous than those in the junior colleges.

All of this means that the normal curve of grades, found in heterogeneous groupings, is usually inapplicable for higher education; the grade curve in colleges is apt to be skewed toward the upper end. In essence, there should be fewer people in the D and F categories of grades than there are in the A and B categories. Because entrance requirements for four-year colleges and universities are generally higher than those for junior colleges, the latter institutions are apt to have a higher proportion of so-called average or C students. Much depends upon the class, however; for very large classes in general education courses, grades may follow the normal curve more closely than would grades in special or elective courses. The smaller and more demanding the class, the higher may be the average grade in that class.

Junior college administrators and counselors frequently study the grade distribution patterns of their own faculties. This study gives them one picture of both student and teacher effectiveness. Occasionally a teacher has been challenged to give evidence in support of his grade distribution. The challenge could come for giving no A's or for giving too many.

Student failures constitute a larger number of a given CJC enrollment than most of us would like to see. One study of a college showed that 43 percent of all students completing a semester were put on probation or were disqualified from further college study (63). Another study of a college reported 30 percent, 77 percent of which were in a transfer program (60:76). Grades affect students greatly and therefore should be carefully derived. To satisfy yourself that your grades are reasonable and consistent with those of other instructors, you should occasionally discuss the process with other department members or the dean of instruction.

The counseling function is not limited to conferring with students about grades. Perhaps you have heard the statement that "every teacher is a counselor." You can counsel a student about professional and vocational opportunities in the area that you teach, about the talents and skills he will need, about course requirements for a major or a minor in your areas, about where he can go to complete his upper division course credits or, in the case of a terminal-vocational student, where he can obtain a job upon graduation. "Faculty involvement in a career conference program is also vital. . . . Faculty members are in a position either to assure the success of the program or to guarantee its failure through their daily contacts and influence with students" (346:41).

Some colleges insist that their teachers serve both as regular counselors as well as teachers. The Fashion Institute of Technology, for instance, is a two-year college that has built this condition into the applications for faculty positions and in promotion and tenure requirements. Duties automatically include regular counseling. Each faculty member is assigned from 5 to 20 guides (students); the average is about 14 per teacher. Duties include academic and technical counseling, counseling for students with psychological or philosophical problems, and counseling for socio-cultural development (84).

Whatever your specific duties in this area, you'll find that students depend upon you for guidance and counseling. Announce to your classes that you stand ready to help them. Announce your office schedule and have interested students make appointments rather than try to catch you in the hurried moments immediately before and after class. Each time you extend a kindly helping hand to a student, you are extending your own usefulness as a teacher and your own reputation as a professional person.

The Class Policy and Orientation

When facing your class for the first time, you must explain to the students the various aspects of your class policy. This is the initial orientation period. Although you may wish to handle this function on the second or third meeting, consider that students generally want the orientation early so as to decide more wisely if they want to remain in the course. It is far better, it seems, to make the course purposes and requirements clear and get all of the class shifting and withdrawals over during the first few days of the course.

What attitude should you demonstrate in the orientation period? Perhaps the best approach is to emphasize positive goals in a realistic way. Describe the work and policy of the course, by all means, but do it in a way which suggests reason and sympathetic understanding. The friendly but realistic approach seems to bring more positive results than the stern and threatening approach.

To orient the class to your course and class policies, the following areas are suggested.* Some of this information can be placed on the blackboard or given to your students on a handout sheet.

Instructor's name and background: Your general background is important here because it establishes your qualifications for teaching your students, it reveals something about your personality and character, and it provides an insight into your basic philosophy and aims. By hearing this information, your students can better understand and appreciate what you have to offer them, and a better instructor-student rapport is established.

Name of course, catalog description, units, etc.: Many students may have been scheduled into your class without their having checked this important information. Take very little for granted. Announce whether the course is general or special education, whether the course is transferable as a requirement or an elective, and other related facts. Although values and appreciations will be elaborated upon later, now is the time to point up aspects of motivation.

Textbooks and syllabi: Avoid great detail here, but provide a general picture of the basic text materials along with information about authors. Describe briefly how much of the basic text will be covered, comment on its basic philosophy and/or organizational approach, and note any other materials students must buy for the course.

---

* Most of these suggestions are for teachers who structure courses in advance of meeting classes. A study of California community college teaching, conducted by Win Kelley during the spring of 1969, revealed that a few teachers tended to let their classes do the selecting and structuring of course content; in this highly unusual case, the students alone or the teacher and class together spend a few days developing the essential facts and policies.

Broad objectives: Refer to your course outline here to make sure you cover the complete list of objectives. Give brief explanations as you go along. Show the reasons for these goals, the values and importance to the students. Let them know if the stress will be on function, theory, or both. Wherever possible, define the course objectives in terms of expected student behavior.

Content outline of the course: Again, follow the content as shown on your course outline. You may wish to show the topics covered week by week or else a general picture without reference to time. Be sure to compare your content outline to the table of contents in the basic textbook to show interrelationships.

Exercises and projects: Show the functional learning activities which help your students reach the course goals. Show which activities will be written and which will be oral or physical in nature. Indicate here only general requirements for reading assignments, reports, term papers, lab work, and the like; announce that the details will be furnished to them later when these activities are introduced into the course.

Evaluation: Explain how many quizzes and examinations you will have, over what areas of the course, and the types to be used, whether essay, objective-type, or subjective observations. Evaluation is especially effective when it is expressed in terms of student behavioral outcomes.

Grading system: Explain how much weight will be given to the various activities and examinations, particularly how much the final will count in the total grade. Announce whether you will use the alphabetical system or the mathematical (points or percentages) system in recording grade credits. You'll find that most students will be more concerned about grades than with the actual good they can gain from course content. Once again, you might reemphasize course values to them. If you can get them into the proper frame of mind about learning, grades may become secondary. A clear cut introductory explanation of student behavioral objectives and evaluation can reduce student anxieties, which are often increased by amorphous instructional objectives and vague evaluative criteria.

Attendance and other factors: Explain the college policy (as well as your own) concerning attendance, withdrawals, and re-admittance. Announce the conditions under which you would excuse them for an absence. For excused absences, it's wise to ask for verification, such as a doctor's appointment card. If you make a policy of accepting an oral excuse from the student himself, you must expect to have some students take advantage of you. If attendance is included in your grading, show the credit to be given. If tardiness is significant to you, mention that also.

Questions and discussion: Don't assume that you have been perfectly clear in the presentation of your class policy. Always include time for answering questions and clearing up misunderstandings. When all of this is done, it would appear that you are ready for the actual teaching of the course.

Other Responsibilities

Thus far we have discussed the major academic duties and functions related to the CJC classroom; listed below are additional common areas of responsibility.

Care of equipment and classroom: You and the colleagues who share your teaching space are directly responsible for the general condition of your classroom. Treat equipment as if it had to last forever. Although junior college students are more mature than those on the lower levels, some have not yet developed a concern for others' needs. You must, therefore, guard against students' destructive behavior. Since junior colleges are frequent victims of thefts and burglary, make sure you secure the classroom when you leave it for more than a few minutes.

Room comfort: You must regulate the heating, lighting, and ventilation in the room if possible. If you have air conditioning, keep the doors and windows closed. Studying will not be pleasant if the room is too cold, too hot, too drafty, or too close. When through with the room, be sure to turn off not only the lights and equipment but whatever else may be appropriate.

Fire orientation: Your junior college board probably has established a policy that requires teachers to give orientation to students on the subject of drills in case of fire or other emergencies. When such a drill occurs in the college, your duty is to usher the students to an outside designated area. To avoid drafts which may aid fires, close both the windows and the doors after you.

Class bulletins and requests: Some colleges may require that you read a daily bulletin to your classes as one way to keep them informed of announcements important to them. Requests for information or miscellaneous reports related to your classroom or your teaching should be completed and returned promptly to the various college offices requiring them.

Teaching of values: Regardless of what subject you teach, a college may expect you to assume general responsibility for the teaching of certain values. In the lower grades, for instance, most teachers must be concerned about good citizenship, patriotism and devotion to country, respect for law and order, the rights and responsibilities of citizens, and so on. In general, junior colleges exhibit more concern for these areas. Many colleges are deeply concerned about moral and spiritual values, in particular. The teacher's behavior is perhaps the most powerful means of instruction in these areas.

Adherence to truthful teaching: We have already mentioned this duty in the previous subject area of textbook selection, but here we mean careful and objective presentation of knowledge. Some teachers may be careless about facts; some may even hide or lie about facts. Nevertheless, both sides of a controversy should be presented as fairly as possible. We should be free to pursue knowledge but not to indoctrinate (236). It is understood, however, that church organized and sponsored junior colleges are often expected to stress values as well as academic content. Under such special circumstances, indoctrination may be expected when it is consonant with the philosophy of the private college sponsor and when the intention is made clear from the outset.

Adherence to class schedule: Every teacher should communicate a positive attitude toward the importance of his classes. Unless a scheduled class meeting is canceled by the administration, endeavor to meet classes on time. Each class should remain in session for the full time allotment. Dismissal of classes for all or part of a period usually needs permission from the proper authorities. If you are ill or become ill on the job, report it to the office as rapidly as possible so that arrangements can be made to notify your classes or to secure a substitute teacher. Let the office know when you expect to return to work. If a sick-leave policy is in effect at your college, complete the sick leave form upon your return.

Establishment of office hours: Classroom duties are extended into your office for the purpose of counseling and helping individual students. Most junior colleges attempt to provide office space for each faculty member. Ordinarily at least one hour of office per day is mandatory. Keep dependable hours so that you can be reached by people who have business to conduct with you.

Instructional improvement: Strive continually to improve your teaching by evaluating and improving your methods and techniques. Such a classroom duty involves trying to understand your students' needs and abilities, advancing their education as far as they can go while you have them in class.

Personal conferences about instruction: When you have teaching problems that you cannot handle alone, it's your duty to confer with proper authorities about them. If you do not receive adequate orientation about your teaching duties and functions, take the initiative. What may seem like disinterest is likely to be a reflection of an administrator's reluctance to seem officious.

Inventory and budgets: At year's end, you may be required to submit an inventory of all equipment and materials under your charge. Normally everything inside your classroom is included on the list except for the common desk supplies. By this time, in late spring, you will also be asked to determine what instructional materials and supplies are needed for the following school year. Whatever you need, whether it is a complex piece of machinery or a simple bookcase, include it on the appropriate form along with the approximate price and where it may be secured. Do not be overly conservative in these needs; let someone else decide whether the material can be afforded. Your primary responsibility is to recommend what is needed to do the best possible job in your teaching field.

Chapter 6

Professional Duties and Functions

Although academic or teaching duties have first priority and effective teaching requires the major portion of time and energy, other work in the college needs to be done. Just as the student's college experience is more than sitting in a classroom, teaching is more than meeting classes. Both the student and the teacher are constantly embroiled in the problems surrounding their out-of-class activities and functions. These various activities contribute to the total environmental experience and complement the basic goals of teaching and learning. The measurement of the student's and teacher's overall effectiveness must be based partially on their performances in the work and fun outside of the classroom.

Important are the following significant areas: Mandatory and Obligatory Duties, Staff Meetings, College Committees, In-Service Education, Club Sponsorship, Faculty Association and Senate, Attendance at College Functions, Professional and Personal Growth, Administrative Relations, Community Relations, Night Teaching, Outside Employment, and Roles in Accreditation.

Mandatory and Obligatory Duties

Professional non-teaching duties and functions can be classified in two categories: (1) those which are *mandatory*, and (2) those which are *obligatory*. By our definition both mandatory and obligatory duties are "required"; they differ to the extent that mandatory duties are those which are officially requested of or assigned to the teacher, while obligatory duties are those which are not officially assigned but are nevertheless obligations. For instance, a teacher is requested to attend a staff meeting (mandatory), but he is expected to attend an important sports event on campus (obligatory). The most successful staff member, we believe, is one who treats both of these requirements in the same manner, one who responds equally to official requests and to reasonable expectations.

There are multiple values to the instructor who participates fully in both the mandatory and obligatory out-of-class activities. By associating with students and colleagues on both formal and informal bases, he gains a greater mutual respect, understanding, and cooperation. He enhances his professional growth by his participation. He sometimes demonstrates administrative potential and is assigned additional college responsibilities for which he receives greater financial remuneration. His physical, mental, and emotional growth is fostered and accelerated by his active involvement in matters outside the classroom. In essence, the better he participates and performs his professional non-teaching duties and functions, the more he gains as a teacher and as a human being.

Certain types of mandatory duties may be assigned more often to new rather than tenured instructors; new instructors are likely targets for such duties as student advisory assignments, dance chaperones, or ticket taking at a sports event. New teachers find themselves with some of these extra duties because tenured staff members may have already served their "time" in these activities, may have teaching loads which rule out extra duty, or may have exhibited persuasive power in escaping the extra assignments. Fortunately, some colleges recognize the danger of overloading the new instructor with these extra duties. Their answer is to defer most non-teaching assignments until the teacher's second or third year; the deferment enables the new person to give his full energies to finding and developing teaching proficiency in an unfamiliar environment that demands many adjustments.

To determine the status of the ten professional responsibilities discussed in this chapter, we asked the specialists in our college-faculty survey to check whether they were mandatory (assigned or requested as a specific professional duty), obligatory (expected), or neither mandatory nor obligatory. Responses of the majority indicated that assigned or mandatory duties are in the areas of staff meetings (88 percent), college committees (63 percent), and college accreditation (65 percent). Classified as obligatory or expected duties by the majority of responses were club advisement (71 percent), faculty association or senate participation (51 percent), attendance at college functions (79 percent), professional growth activities (65 percent), administrative relations (60 percent), and community relations (75 percent). In the last two areas, almost all respondents indicated by their answers that faculty members were obligated to maintain satisfying roles and relationships with administrators and the community in general.

When we checked the majority of responses in each college, we found that three of the professional responsibilities were required and the other seven were obligations. Assuming that most of the respondents were accurate, we can say that 20 colleges required participation in staff meetings, 13 required duties in the area of college committees, and 14 required participation in college accreditation when the colleges were involved in this function. The greatest number of colleges in the "Obligated" category was 19 for "College Function Attendance." The greatest number in the "Neither" category was 7 for "Faculty Association or Senate."

In summation, the results show that all 10 areas are either mandatory or obligatory in most of the colleges studied; we presume the same would be true if a much wider sample had been taken. These professional responsibilities are representative of those you are apt to find wherever you work in a CJC.

Staff Meetings

As a beginning instructor, you may come to regard junior college faculty life as one long series of staff meetings. Even before classes begin, you will be requested to attend orientation meetings for new staff members. In addition to on-campus orientation, you may also have district meetings to acquaint you with policies and procedures, especially those in a multicampus district. These meetings for new staff members are extremely important, since they are designed to help you meet your responsibilities as effectively as possible. Most colleges operate on the assumption that you know your subject and how to teach it; however, as a new member, you will not know the various campus routines and procedures that are discussed in some detail in Chapter Five. Each campus has evolved unique variations of the general administrative procedures. Consequently, every junior college has to provide briefing sessions for new staff members. Harris says that "The tenure faculty ought to participate as well, in order to get some of the collected smog removed from their brains and restore their sensitivities to the needs of students and community" (157:11).

Quite often the meetings for the new staff are followed by general faculty meetings. These sessions usually review any new procedures that are to be introduced in the fall semester. At the combined meetings the superintendent and the president, the deans, and the librarian usually make use of the opportunity to address the whole staff, to draw their attention to new developments of general interest. You are likely to be introduced at the general meeting, which often will be followed by a tea or coffee hour.

After your initial orientation period and the general staff meetings, you may find that department staff meetings will be scheduled next. This may be your first opportunity to meet the other members of the department. These, as well as all other staff meetings, are considered mandatory, at least in 20 of our 22 colleges studied. You will be wise to be prompt as well as continual in your attendance. In terms of your class-room responsibilities and teaching skills, department staff meetings have the most immediate impact. The choice of textbooks, the planning of courses, the coordinating of sections and sequences—all of these are likely to be discussed and decided at department level. These meetings have the added dimension of acquainting you with colleagues teaching in your field. They can be of appreciable assistance to you, not only in your first year but in the semesters or quarters thereafter. Senior faculty members are likely to take their cues from you in the matter of offering assistance; they may prefer to tender help only if you reveal a desire for it.

Staff meetings usually continue in a logical pattern through the remainder of the school year. At the beginning and end of each semester or year the greatest number of decisions are to be made and the largest amount of information is to be disseminated. Among these peaks of activity you may find distributed other meetings which have been timed to avoid the rush periods. Like the opening meetings of the year, the final meeting will probably involve the general staff, mixing together a social occasion with information on faculty summer plans, check-out procedures, and announcements of staff changes.

A person's absence from a mandatory staff meeting is silent communication. Absence implies "You and your meeting are of little import to me." Of course, there will be times when illness or some other problem will prevent your attendance. In this event you should make known to those responsible for the meeting the reason for your absence. In a sense the situation is analogous to your relationship to the student who is absent without excuse; unless he takes the time to explain to you the reason for his absence, you assume he had no legitimate excuse. When there is no explanation, the logical assumption is that the absence is of little concern to the absentee. The instructor who is habitually absent from staff meetings announces silently but clearly his attitude toward his colleagues, the institution, and the profession; furthermore, in most colleges he may be inviting dismissal as a teacher.

College Committees

An official assignment to a college committee is also a mandatory duty for teachers in the CJC, although the majority in 9 of 22 colleges of our survey reported this duty as obligatory. Such an assignment gives the teacher an important voice in the decision-making machinery of the college. Decisions which represent the end product of faculty study and discussion can bat a higher average than those represented by the thinking of only one person. A committee or group decision is more apt to consider justly those whose lives are affected by the decision; the affected people are more apt to accept a decision when it comes from the consensus of a well-trained, professional group concerned about their welfare. Faculty participation in group decision making increased greatly during the 1960's. Committees have been criticized and satirized; despite their shortcomings and weaknesses, they have demonstrated their values, chiefly in offering an alternative to decisions by autocracy. There are still numerous decisions which have to be made administratively and individually; nevertheless the committee is established as a vital complement to CJC administration.

Administrative Committees

Many college committees are related to the institution itself. Members, sometimes ex officio, usually include the president and one of the deans. These committees represent the integration of the faculty into the decision-making process. The president is responsible ultimately for the decision, but he acts with the recommendation or advisement of the committee. He often has a "cabinet," composed commonly of deans, department heads, and the president of the faculty club or senate; very frequently, the chairmen of the various committees—if they are not already administrators—serve on this cabinet. The title of this cabinet committee is frequently President's Advisory Council, the title varying with each campus. Its essential task is to bring together those staff members who are directly involved in policy decision and implementation. They function also as liaison between the president and the faculty and the board of trustees and the faculty.

Ashmore discusses some of the basic principles of organization of the committee in administration (11). First, the purposes and problems of the committee must be clearly defined and understood. The committee must also understand procedures of when and where reports are to be made. To motivate committees and to produce satisfying results, the administration must consider all committee recommendations. We should add the fact that such recommendations are binding upon the president who delegates administrative power to these committees. Reports should be completed on time and based upon the best knowledge and judgment of members. There must be specific organizational and administrative regulations relating to committees. Ashmore supports the right of administration to override a report when specific reasons exist, but such a principle would be operative only when the president has clearly reserved for himself the right of veto. Legally, he does not have to eliminate his veto rights, but he should adhere to the policy he selects.

Subordinate to this central committee are the various subcommittees, composed largely of faculty members. Although each campus may have several of these groups peculiar to the specific college, there are others which seem to be rather standard, at least in function if not in title. The most common committees are those concerned with curriculum, research and development, community liaison, student activities, instruction and in-service education, library, and faculty employment (screening).

Curriculum Committee

Perhaps the busiest committee is the one concerned with curriculum. Because of the constant need to consider new courses, changes in old courses, textbook changes, the preparation of lucid course outlines and catalog description of courses, the committee meets more often than most other committees. Working closely with the dean of instruction, members study and approve changes or additions which continue on through channels to the administrative cabinet and finally to the board of trustees. Membership not only admits contribution; it is also valuable as a means of learning more about the curriculum patterns and needs outside one's own discipline. Studying other course outlines offers an opportunity to improve one's own outlines. Whether or not a member, you may meet with this committee to present your proposals; your presentation forces you to examine thoroughly your reasons for adding or changing a course.

Research and Development Committee

Sometimes titled the *planning committee,* this group works directly with the president or whoever has been designated as the director of research. The group has the interesting and somewhat disturbing responsibility for deciding what questions the junior college should be asking, how the answers can be found, and how they can be communicated and accepted after their discovery. Many of these decisions have much to do with the future of the institution, inasmuch as their anticipatory guesses commit the college to program and facilities aimed at the needs of the next decade. Concerned with the discovery and interpretation of current facts relating to status, the committee plans accordingly, involving in the process all in the college and community who can contribute to their findings.

Community Liaison Committee

This group includes as members both college and community people. It works closely with the president or an administrator designated by him. The chairman is very apt to be a layman in the community. In many cases there may be several of these committees, each serving some special need to develop better articulation between college and community in one particular area. These groups also include the category of community advisory committees. These citizens serve as a source of vital information from the "consumers" of the CJC "product." The common procedure is to appoint representatives with mutual vocational concerns, such as business, nursing education, or a technical-vocational field. These meetings provide an opportunity for communication between the college and the community, for employers to voice their concerns, and for college staff members to describe and explain the programs and policies of the college.

Student Activities Committee

A dean may head this committee or at least be a member of it; he is usually in charge of student affairs, or he may be the dean of men; in the latter case, a dean of women may also serve on the committee. The group's job is to study and recommend policy for the supervision and governing of student conduct and activities outside the classroom. In this, as well as in other committees, students themselves may be represented by student officials, usually the president of the student body or the chairman of the student activity council, composed of club representatives and student body officers. Numerous student problems are discussed for the purpose of establishing guidelines, rules, and regulations. Official recommendations are sent to the central administrative committee and the board of trustees for final approval.

Instruction and In-Service Education Committee

Usually headed or chaired by the dean of instruction, this committee concerns itself with the problems and improvements of instruction. Any aspect of instruction is fair game for the group's deliberation. Many of the college's philosophies and regulations concerning the teaching function are given birth by this committee. To help instructors do their jobs more effectively, in-service education programs are created and scheduled, teaching schedules and loads are improved, facilities and teaching aids are increased.

Library Committee

Even if a librarian has a large staff working in the library, he or she needs guidelines and special asistance of the administration and total faculty. Serving as chairman or member of this group, the librarian seeks leadership and decisions in the choice of periodical subscriptions and criteria in the selection of books. The holdings of the library frequently include other materials such as magnetic recording tapes and motion picture films. The library budget is also discussed frequently. In these days of federal funding, this type of committee serves as liaison between the faculty and the library for establishing project areas and priorities. If we accept the premise that the library is central to the life of the CJC, then the work of this committee is essential to faculty and students.

Faculty Employment (Screening) Committees

You may become acquainted with the screening committee even before you join a faculty. The committee interviews prospective candidates for employment as instructors. The membership is usually a very select group, including a department chairman, other members of a department, the dean of instruction, other subordinate administrators, and the presidents of the faculty association and the college. In a few colleges, students are admitted on the committee. The formation of such a committee is an expression of the administrative acceptance of the faculty's selection of its new colleagues. Duty with this committee is very important, because it combines the responsibility for selecting one's colleagues with that of making decisions that may have a profound effect on the applicant's future. The committee must realize that interviews, even at best, are somewhat artificial situations. Wise decisions require as many criteria as possible to reduce the likelihood of any one criterion overwhelming the others.

Faculty Association Committees

Occasionally there is some duplication of committees, particularly if the college president's style involves committees and if the faculty association president and senate create their own committees. Often the administration and faculty leaders will evolve an amicable arrangement that allocates duties on the basis of interests and abilities. College committees are, of course, usually assigned; they can, therefore, be classified as mandatory duties. On the other hand, faculty association committees are obligatory assignments for members. These faculty committees usually include such categories as professional ethics and faculty salaries, to cite only two. Professional ethics committees may act as arbiters or "policemen." In a situation where an issue arises between faculty members and administrators, it may be necessary to have a third body study the problem and make a recommendation. Or it may be that a staff member's conduct is jeopardizing the reputation of his colleagues and the college. These problems require a combination of varying proportions of tact, concern, and force. On the one hand the committee has to protect the freedom of the instructor; on the other hand it has to be concerned for all of the instructional staff. Self-policing of one's own profession should be one of the characteristics of its members.

Three Simple Rules

Any member of these or other committees may request your service; our discussion has been limited to examples of those which you are most likely to encounter. Your service on any one of them can be useful training for you and valuable service to your college and your profession. To be an effective member you should observe at least three rules:

1. Do your homework; prepare for the meeting.
2. Listen carefully and speak effectively.
3. Keep personalities out of the discussions; staying with the issues is the best insurance against gossip, bull sessions, or strained relationships.

In-Service Education

Many CJC districts and campuses maintain in-service training institutes. These are commonly designed to continue the professional training of faculty members after they have completed their formal preparation for teaching. When administratively conceived for the general staff, in-service training programs are generally mandatory insofar as faculty attendance and participation are concerned. These programs have to do with teaching techniques, new curriculum programs involving the total faculty, and the latest information about technological aids, among other subjects. Off-campus speakers are used frequently; field trips are taken. Sometimes professional credit is given for attendance at cultural affairs and professional association meetings.

An unusual form of in-service education is that offered by Monterey Peninsula College in California. Financed by a grant from Ford Foundation's Fund for the Advancement of Education, members of the college faculty visited other colleges across the nation to find out whether travel seminars are worthwhile. Results showed that the answer was "yes." Fletcher, reporting these results, said, "But we . . . are not alone in pointing to specific values of a travel seminar. Last year the Systems Development Corporation of Santa Monica completed a contract with the United States Office of Education 'to conduct a study of the effectiveness of traveling seminars.' Their primary finding: the traveling seminar 'is a highly effective dissemination method for stimulating and facilitating educational innovation.' Their leading recommendation: 'The traveling seminar technique should be expanded and actively supported as an effective dissemination activity by the U.S.O.E., state departments of education, and local school districts'" (116:21).

Apart from college-sponsored institutes and training programs where attendance may be required, are those activities in which faculty members participate voluntarily—summer school attendance, night courses, independent study, educational travel, and so on—but all of these are more properly discussed under the subject heading of professional and personal growth. The whole idea of mandatory institutes and training workshops is to help guarantee that teachers increase their knowledge and skills as conveniently as possible. Knowledge is perishable, in that much of it becomes obsolete rapidly. Mandatory attendance and duties related to excellent programs which bring all faculty members up-to-date in general knowledge and competence seem to be justified.

Club Sponsorship

A fourth area involving mandatory duties is club sponsorship or advisement. Not all faculty members are assigned as sponsors; once assigned, however, teachers are duty-bound to understand their functions and perform them well. In most cases you would be assigned to a club that falls naturally into your academic discipline or interest area. A speech teacher, for instance, would be assigned to the forensics club, an English teacher to the creative writing club, a physical education teacher to the athletic club, and a social science teacher to a political club. Along with such special interest clubs are those much broader in scope, such as the freshman and sophomore classes, the associated student body organization, and honor societies. Most colleges require that each student organization have a faculty sponsor or adviser.

As a club sponsor, you should fulfill your role according to the valid expectations of the college and students. As sponsor you represent the official voice of the college; you provide the students with a responsible source of opinion concerning college and community activities. In your relationships with the college and the community, you also represent the club's official voice. The club's activities, its prestige, its general public image reflect upon you as well as upon the club members and officers. You usually hold the power of executive veto over the activities and functions of the club. Club actions must receive your approval, followed by the approval of an inter-club council or central body that regulates clubs and their activities.

Let us discuss this matter of veto in more detail. Veto should be used as a kind of last resort, when it would seem impractical or virtually impossible for the club to continue in a certain direction. For instance, a club, without a penny in its treasury, wants to have a dance and hire a particular band that charges five hundred dollars for its services. A few leaders in the group have sold the membership on the idea of having the dance and contracting for the band in the hope that attendance at the dance will be sufficient to pay all the expenses. The sponsor correctly uses persuasive reasoning at first. He shows the gamble involved. What if ticket sales at the dance are not sufficient to pay the costs involved? Where will they get the extra money which, according to the band's contract, must be available to the band on the night of the dance? Shouldn't the club raise the money first through other methods so that the band's guarantee can be met? After much discussion involving the adviser and the members, the latter still feel that attendance at the dance will more than pay the costs involved. As a last resort, the adviser may decide there is no way to curb their plan other than veto.

Of course, your assignment is not to run the club but to help the students operate it and to offer assistance and advice wherever necessary. Clubs with excellent student leadership tend to keep advisers as passive, happy observers. Most club members, however, are in the process of developing their social skills and leadership potentials. Your main tasks are to foster that growth, guide indirectly as often as needed, and serve upon request as a source of information. You will also bring continuity to a club group which is likely to have a complete turnover every two years and even as often as every semester in some cases. Club sponsorship affords you opportunities to know students outside the formality of the classroom; especially when the club relates to your discipline, you can offer the most enjoyable aspects of the subject matter. As clubs combine social activities with service projects, your imagination and enthusiasm can make a significant difference in the club's success.

Faculty Association and Senate

A new faculty member is almost certain to be invited to join the faculty senate or association; the invitation is obligatory rather than mandatory. If you want to be identified as a professional, join the group, even though you may feel a slight financial pinch from dues. Serving your profession through active membership adds to the strength of the faculty association. There are social values in your becoming acquainted with colleagues in an informal fashion. Constant opportunities exist for your leadership and for you to become an officer in the organization. You can gain personal satisfaction and growth as an officer and acquire experience in peer group activities and professional business.

In recent years many articles have appeared on the subject of the academic senate, especially as it relates to policy making (381) and faculty power and participation (177). Honer supports the senate as an opportunity for growth if it doesn't bog down in trivia and over-participation. He states that effective exercise of faculty senate power requires four principles: simplify the power, select wisely the proper areas of concern, localize the function to the one school rather than attempt to imitate others, and innovate—or else one might as well do better through official channels of the formal structure. There must be mutual concern, open lines of communication, and shared respect: administrators should encourage faculty participation, and faculty should involve itself only in important or relevant educational issues (177).

The faculty senate differs in several ways from the faculty club or association. The senate is ordinarily unconcerned with any social activities. It relates to the administration as the advisory voice of the faculty. It is smaller than the club. Members are elected usually from each department in a ratio to the number of faculty members within the department. Committees are chosen by the senate to explore the problems and improve the welfare of the college as well as of the faculty itself. If elected to the senate, you will be thrust into a position of double responsibility; you will need to interpret the actions of the senate to your department colleagues; and you will need to encourage department members to maintain your awareness of their attitudes and desires. Caught in the middle, you may feel periodically that service in the senate is rarely appreciated or understood; nevertheless, the senate is potentially a powerful and significant voice that exists for the good of the total institution.

An extensive paper on the subject is that prepared for the California State Federation of Teachers (288). This paper states the belief that the CJC is a shared responsibility of the public, the governing board, the administration, the faculty, and the students. The outstanding junior college, the report says, requires the utmost utilization of faculty resources in the development and implementation of policies and procedures. Suggested are the following areas of delegated authority where academic senates may legislate policy: (1) student relations (conduct, discipline, activities) (2) faculty relations and personnel policy (including appointments, retention, tenure, promotion, dismissal, leave of absence, evaluation, professional growth opportunities, and sabbaticals), and (3) academic policy and standards (admission, honors and degrees, college organization, financing, and budget).

Attendance at College Functions

Among your obligatory duties in the CJC, perhaps the most important is attendance at various college functions. Seventy-nine percent of our respondents, the largest number, classified this duty as obligatory. Three major spheres of college activities require consideration: those related to faculty, those related to students, and those related to the general community. Often they overlap and resist classification. Each looms large in the eyes of those who originate it; each has a claim, in varying degree, to the attendance and support of faculty members. No staff members can attend all the functions in a busy community college. Thus, it is essential that you be familiar with the patterns of college functions in order to lend majority support in a selective fashion.

Those functions related to faculty are often social in nature. The occasion may be a retirement banquet or a going-away party or a special tea for a distinguished visitor. Or the function may be a special faculty lecture or recital, especially when there is an eminent staff member available. Frequently, there are faculty dances or parties. Some of these events could be off campus, perhaps in some staff member's home. No one should require you to attend these functions, but it is a diplomatic gesture of good will and interest when you do so.

By far the most numerous college functions are those growing out of student activities. Despite the impressions created by newspaper and television reports, the majority of CJC student activities are peaceful and orderly. Athletic events in themselves create a special occasion on what may seem to be every weekend. Add to this the dances which commonly accompany a game, and the result is a pattern of student activities that seem to be continual. Athletic functions require much supervision, and supervision demands faculty participation. Consequently, you may be asked to serve as a gatekeeper, ticket taker, or dance chaperone. At some colleges, these duties can be a source of extra income; at other campuses, the duties are passed around, most often devolving upon new faculty. In many junior colleges, students are given some of these duties, and teachers are, therefore, free to enjoy the games.

Other student activities involve plays, concerts, carnivals, art exhibits, assemblies, pep rallies, and conferences. Even if you are not requested to serve in some official manner at these student events, you should attend as frequently as your schedule and stamina allow. Your presence has many values. You and the students can become better acquainted on an informal basis. You gain respect and appreciation from the students. You give more pride and awareness to the students. You may even find that you enjoy yourself. In essence, everyone wins something by his presence and participation, and everyone stands to lose something by non-attendance and non-participation.

The CJC itself is a generator of various events and ceremonies; and here we are not talking about student activities that are performed before the public. Athletic events, plays, concerts, and the like—all may be student activities designed essentially to provide students with experience, either among themselves or before audiences. On the other hand, the college may direct or inspire activities chiefly for the experience and benefit to community participants and audiences. Thus, the college may have community athletic programs, community dramatic societies, and community concert associations. Guest speakers, foreign films, and social and political affairs may be staged by the college. Although students may also attend and enjoy these events, the programs are primarily oriented toward community enlightenment, persuasion, or entertainment. Community college service events vary widely in their nature and frequency across the United States.

Of course, there are many college functions that benefit both the students and the communities. Baccalaureate and commencement exercises, for instance, are official college activities that involve students, parents, and the faculty. Some junior colleges may omit the baccalaureate ceremony from pre-commencement activities; others may allow the community council of churches to serve as coordinator, while the college serves as liaison between the ministry and the graduating students. The most formal approach is that planned by a college staff chairman and faculty committee. For both students and faculty, attendance requirements vary from compulsory to optional.

Commencement ceremonies may be relatively informal, with only the graduates wearing caps and gowns. A few junior colleges bestow a hood as part of the ceremony. Academic gowns for faculty are often required; some colleges avoid them, because many of their technical and vocational staff are qualified by their specialized occupations rather than by academic degrees.

Your attendance at these year-end ceremonies may be required. Surely it is obligatory. Commencement is an outstanding event for the student, especially one who remains in the community instead of continuing on for a further degree. Unfortunately we are prone to minimize the status of the Associate in Arts or in Science degree, when our own subsequent degrees change our perspective. When faculty members attend commencement at the community college, they imply by their presence that they respect the degree and those who earn it.

In conclusion, here are a few words of caution. Some faculty members sponsoring programs and events may be extremely sensitive about your lack of presence at their functions. If you know that you may hurt or insult a colleague by your non-attendance at his program or event, apologize for your absence. Sometimes a brief note in his mailbox may help if you cannot see him immediately.

A second caution to observe is to give some word of appreciation or praise to the colleague after you do attend his program. Too often staff members struggle for weeks to present a fine event, only to be disappointed when their colleagues offer no comment or give no word of encouragement and appreciation.

Finally, if you have charge of a program that in some way competes for attention with a colleague's program, avoid an active rivalry. Faculty feuds are caused in many ways, but bitterness between departments or staff members is often a result of jealousies and competition surrounding college activities.

Professional and Personal Growth

One measure of the professional competence of a CJC instructor is that of professional growth, defined both as increased mastery of one's professional discipline and improvement as a member of the teaching profession. While your duties toward self-improvement as a teacher and person are not specifically stated or demanded in many faculty handbooks, the duties are nevertheless implied. Only 3 of our 22 colleges required some form of professional growth activity, while 16 others merely expected growth to occur. The college may help growth through its in-service training programs. These programs are economical and convenient, but they are quite general and certainly inadequate alone; they cannot focus on the special interests of each participant. By necessity they serve only as a supplement to the more important individual programs and self-initiated activities.

In designing your own personal program of professional improvement, you could establish as a core a systematic reading program. Appropriate periodicals and books may be available in the CJC library. Many of the special materials relating to the junior college, such as the *Junior College Journal*, are apt to be found in a small section reserved chiefly for faculty perusal. Undoubtedly you will have to complement these materials with subscriptions to periodicals and acquisitions of books for your own shelves. Fortunately a growing number of universities are recognizing these needs and are making available their facilities to CJC faculties.

Besides your personal reading program, a second common method is membership in an appropriate professional organization. (See Chapter Two.) Major goals of most professional societies consist of keeping their members up-to-date in their fields, as well as the sharing of ideas and comradeship. At the local level of association meetings, you have easy access to the development of leadership. The local groups feed leaders into state and national offices. Consequently you can combine professional growth with the development of leadership skills if you are an active participant in your professional organization.

A third standard method is to take additional graduate courses at a university. If you already have your master's degree, you might decide to matriculate for a doctorate. Many universities have special programs designed expressly for the CJC teacher. Other professional projects and studies are sponsored by such as the National Science Foundation, the Ford Foundation, and federal agencies.

There is no endpoint to professional and personal growth. It is a natural outgrowth of the desire to learn and the drive to improve. You will encounter a wide variety of attitudes among your colleagues, some of whom will be relatively unconcerned about growth of any sort. Fortunately most CJC instructors continue to increase their professional competence.

Relationships with Administration

There seems to be a growing strain in the relations between faculty members and administrators. This strain or faculty unrest sometimes comes from trying to shed the "yoke of secondary education status" and of seeking "acceptance as a peer with the other segments of higher education" (292:8). Central to the problem is the struggle for power in college governance. The tenseness of the situation caused one recent writer to say, "Regret it though we might, it appears that the 'We-They Complex' becomes more serious with each passing year, and as tensions draw up tight to the breaking point, an outside consultant is sometimes the only resource for solving administrator-faculty problems" (157:12).

A shift in roles is evident as administrators introduce, sometimes reluctantly, democratic processes. Simultaneously junior college faculties acquire a larger role, still primarily advisory, in college governance. In distinct minority is one extreme attitude, that of the paternalistic administrator who clings to the unilateral authority, albeit benevolently. At the opposte end are the faculty minority who express a desire to place in faculty hands the entire control of the college. Under this arrangement, administrators would serve as clerks and messengers. In contrast, most CJC faculty members appear to be concerned mainly with their teaching responsibilities; they would leave administration to those employed for the tasks. Most administrators appear to be in favor of sharing their problems and policy decisions with their teachers. They are, after all, former instructors themselves, and many of them undoubtedly remember their own dissatisfaction with dictatorial leadership. It is significant that after trying administration for a time, some of these people finally decide that they prefer the classroom after all.

The new generation of CJC administrators seems to be oriented more toward the lecture room as the focus of the college operation. There is a growing pressure on the requirements of successful teaching experience coupled with an academic major for qualification for the top administrative positions. This situation is in contrast to the earlier patterns of lateral movement from training and experience neither academic nor junior college related. The new administrators seem to be more sympathetic to the problems of instructors and more willing to share authority with those who are affected most by administrative decisions.

Teachers and administrators seem to relate well if they accept as their common purpose the academic and personal welfare of the students. Relations are more likely to deteriorate when either group feels that its primary function is other than to provide the highest possible quality of higher education for the supporting community. When administrators perceive their contributions as valuable only insofar as they support the student-instructor relationship, and when teachers accept this motivation as one common to administrators as well as teachers, there is far more likelihood of a unified educational effort.

Any disruptive force in the harmony of teacher-administrator relationship should be immediately corrected so that there is no unpleasant distraction in the process of educating CJC students. Most respondents, 60 percent, and most colleges in our survey, 15, regarded this aim as an obligation. The implication is that friendly relations with administration are needed, if not for professional duty then for the practical matter of holding a teaching position and gaining tenure.

Relationships with Community

One of the criteria used to evaluate a new instructor is that he have a desirable relationship with the community. That this duty is significant is demonstrated by the fact that 75 percent of our respondents and 18 of 22 randomly sampled colleges considered it obligatory. There is often a mutual benefit to many community activities; the community gains from college staff participation, and the staff member benefits from associations and communication with the non-academic community. There is no checklist of required activities. No two instructors have the same opportunities or inclinations. Choices range from service organizations to dramatic societies to political committees.

The junior college instructor has available the majority of the avenues of activity afforded other citizens in the community. And like the employee of any corporation he is, in effect, an extension of his employer, even when off the job. Consequently the CJC instructor *is* the college to his neighbors and friends in the community. This role can be inhibiting; on the other hand, the teacher serves as a valuable liaison—he interprets the college to the community and relays opinions and reactions from the community back to the college.

Community involvement varies both in kind and degree, depending on the instructor's personality. Instructors in certain fields and particularly administrators join service clubs quite often to maintain close contact with the leaders of the community. Recreational activities have worthwhile side effects in community relations. Outside the lecture room, teachers turn into rock hounds, coin collectors, amateur photographers, church choir singers, little league baseball coaches and managers, artists, and a vast array of other pursuits. As you participate in these community activities, you develop lasting friendships and associations that complement your professional life.

More serious than the above-mentioned activities in community relationships are those that exercise freedom to speak your mind on controversial problems and issues, particularly politics. College instructors have been elected to local, state, and national office, and teachers have campaigned vigorously for many causes and candidates. By engaging in politics, teachers risk antagonizing people in the local community, especially when these teachers represent a group unpopular with the general community. Teachers, however, have a right to function as citizens, to develop political opinions and action in open society; clearly the risk must be taken if the right is to be exercised.

The matter is entirely different in the classroom and on the campus. In discussing the political activity of teachers, Marsee states that, while teachers should be free to work on political matters away from school and when off duty, they may not participate on campus and during duty hours (226).

There, the most valuable single guideline for instructors is painstakingly to avoid bringing their biases into their instruction. Carrying an authoritative political message and prejudice into the classroom or onto campus may be what laymen really fear about teachers' community politics. Communities vary widely in their sophistication and ability to allow a dissident viewpoint, particularly from someone responsible for teaching CJC students. You will need to know your community rather well before embarking on an unpopular campaign of any sort. Colleagues and the dean of instruction can often save you needless cuts and bruises in this especially sensitive area of community relations.

Your obligation to the community is essentially that of any responsible citizen: to accept your share of the activities that enable democracy to operate at its several levels. Relatively few junior colleges and communities can accept from their faculty behavior without bounds. One of your inital assignments will be to learn the boundaries of acceptable teacher conduct. Each decade they coincide more with those of the general community.

Night Teaching

Some colleges require their teachers to instruct night classes as part of their regular load, particularly if qualified personnel are in short supply. Sometimes known as extended day classes, these courses are very much the same as those taught during the day. In fact, junior colleges tend to require the same quality and standards for both day and night instruction. Instructors tend to differ in their acceptances of night teaching, especially when it is required as part of the regular load; some like it, and others abhor it in varying degrees.

In our college-faculty survey, the question about night teaching was asked of the respondents. According to majority views, 18 junior colleges had night teaching policies while only 4 had no policy. Thirteen of the 22 colleges in the survey included night teaching as part of some faculty members' regular load. Fifteen of the institutions paid extra for any over-loads. Thirteen colleges placed limitations on night loads; 6 of these limited the load to one class or three hours, 5 to two classes or five to six hours, and 2 to three classes or seven to nine hours. According to the majority, the general faculty accepted the situation on night teaching in each of 12 colleges; of the 18 with a policy, faculty in 10 colleges were generally satisfied.

The results of the survey suggest that many faculty members do not know what their night teaching policy actually is, for 15 of the 118 re-spondents said they didn't know and respondents in 18 colleges conflicted to some extent in their answers to the basic questions. A second con-clusion was that there is a fairly large group of discontented faculty in-sofar as night teaching is concerned. These two conclusions alone lead us to suggest that (1) specific policies should be established in writing, (2) faculties should be thoroughly oriented concerning these policies, (3) policies should be liberal, perhaps allowing for freedom of choice for the instructors, (4) policies should include a more generous pay schedule for night teaching, approaching as nearly as possible schedules paid for day teaching, and finally (5) policies should include representa-tive faculty members in their formation and approval.

Outside Employment

Any employment outside the college is usually an instructor's own busi-ness; therefore it is neither mandatory nor obligatory. Ironically but understandably, the beginning instructor discovers that when his salary is at its lowest point, his expenses seem to be approaching their peak. This dilemma can be awkward, particularly for the married man with children, although single teachers have financial burdens also, some-times dependent parents or debts remaining from the years of college training. A new teacher may thus feel it mandatory to supplement his professional earnings with some form of outside work. The immediate questions relate to what kind and how much work. The questions must be examined carefully, for they relate to your evaluation by the institu-tion and the community. Let us consider briefly the implications of these questions.

First, there is the problem of how much work. From the institution's standpoint, a teacher who engages in too much outside employment—say a full-time second job—usually finds that his professional duties suffer to some extent. The college ordinarily feels that the teacher's contract should have first priority; consequently officials are apt to have a policy which limits or prohibits outside employment, especially that which hinders or conflicts with teaching duties. Obviously, a teacher cannot pursue outside employment to any great extent without having it interfere with his main profession. Other writers give evidence of this fact (29:143).

From the teacher's standpoint, outside employment may be such a burden that health is impaired or problems and conflicts develop. The community may be very sympathetic about teachers having a second job in order to support themselves and their families, but they, too, may be concerned about the extra work competing with teacher duties. Regular outside employees may resent instructors coming into the community for extra employment. The resentment seems to stem from the attitude that an instructor is taking a job and income which should go to someone not already employed full time. While this attitude may not be representative, the instructor should be prepared for it. Facts are usually the most effective defense. When the critic discovers what the beginning instructor receives in take-home pay, he is likely to be sympathetic rather than hostile.

Second, there is the problem of the type of outside employment. There are a few occupations which are by nature somewhat questionable for the CJC instructor. One example is that of bartender, in some communities a skilled, well-paid position which, nevertheless, puts the teacher in an awkward relationship to members of the community, but particularly to his students. Most communities are not yet ready to accept the teacher in such a role. Of course, no instructor should accept outside employment which violates the policies or customs of his college which, like the community, may object to the teacher's bartender role. It is the instructor's responsibility to determine from his colleagues or the appropriate administrator the guidelines to acceptable types of extra employment. Discretion, moderation, and diplomacy are essential in combining outside employment with a full-time CJC teaching assignment.

The specialists in our college-faculty survey indicated the kind of outside work which colleges tended to favor most; mentioned most frequently was work which related to the teachers' specialities and which provided desirable services to the community or some portion of it. Consulting services ranked highest in the general comments. Examples mentioned were technical-vocational teachers being paid for consulting in business and industrial enterprises. Mentioned also were religion and music teachers serving in local churches, art and drama teachers creating and performing for art shows and theatrical endeavors, and social science teachers serving part-time in government offices. In appropriate part-time, outside employment, teachers appear to be encouraged by their colleges, because added prestige and status come to both teacher and college.

During your free summers, you may also find employment that is linked to your academic discipline. The technical-vocational instructor who spends a summer in industry can give to his students practical, up-to-date information. The business education specialist needs to keep in close touch with the practitioners and the employers in his field. A summer on the job can combine valuable training with extra income.

As shown in the section on night teaching, colleges tend to try solving the new teacher's financial problems by offering him extra teaching that carries with it extra income. If there are no opportunities available on your campus, you may want to investigate extra teaching assignments at other institutions. Some communities have evening high school programs. The principal of the adult school is usually looking for extra teachers. Most colleges permit a teacher's taking this kind of job in another institution, but you should check with your college before committing yourself.

Roles in Accreditation

All of the duties discussed in this and the preceding chapter are, of course, subject to evaluation in accreditation. The accreditation process, widespread in acceptance, is likely to involve you with another very important duty area. If you teach in one CJC for even a few years, probably your institution will be visited at least once by an accrediting team. Accreditation is not just an administrative responsibility. Your administrators must depend upon your efforts and cooperation to see that the process results in success.

Any analysis of accreditation indicates at least three major roles for individual faculty members: (1) serving as a visiting team member, (2) serving on the college committee which prepares the status report for the visiting team, and (3) serving as a professional teacher and faculty representative in confrontations with the visiting team. Each of these merits at least brief discussion.

The Visiting Team Member Role

In many parts of the nation it is now common for CJC teachers to be selected for an accreditation team. Selection is considered to be an honor for you and your college; service is considered to be a professional duty. In the role of team member, you should meet at the proper times with your colleagues, some of whom will be representatives of universities, community college administration, four-year colleges, and state departments of education. During the meetings you prepare for your campus visitation under the guidance and leadership of a chairman. On the designated dates, you accompany the team to the college seeking accreditation. You study the report prepared by this college, have conferences with various members of the college and community, visit classrooms, conduct informal interviews, and make pertinent observations. After approximately two or three days—or whenever the visit is concluded—the team may make a preliminary appraisal to the college.

After leaving the campus, the team soon begins its final accreditation report. Although styles vary somewhat with each chairman, each member has responsibility for one particular report area, and all members contribute information and general cooperation in the final writing. In each section of the report, care is given to commend the strong points and to recommend improvements in the weak areas. Your job is completed normally when the report is sent on its way through accrediting agency channels. Subsequently a copy of the report is sent to the college for perusal. Along with the report goes the decision of the agency for or against the college's accreditation. The period of accreditation ordinarily ranges from one year to five years.

When serving on the visitation team, you should endeavor to display a constructive attitude toward the college and its personnel. The staff members believe in their institution in most cases and are very anxious to present their situation in the most favorable light. Be most courteous in dealing with the people, give no impromptu criticism and take great care in wording your part of the written report after the visit. Your team chairman should give you ample guidance concerning your attitude and job.

The Report Committee Member Role

A second major role, more apt to come your way, relates to your being selected to serve upon the faculty committee whose job is to prepare the report for the visiting team. The report is actually a part or the whole of an application for accreditation and includes vital information about all phases of the college. The organization of the report will follow undoubtedly the guidelines of the regional, state, or other agency which is responsible for the accreditation. In Chapter One are some of the common areas of evaluation.

Staff members are assigned to various areas of the application report. As a member, you must secure the necessary facts for your assigned area, whether it be a statistical analysis of enrollment or a description of institutional goals. Usually you have the help of others in gathering these facts. You must meet with the report committee frequently, make various decisions as a voting member, and generally help to complete a final report that is accurate and that substantially shows your college in an honest but favorable light.

The Representative Faculty Role

The third major role, which is every faculty member's responsibility, is that of serving as a representative of the staff in relationships with visitation team members. Many staff members work through a team visit without ever confronting a team member; nevertheless, the possibility of a team member's visiting your class is fairly good. You will be alerted to the possibility by your faculty committee or administrators, and you should be prepared to have a team member walk into your class at any time during the visit. He is there, naturally, to observe the quality of classroom instruction, which is one of the common areas of evaluation in accreditation. The best thing for you to do is to greet the visitor and conduct the class as you do normally.

A team member may also discuss with you some aspects of the college and its programs. Your comments should be constructive and unemotional. This advice is sometimes needed, for there are cases where teachers downgrade some aspects of their colleges, complain bitterly about conflicts or deficiencies, or display unjustified feelings and observations. Such a staff member often reflects more of his own inadequacies and maladjustments than those of the college.

Sometimes pressure is applied for a teacher to praise the college and to avoid mentioning any of its defects, but this pressure should be resisted. Like any objective professional, you should answer questions with facts more often than with opinions, but show your fairness by weighing possible college inadequacies with the many possible good points. To engage in discussion at all, however, you should know enough about the philosophy and objectives of the college to speak with some authority.

Chapter 7

The Art of Junior College
Instruction: Philosophy

A discussion of the art of teaching is appropriate in a book addressed to new teachers and students in the CJC field; the discussion may be considered by some readers as the very heart of such a book. We believe that the following topic areas are most significant in teaching effectiveness: The Nature of Art in Teaching, The Importance of Communication, Perception of the Student, Philosophy of the Instructor, Philosophy of the Institution (Topics in Chapter Seven), The Psychology of Learning, Some Methods and Techniques, Evaluation of the Student, Evaluation of the Instructor, Evaluation of the Course (Topics in Chapter Eight).

The Nature of Art in Teaching

The word "art" to describe junior college instruction was chosen carefully. Gilbert Highet (170) and many other teachers have compared teaching to an art. Although there is a growing amount of scientific knowledge applied to college instruction, the application of this knowledge resembles the work of an artist. The class—even one student—is the instructor's audience. If there is no effect or an undesirable effect upon the audience, we consider the art defective, in essence a failure. The goal is to create a response which produces a desirable behavioral change related to one or more specific goals. A person listening to a fine play is caught up in the sights and sounds from the stage. He is involved in what happens: he departs a different person for the experience; his subsequent behavior is altered even if slightly or subtly. And so it is with the art of teaching.

We maintain that the best, most inspired teaching at any educational level is an art. Concurring with this point, Kegel suggests that the teacher is both mirror and lamp (198:102). Knowledge of subject matter, of media and techniques is not enough. Art uses this knowledge as a means of creative communication, the creativity being the unique addition of the artist, the manner in which the artist uses the variety of materials and techniques that affect the behavior of his audience and establish his art form or style. His imagination and personality combine with the means of teaching to determine his effectiveness as a teacher.

The role of personality is underlined by Pullias: "If one tries to understand the power of the world's greatest teachers, he is steadily led toward the conclusion that life and meaning were given to their teaching by a special quality of their personalities. These personalities are greatly varied, but a common thread seems to run through all examples of powerful teaching: that to be considered or learned, mediated through the teacher, becomes alive and meaningful in a special way and reaches the learner as vital, direct experience. This quality is manifested by Socrates, Hillel, Abélard, Mark Hopkins, William James, William Rainey Harper, Woodrow Wilson, Frederick Jackson Turner, Louis Agassiz, Anne Sullivan Macy, Alfred North Whitehead, Mahatma Gandhi, and a multitude of other less celebrated but perhaps equally great teachers. The essence of the teaching art lies in the character of the person" (298).

There is no formula for the art of CJC instruction, but we can at least present some descriptions of qualities and techniques that emerge most frequently in successful teaching. All of us remember various teachers and professors whose teaching combined quality with popularity. Those who stand out tend to have several characteristics in common:

1. They were keenly and obviously interested in and enthusiastic about their subject matter.

2. They were thoroughly prepared. Most of them worked from notes rather than from manuscript, a practice that indicated their mastery of subject matter.

3. They were organized. Material was presented in segments that moved forward to an integrated whole.

4. They communicated. That is, they spoke clearly, forcefully, and logically; listeners could hear and follow the thread of the material.

5. They changed pace. They provided variety in communication to hold attention and to avoid restlessness and boredom.

6. They presented live, vital facts that stimulated and motivated the students.

7. They emphasized instruction rather than persuasion. Students were free to decide for themselves in a controversy.

8. They took a personal interest in each student.

9. They had exciting and interesting personalities.

10. They had character that could be admired by students.

One psychologist reduces the list of personal characteristics to eight qualities: enthusiasm, initiative, curiosity, creativity, ability to see rewards in the intangible, high morals, discipline, maturity (8:115). You may find particularly interesting his discussion of the various tests to analyze personality traits.

Our outstanding contemporary teachers do not necessarily possess the above characteristics to the same degree. Teachers who are considered "great" (286) often lacked what we might consider an essential quality; yet they achieved greatness. Their achievements rested on other qualities so outstanding that their shortcomings could be ignored. "Teachers whose personality and character elicit admiration and emulation and invite personal contacts beyond the classroom will radiate influence of which they may scarcely be aware" (357:271). People with above average potential are, to be sure, "born"; their teaching lives unfold as their latent abilities are developed. However, the majority of us rarely perceive or achieve our potential in all of the qualities which enhance college teaching.

The "art" in teaching contains remarkable elements; it is creative, it is an expression of personality, and it offers endless avenues for improvement. "Teaching is a tough, complex, often delicate activity of human relationships in a special kind of setting" (125:524). Creative teaching brings together style and imagination in a process not unlike painting or sculpturing. Teaching styles vary widely, from the benevolent to tyrannical, organized to chaotic, dramatic to austere. In an art where knowledge decays and expands, and students provide a constantly changing media, there can be no end point, no complete mastery. It is ever-changing, ever-improving, ever-reflecting the uniqueness of the personality.

Among the institutions of higher education, the junior colleges have the conditions perhaps most conducive to artistic teaching. While the senior institutions have many professors who are outstanding teachers, the emphasis and awards in research and publication tend to distract professional attention from the teaching function. Senior staff members are sometimes urged to teach lower division classes, but the typical assignment of the full professor is likely to be several small upper division or graduate seminars, which reduce his teaching load and allow him to pursue his research and publication. His success has the effect of withdrawing him from consideration for teaching the lower division courses, which are more often taught by graduate students or faculty without seniority. The graduate student must give priority to his own graduate studies, while the new professor usually wants to establish his reputation in the areas of greater recognition: research and publication.

In contrast, community college faculties have been relatively free from pressures of research and publication. Tenure, salary increases, and promotion have been virtually automatic. While the colleges are becoming more concerned with research, particularly at the institutional level, and more and more teachers are publishing, the paramount goal of the CJC continues to be excellent teaching and learning. As a consequence, CJC teachers as a group tend to be vitally concerned with the teaching function and tend to be excellent teachers. As Blocker stated, CJC faculties are competent, as competent and even more so than lower division university instructors (26). Even more glowing praise is given by other writers on the subject.

In previous chapters you were provided with information that was important but more peripheral than central. The core of your success remains the art that you practice in the classroom. Relating where needed the scientific basis in teaching, the remainder of this and the next chapter explore the dimensions of this art.

The Importance of Communication

Communication is of primary importance to all teaching; it is the most significant tool in the teacher's employment of his art. The teacher's effectiveness relates directly to his proficiency in the communicative skills; speaking, writing, reading, listening, and thinking. He is immersed in communication; so are his students. The classroom resembles our own total society; both are suffused with useful and useless communication, all of it competing for attention. As communication is both the cause and effect of dynamic change and progress in a society, so is it in the smaller environment of the classroom. In essence, communication is the major process through which we affect other persons' lives.

Speaking

Speech is commonly regarded as the essential core of communication, although the other four communicative skills are, in their way, equally important. Speech employs both physical and vocal effects. Physically, we communicate our thoughts and feelings by the way we stand, gesture, walk, or even breathe. A teacher who stands still all the time, sits constantly at his desk as he talks, or paces continually, invites student responses of boredom and undesirable distraction. Even the way a teacher dresses may create distraction or even hostility. The important fact about "silent speech," sometimes called *animation* in speech, is that all animation in speaking should reinforce and strengthen the vocal aspects of speech.

Vocally, a teacher needs to be effective in volume, rate, pitch, and quality. Any great weakness in any of these can interfere with or even destroy communicative goals. Volume, sometimes called vocal projection, requires the teacher-speaker to speak loudly enough for all in the audience to hear and yet not so loud as to deafen the listeners. Rate of speech by the teacher-speaker should be slow enough for all to understand the words and ideas in the message; the effect should be smooth and rhythmic rather than choppy and staccato. The speaker should not pause too much, especially for long periods of time, nor should he race through the material. In all cases his rate should be varied, appropriate to the speech material. The pitch should be flexible in range and have enough inflection to excite interest in and interpretation of the speech material. Monotone, a pitch too high or low, or an unnatural inflection are distracting. The teacher-speaker should have a pleasing, resonant voice, without harsh, nasal, throaty, breathy, raspy, thin, or guttural qualities.

Teachers in all levels should also be careful of their articulation, pronunciation, language usage, and grammar. There is little excuse for a teacher's sloppy diction. Inarticulate teachers cannot be the most effective educators, no matter what their mastery of subject matter. Anything that stands in the way of concentrated and successful communication, in fact, is a handicap to learning. Morton sums up the bad effects when he says, "Voice levels and characteristics can vitiate much good scholarship by discouraging attentive listening and draining out many potential values from the lecture" (265:121).

Teachers who have effective physical and vocal characteristics enhance their success in communication. Too often we see teachers, however, who have developed inadequately their skills in speaking; they can never become the best examples of great teachers until they master the art of public speaking. Every prospective CJC teacher should take a course in speech in order to accelerate his development of these vitally needed communicative skills; he should practice and improve them throughout his teaching career.

Writing

The art of teaching also includes written communications. Your written communications include any reading material given to your students as a teaching technique; guidelines, examinations, and comments placed on student papers are prime examples. Several writing skills need to be developed if effective communication is to result. Needed for both speaking and writing are appropriate style, usage, and word choice. The best writer and speaker uses language appropriate to the students' levels of learning, usage that is acceptable, and word choices that are exact. An ignorant or negligent teacher inevitably displays language errors in his writing and speaking. To the students such errors are distracting.

More than a few times teachers have returned student papers with the teacher's comments misspelled, mispunctuated, or incorrectly capitalized. The teacher must provide proper models for the students. It has been said that every teacher, regardless of his academic discipline, is a teacher of English. The best teachers are usually those who have mastered their written and spoken native language.

Another writing skill relates to the semantic aspects in the writing of an examination. Perhaps, as a student, you have had the experience of trying to decipher a poorly written examination. Examination questions form a kind of dramatic communication; their quality can have a profound effect on a student! Questions that are ambiguous or misleading interfere with the learning process, causing the student and teacher to talk past each other. Many hours must be spent in preparing examinations if they are to be clearly written and clearly communicated to the students. Other important aspects of examinations, such as validity and reliability, are discussed later. Here, we wish to emphasize only the need for clear writing.

College instructors are frequently taciturn or cryptic in their written comments on student papers. Most of us are interested in what someone else, particularly a teacher, thinks of our efforts. A paper with nothing more than a grade, even an A, is disappointingly impersonal. And a D paper without comment gives no guidelines for improvement. Most students thirst for response to their efforts. Consequently, the instructor's comments are essential to effective teaching. These comments should be constructive as well as clear; they should be stimulating as well as encouraging.

Reading

The CJC instructor is a major consumer as well as producer of communication. He is constantly called upon to read an enormous amount of material related to his discipline. Student papers, professional journals, new textbooks, and committee reports seem to flow inexhaustibly onto his desk. There is no question about whether he should read all this material; he must. The task before him demands that he read rapidly and comprehend precisely.

You may already be an effective reader, capable in speed, comprehension, and interpretation. If you are not, then you must improve these skills in order to round out your communicative function. Doubling your reading speed can increase your teaching effectiveness by providing you with additional hours to use for preparation. Increasing your comprehension enables you to derive more from your professional reading, the wellspring of your teaching. Improved interpretation of your reading offers you greater accuracy in your classroom. All three of these special reading skills affect the quality of your analysis of students' writing. The appropriate response to their efforts can play a major role in your relationship to them. If you need assistance in improving these skills, enroll in a reading improvement course.

Listening

Listening is a communicative skill chiefly for one reason: It requires a physical response properly communicated in terms of the stimulation provided by the speaker. Listening, as well as reading, gains effectiveness by its degree of present attention; both are responsive, not passive, communications. The speaker who does his part well usually expects the listener to do *his* part well. Responding freely to the stimulation, the listener may smile, nod, frown, lean forward or back in his seat, applaud, or do a number of other physical things—all of which prove that he is reacting through attention and interest. Although hearing is the essential pathway to listening, the listener reinforces what he hears through his observation of the speaker. The good listener concentrates upon what the speaker is saying. He tries to avoid all distractions that may interfere with listening. He forces himself to comprehend, appreciate, and evaluate the message transmitted to him. In short, listening is a vital process that aids or interferes with communication (320:139).

The CJC teacher must watch his listeners carefully in order to determine his degree or success in getting across his message. If responses (feedback) are missing or inadequate, he must change or vary his approach to secure better listening. He should give each student the kind of attention he would give to his colleagues. His response to student questions or comments should be respectful. The teacher who listens reluctantly or halfheartedly to students is communicating unmistakably his apathy or hostility toward them, even though he may claim to be student oriented. The best teacher listens carefully; he does so by comprehending, appreciating, evaluating, observing, forcing himself to listen, opening his mind to the message, making mental notes, analyzing, and responding correctly in a respectful, courteous manner.

Thinking

The fifth communicative skill, thinking, is the heart of all effective communication. The value of any means of communication is unlikely to transcend the quality of the thought. Effective thinking requires a trained mind, an intellectual capacity for analysis, common sense, and reasoning. These abilities being present in a person, other requirements include the need for concentration, attention, and interest, plus a certain amount of factual knowledge in the subject or topic area under contemplation.

The results of excellence in thinking are numerous. For instance, the instructor analyzes thoughtfully the content of the material he wishes to present to his students. By careful study he can properly determine which materials to select; he will know that no semester or term is deep enough or long enough to include more than a fraction of what is known about biology, history, or geology. His immediate problem is that of limitation. He also uses careful thinking to determine how he must organize the material he has selected for class instruction. If he thinks well, he should organize well. After selecting the material and organizing it, he must plan the best way to deliver (present) it to students. The careful thinker will realize that speaking to students (perhaps from notes or an outline) is far better than reading a lecture to them. He will also be aware that learning can take place with the instructor's speaking. In essence, he will think through all aspects of the art of CJC teaching and utilize those tools which suit him best and create the most desirable learning among his students.

To improve your ability to think clearly and correctly, study the various forms of logic, the process of analysis, and the varied patterns of organization in oral and written communication. There are formal exercises in the development of thinking abilities, but the most common method is that of listening to dynamic and lucid speakers and of reading works by those who have developed a reputation for unusual insight and expression. The ultimate test, however, is in your own speaking and writing. The essential critic, your listener or reader, should give you ample clues as to your overall effectiveness.

All of us are constantly engaged in the five communicative skills just discussed; no two of us are alike in our degree of mastery in these skills. Some of us make better speakers than listeners; others find that listening often has greater value than speaking. It is doubtful if any instructor ever reaches *complete, total* proficiency in all five communicative skills; nevertheless, we should all be aware of the pervasive effects which communication has on our teaching quality. Along with that awareness should come a steadfast determination to increase our potential as communicators, that we may reach a higher level of excellence in teaching.

Perception of the Student

An important weakness of any present-day instructor, whether in the CJC or in some other level of education, is lack of knowledge of his students. One may sympathize with the instructor who tries but fails to understand and know his students, but the teacher who makes no conscious attempt to become informed about his students is to be deplored. In fact, Bossone suggests that he is bound to be ineffective, especially when dealing with students from underprivileged social classes (37).

Like the public speaker who analyzes his audience to select a proper subject suitable for their attention and interest, the most efficient instructor will try to uncover certain facts about his students. Such facts need to be employed in the modification or improvement of his instruction, particularly his communication and rapport. The instructor is likely to discover from the facts that, as Garrison suggests, "Instead of relative homogeneity of background and abilities, the instructor faces heterogeneity of a really extraordinary sort. Instead of 'usual' collegiate motivations in students, teachers deal with motive-for-being-in-college ranging from immediate employability to fantasy notions about careers wholly unrelated to the obvious abilities (or lack of them) brought by the student to his college experience" (126:16). Certainly; to lead "the collegiate horse to water" requires motivation, and student motivation seems unlikely unless the teacher is aware of student background and characteristics and makes use of this knowledge (127:26).

Although each group of students will include different degrees and varieties of backgrounds and characteristics, a few generalizations can be made about all students at a given level of instruction. One of the most revealing discussions of the junior college student was written by Medsker. The following group of facts, supported in Medsker's book, should provide you with a general understanding of the type of junior college student you are apt to face in the course of your teaching (247: 29-50).

1. Junior college students are characterized by diversity; they are of all ages, abilities, philosophies of life, levels of knowledge, degrees of wealth or poverty, races, faiths or creeds, purposes, etc.; they do not necessarily have the same characteristics as their counterparts in the four-year colleges.

2. In general, the mean scores on aptitude tests taken by junior college freshmen are somewhat lower than the means scored by freshmen in four-year colleges.

3. Transfer students are generally more able in aptitude than terminal students in junior colleges, although there is a great overlap of superior ability in some areas.

4. Junior colleges that tend to draw superior transfer students also tend to draw superior terminal students.

5. Junior colleges tend to have a significant number of students who are well able to engage in college work as rigorous as that offered in four-year colleges and universities.

6. Junior college men and women students are about equal in their aptitudes, men having scored slightly higher than women in some cases; women transfers, however, tend to outperform the men transfers in several respects, perhaps because women tend to utilize their aptitudes to better advantage.

7. In general, junior college transfers seem to do about as well or even better than their classmates who spend their entire four years at four-year colleges.

8. Public junior colleges, because they are usually local and inexpensive to attend, tend to draw most of their students from the lower half of the socioeconomic distribution; high tuition junior colleges tend to draw most of their students from upper-middle-class and upper-class groups; most junior colleges, however, tend to draw students from a cross-section of the population.

9. Student ages range from 16 to 60 or more, although at least half are usually in the 16 to 22 age range.

10. In general, the majority of junior college students are high school graduates; one study report showed that only 6 percent of the students were non-high school graduates.

11. A large percentage of CJC students are married; one study showed an average of 23 percent married students.

12. The ratio of men to women students in junior colleges is about two to one; in the case of two-year technical institutes, the ratio is much higher.

13. Many studies show at least three reasons for students entering the junior colleges: persuasion by parents or others, proximity of the institution, and the lower cost.

14. Students withdraw from junior colleges most frequently because of full-time employment; other reasons include personal reasons and health, moving or transferring, non-attendance, academic or faculty action, entering armed forces, dissatisfaction with school, financial problems, marriage, and completion of education goals.

Blocker, Plummer, and Richardson make an especially useful supplement to Medsker's study. Their summary of findings, remarkably consonant with Medsker's earlier work, follows:

1. There are two classes of college-age students: 17 to 21 college-age youth and adult ages from 21 to 60 or 70. The latter make up about 50 percent of the total number of two-year college students in the United States. Unlike the younger students, the adults concentrate upon their classes and achievement of their immediate goals; they are not interested in school activities, etc.

2. The ratio of men to women is about 3 to 2.

3. More than half hold part-time jobs.

4. A study of educational background shows a variety of abilities, with junior college freshmen scoring at about the 25th percentile in median score as compared with college freshmen in four-year colleges. Junior college freshmen enter with generally lower personal motivation and less academic ability as measured by standardized tests.

5. More two-year college students come from lower socioeconomic

backgrounds than do their counterparts in four-year colleges and universities.

6. There are several student views of junior college: Seeing the CJC as a "right," wanting personal identification as a college student, wanting identification with a status occupation or curriculum, wanting emancipation from home and parents, seeing the junior college as a milieu where he can live and be treated as an adult, seeing the CJC as a place to help him qualify for a vocation.

7. The main reason for attending a junior college was lack of financial resources to do anything else, but many also wanted to remain in the community, to continue work in the home town.

8. Two-thirds of the students who enter two-year colleges do not go beyond the sophomore year, although the aspirations of junior college students are largely limited to college transfer.

9. As for student mental health, three groups are evident: low, middle, high; the CJC has students in all three groups.

10. There are three types of women students: single college age, single adult age, and married women, each having slightly different reasons for going to junior college.

11. There is a great deal of mobility in the junior college, and the attrition rate is usually high.

12. The junior college filling station concept has some truth.

13. Faculty rank abstract and intellectual college aims higher than do students or administrators; faculty see visionary aims as highest rank and practical aims as the lowest. Administrators rated all aims of the college high but considered the practical aims most essential; students rated abstract aims least essential and practical aims most essential. Students rate guidance as more essential than do either administrators or teachers (29:106-131).

The implications of such studies as the above are extremely important in considering the analysis and proper use of the art of teaching. If the teacher remembers the diverse backgrounds, interests, and abilities of CJC students, he will employ a variety of instructional methods and subject content. A teacher who thinks that one content or method works equally well for all students finds his experience refuting the thesis at various points during the school term. The truth is that the most efficient instructor employs a teaching art form that suits the general needs of the greatest number of students. To employ figurative language at this point, the *door* to education and learning is "the fulfillment of students," and the *key* to that door is the teacher's "varied responses to these needs."

But even if the instructor applies the key to the door, he may still fail to unlock it in certain situations. He must then apply his knowledge of students to the process of planned motivational devices. If the student does not react sufficiently to the teaching procedure which ordinarily should satisfy his need, then the instructor must provide special motivation. The CJC has a rather high dropout rate among students; if only a few of these dropouts can be saved through special interest and motivation, it is the teacher's prime obligation to utilize these devices. By encouraging a potential dropout to remain in college, the teacher aids our society as well as the individual.

In review, teachers, like public speakers, must know their audiences; they must use this knowledge to determine the proper approaches to learning. The best methods are those that reach as many of the students as possible, regardless of student differences. If the key does not unlock the door, the teacher should try a bit of graphite in the form of motivation. Periods of frustration and anxiety in teaching are compensated for when the graphite works. Knowledge of students is the necessary prelude to the establishment of one's philosophy of teaching.

Philosophy of the Instructor

Your career as a junior college instructor is largely an expression of your own philosophy, tempered by the philosophy of the institution. Your philosophy may have a profound effect on your students, whose lives are affected by your perception of such issues as the purpose of education, the roles of tests, and the importance of grades. You may find it worthwhile to analyze your beliefs systematically, to establish an orderly structure in your relationship with the college, the students, and your discipline. Another teacher's "credo" may stimulate your own philosophical growth (200). A major step in this growth is to determine answers to at least three of these issues.

1. What are the purposes of education? Do you believe that each human being has value as an individual, regardless of who he is or what abilities he may have? The question is especially important in the CJC, where the population is not screened generally by entrance examinations or academic motives. You know, from the previous topic discussion, that many students achieve their goals—frequently a job in the community—in less than two years. Do these students have value equal to those who go on for degrees or do fewer academic aspirations make them second-rate?

If your philosophy attaches special merit to students in the transfer program, your relations with terminal students and those who teach them are likely to be affected adversely. Academically oriented faculty attitudes toward non-transfer students and programs are a common problem in the junior colleges. Some of these instructors perceive themselves only as potential lower division university professors whose purpose is to winnow from their campus all those students who are not university material. This philosophy can be disastrous in, for example, an English course established for non-transfer students. A negative attitude from an instructor discourages such students from developing confidence and pride in themselves. If these students find that their transfer colleagues receive special favors and praise, they may endeavor to switch to a transfer program even though their interests and abilities do not qualify them for such a change. If they are not able to compete successfully, they discover that their morale and even alternate careers may be distorted or destroyed.

On the positive side, if your philosophy includes the tenet that further education is of vital importance to the general community and that general education has as much basic value as special education, you may find more pleasure in your work and possibly uncommon opportunities for curriculum design. The growing proportion of students with lower ability has created extensive demands for instructors who are interested in designing programs for students who will remain in the community. Such students become the leaders and the taxpayers who are necessary for the support of junior colleges for subsequent generations. On the other hand, transfer students depart for senior institutions, frequently never to return to their local communities.

2. What should be the personal relationship of the instructor to his students? Of course, in a class with hundreds of students, a general student anonymity is virtually unavoidable. However, many classes—probably the majority—are small enough so that an excellent contact and relationship can be maintained. As you may know from experience, some college instructors make little attempt to develop a relationship with their students in these smaller classes. Moreover, there are a few instructors who deliberately try to keep their students from becoming more than names or numbers. In contrast there is a philosophy that, historically, counseling has been a central part of the tradition of teaching. Garrison maintains "The best counseling is within the limits of the discipline that is the teacher's responsibility" (131:13).

Junior colleges have traditionally presented themselves as institutions where there was student identity, in contrast to the anonymity felt by students at some of the large universities. Student-faculty relationships consume time and energy; they also help to inspire better student achievement and to make grades more personal. An attempt to develop rapport with a whole class is not the same as rapport with an individual student; frequent face to face encounters with individuals need to be made if rapport is to develop. Certainly every instructor should see each of his students at least once privately during a term; ordinarily the instructor's office is the best place for these appointments, but sometimes a casual conference-walk across campus is most effective. Only you can decide the degree or amount of personal student contacts; the hope is that you will make them as frequent as possible, even though the humanization of teaching increases its overall complexity.

3. What should be the instructor's attitude toward tests and grades? Studies show that there are almost as many attitudes as there are instructors. The problem is particularly annoying when grades are transferred with the student to another institution. Questions asked are these: What does this grade really mean? Is the grade comparable to the same grade given at our own institution? How did the instructor arrive at the grade? How many tests did he give, and what kind of tests were they? Is the content of the course parallel to the content of the same course in our own institution? Compounding the problem is the fact that instructors teaching the same course in the same institution may cover different ground and apply different grading scales.

Testing styles range greatly from daily quizzes to one final examination; they may be either subjective or objective in nature. Frequent quizzes prod the student into staying up with his assignments and preparing himself for class discussions. Some instructors consider this to be spoon feeding. Others claim that such instructors are merely trying to make a reputation as a hard teacher. Still others say it is mere busy work to make the teacher look good. Apart from these criticisms is the fact that the overuse of daily quizzes can affect adversely the student's general academic performance. Students have other classes, too; they also have their families and need recreational time. There seems to be ample justification for a stand against the policy of daily quizzes.

The other extreme, that of no examination other than the final (and sometimes not even that), puts the responsibility for discipline almost entirely on the student. Opponents of this plan insist that the responsibility is too great, for the vast number of students, they say, are not disciplined enough to rely upon themselves. They say that a few quizzes during the semester are necessary to keep students motivated to learn course content. Certainly most of us will not work as hard in a course if we know there will be no quizzes and frequently no final examination. Philosophically, both extreme patterns exhibit the instructor's determination that the student demonstrate some form of achievement, whether orally, by testing, or by written papers (themselves a form of testing). The resultant amount of student dependence varies substantially.

Grades also reveal the instructor's philosophy and personality. Grading has been described as the most difficult step in teaching. Drawing lines among students can be painful; nevertheless it is necessary, if there is to be a variation in recognition. The more difficult question arises when the instructor has to decide whether the standards are fixed or related to individual or total group effort. In the case of the student who starts with unusually low ability, demonstrates substantial progress, and yet falls below the average, recognition of effort as well as achievement becomes very important.

Should the instructor assign a barely passing grade to such a student? One instructor will say "no," that work which does not meet minimum college standards is unquestionably F. On the other hand, the instructor who is concerned with subsequent academic achievement may argue that a D will elicit greater effort in the next course, especially if the student feels that his achievements were not classified with those of students who did not work up to their abilities. There could be many high ability students who top their classes with A's and still fall considerably below their potentials. And what grades should *they* get? The instructors interested only in achievement would give such students A's while those interested only in effort would give them much lower grades.

Once again, it would appear that the most reasonable teacher would consider both effort and achievement in grade determination. Care has to be taken, naturally, to avoid a "halo" or reverse effect from the instructor's perception of the student. A student should be able to disagree with the instructor without feeling that the grade has been jeopardized. At least one study indicates that student agreement with the instructor's position did not predict student grades (320). Another guide for the thoughtful teacher is a report that current grading practices are inconsistent, damaging, and badly in need of revision (63).

Philosophy of the Institution

You may have discovered already that virtually every CJC bulletin has an introductory statement of its philosophy. The statement is usually general, sometimes labeled as aims or purposes rather than philosophy. To illustrate, Trenton Junior College's bulletin says "this institution exists to serve the individual man, whose development to his fullest potential augurs well for all of society." Phoenix College's bulletin says the aim is "to aid in the development of the whole student." Sullivan County Community College's bulletin shows a program which "—will enable each individual in attendance to 'become all he is capable of being.' " Freed-Hardeman College's bulletin says, "Emphasis is given to the four-fold development of youth—the spiritual, intellectual, social and physical aspects. Effort is made to teach the students 'how to live and how to make a living.' "

These philosophies are consonant with most of the expressions of belief found in community college bulletins. The phrasing and details differ: nevertheless most junior colleges aim at the realization of the unique human potential in each of their citizens.

Philosophical generalities, however, derive their meanings from campus application. The governing board, the president, the deans, the department heads, and the faculty translate the aims and purposes into programs and courses; it is in the teacher's classroom that the most important translation problem may develop. For example a college may declare itself as an "open-door" institution, one which welcomes any student beyond the high school, or over eighteen years of age. Such a policy implies that each instructor must help not only the high ability but also the low ability student to "become all he is capable of being." It is an ambitious and challenging order for any instructor. He is greatly aided if the college backs its policy with teaching programs appropriate to various levels of ability among students. Such programs are tangible evidence of the real concern of the institution; they key downward from the board members (who must approve the allocation of staff and funds) to the administrators (who must direct and supervise the transformation of the philosophy into teaching programs) to the teachers (who must expedite the transformation into the realities of the classroom).

You will learn rapidly that the institutional statements of philosophy usually represent the work of a committee. Committee work often represents a sum different from its parts. Consequently, the group may arrive at a statement which does not represent the views of any one of the individuals and yet which is acceptable as not violating the beliefs of any one of the members. The beliefs of individual senior faculty members can be valuable sources of information for this committee, as well as for individual faculty members. They know from direct experience the admission, retention, and grading practices of the institution. Admission determines who enters, but retention determines how easily and how rapidly the student leaves. These policies may vary from year to year with the supply of faculty and students.

Institutional probation policies are also significant in the teacher's determination of his own philosophy. Students may be placed on probation easily, but they often may be removed only with difficulty. Petitions for reinstatements may be routine or rare. The registrar or admissions officer can play a major role in the interpretation of institutional philosophy.

Another sensitive area of institutional philosophy is that of grading. You will usually find this policy established at three levels: the dean (frequently with the assistance of a committee), the head of the department, and the individual department members. Quite often the dean coordinates grading practices by furnishing department heads and faculty members with institutional analyses of grade distributions. These studies can furnish you with valuable guidelines, in that they reveal how your colleagues apply the grading standards of the institutions. Definitions of grades are only the first step; the frequency of A's and F's has greater significance. Different standards among departments are sometimes logical. Grades in advanced mathematics courses, for example, will average higher than those in beginning algebra, for algebra classes are relatively unscreened. Calculus students represent the survivors of various screens; consequently they merit a different standard. Generally, there are higher averages in the second year courses; conversely, the institutional and individual philosophies establish the first year of CJC as one of lower grades and more frequent probation.

Institutional philosophy also has much to do with your time in the classroom. Some junior colleges allow a remarkable amount of freedom, while others tend to demand certain teaching procedures or approaches to learning. Your degree of freedom as a teacher relates directly to the college policy of instructional supervision, which may or may not include classroom visitation by administrators or deans. Your junior college may pattern its philosophy after the senior institutions, where new instructors are frequently ignored as teachers but scrutinized as writers and researchers. Or you may be treated in a fashion more akin to the high school, where there is great concern about visitation and evaluation. These patterns are often determined by the chief administrator and his perceptions of the CJC staff.

Institutional philosophy is much more than the combined thinking of the college staff and board members; it also represents the aspirations of the community—parents and students as well as interested citizens. The philosophy as stated and practiced must stay within the latitudes acceptable to the community. The boundary lines vary with each college: some are restrictively narrow, especially in the small isolated communities: others are remarkably sophisticated, like those found on the university campus. Your task is to perceive the actual institutional philosophy, delineate your own philosophy, and reconcile the two in an operable manner. This manner is manifested chiefly, perhaps, in the application of teaching methods and techniques, and by recognition of the "laws" of learning. These topics are discussed in the following companion chapter.

Chapter 8

The Art of Junior College
Instruction: Application

To be an art, teaching must be applied. Consequently this chapter combines the philosophy of the previous chapter with brief excursions into the psychology of learning, methods and techniques, and evaluation of the student, the teacher, and the course. Hopefully, you will pursue further reading or graduate work in these areas. Certainly educational psychology has become a highly specialized field in university research as well as in business and industry. Teaching methods and techniques have expanded dramatically by a growing acceptance of alternatives to the formal lecture; simultaneously a burgeoning electronics industry has made available a host of new communicative techniques. Research has also provided the college instructor with increasingly sophisticated methods of evaluation.

As some authors have stated (29), the CJC has established a reputation for special competence in lower division college education. In these colleges all the concentric orbits of education relate to the nucleus —the student, the instructor, and the subject. The velocity and direction of your role will be determined by how rapidly you master it. As in many other arts, a trained and experienced college instructor is far more effective in his fifth year than in his first, especially if he has worked systematically at improving his techniques. You may never be a "telly-guru," as described by Kamrath (195); nevertheless, as your potential continues to grow, it will approach ever closer to its ultimate boundaries. This chapter is only a starting point toward direction and acceleration.

The Psychology of Learning

Numerous books have been written on the psychology of learning. These books and courses center around a number of "laws" of learning, such laws to be used in the teaching-learning process. In attempting to select some of these laws of major importance to the new instructor, we have sometimes applied our own terms. The list below is by no means inclusive; nevertheless, its simplicity may increase its usefulness in your introductory semesters. We call these items the six R's in the psychology of learning.

Receptivity

A few decades ago, if an instructor had been asked "How do we learn?" he might have answered "Through the discipline of our faculties." His statement would have been an expression of the concept that the more painful the experience, the greater the learning. Thus, mathematics was an ideal subject for general learning, especially if the student found it difficult. Making learning too easy was construed as a disservice to the student, because ease diminished the amount of pain, and the less pain, the less learning.

The psychology of learning changed in the ensuing decades. Psychologists have long since demonstrated that we learn more from those activities wherein we achieve success and from which we derive pleasure. We call this phenomenon *receptivity*. Before students can learn effectively, they must be in a mood to learn—they must be receptive to learning; to be fully receptive, they must find a certain amount of joy and pleasure in their learning. They must have some reason for learning.

Test this law against your own experience. Don't you prefer enjoyable situations? Weren't your best classes those in which you found the greatest pleasure in learning? And wasn't your level of achievement greater in these classes than in others that gave you less pleasure?

Learning is frequently a difficult and lonely process. There are painful realities, both for the student and the instructor, but " . . . the reality of the study of any subject is in the student's response to it . . ." (128:19). Hard work and loneliness can be relieved by the degree of pleasure in the learning environment. CJC instructors can, within broad limits, do much to minimize psychological hurdles which are often set up inadvertently in the classroom. They can do more to establish receptivity in students than can the students themselves. Instructor attitudes should be geared toward the development of student receptivity, one of the psychological principles which can be applied to facilitate learning. Twitchell describes some obstacles to receptivity in learning. Among these are cynicism, narrowness, confusing purposes, distorted conception of students, clutter and crowdedness, pedantry, authoritarianism, antipathy to change, ineffective communication, lack of respect for the learning process and humanity (373).

Reinforcement

Reinforcement is the process of encouraging the student responses that we desire, making those responses more likely in subsequent behavior. Thus one knack of a master teacher is that of finding some way of structuring success into the experience of the student. Often the avenue is that of a favorable comment on the student's achievement. Highly motivated students are accustomed to academic success and can sustain their efforts; the student whose tastes of success have been slight or nonexistent needs to develop the habit of succeeding. The teacher can develop that habit by employing reinforcement through designed successful experiences.

The adult CJC student, often returning to school after several years away from a campus, may be especially apprehensive; consequently, he is likely to respond dramatically to reinforcement that allays his fears of inadequacy. The art of teaching is illustrated by the instructor who can be critical with such a student and yet find something to commend. The timing of reinforcement is important, too; it can establish an initial receptiveness to subsequent comments. Our hearing and success tend to improve as a result of pleasant communication serving both receptivity and reinforcement at the same time.

Respite

Another psychological principle that can improve communication and learning is related to *respite.* There are various terms to describe the decline of attention; respite describes what the student longs for after trying to sustain his span of attention beyond twenty minutes or so. Respite, then, is rest. One of the characteristics of maturity is the ability to listen intently for a lengthy period; in contrast, a child's attention is very apt to wander when he is thrust into a passive role. But even the strongest adult welcomes a change of pace, a respite from unrelieved listening to one voice or from unrelieved tensions within one concentrated activity.

An occasional respite reduces fatigue and creates better learning. Perhaps you have noticed how, after a brief rest period, you have returned to an activity with renewed vigor. Perhaps you have seen how a change of pace—a student question or the switch to a different teaching method—can suddenly renew your eagerness. We do not suggest that a skilled professor cannot keep a class rapt for fifty uninterrupted minutes of lecture; we do suggest, however, that the budding instructor introduce an occasional respite for his students, if not for psychological reasons, at least for physical reasons.

Relevance

Students also appreciate *relevance*, the quality of being applicable or pertinent. If someone suggests to you that you should learn the names of, for example, the Japanese political parties of this century, you would probably respond with one word—why? If you perceive this knowledge as relevant to your interests or needs, the odds go up for your learning. On the contrary, if there seems to be no justification other than a demand at grade point, your learning will be much more difficult.

Thus, a basic psychological learning principle is the need to help students perceive the relevance of course learnings to their lives. Accepting the value of this need may occasionally prove embarrassing, for we frequently discover that some of what we teach is difficult or impossible to justify.

Romance

Romance, the first step in Whitehead's cycle of "romance, precision, and generalization," is similar to relevance in that it should come early in the student-instructor relationship. The romance of learning, includes the dramatic, interesting, and intriguing. In our opinion there is no field, no academic discipline without facts and ideas which are of special interest to the newcomer. Thus, the skillful teacher establishes the launching pad for further learning by capturing the student's interest and imagination as rapidly as possible and by giving him a sense of excitement and adventure as he explores an unknown field. The principle is to make learning dramatically interesting with greater learning as a result.

Retention

Finally, we urge you to consider and accept human memory as it is— similar to a leaky bucket gradually losing and mingling its contents. The "law" of memory, *retention*, is rather exact: most of us forget much more than we remember. Your inspired introduction to the semester will be faded and warped by mid-semester as student memories grow dim and their aging notes become increasingly cryptic. Frequently, an apprehensive student betrays his weakness and asks for a review. Ordinarily he is voicing the uncertainties of others. Your anticipation of these concerns can help to establish a better learning climate.

One way to anticipate retention problems is to use frequent summary and review sessions. Retention requires much repetition. Another approach is to engage in various kinds of drills and exercises so that facts can be put into practical application. Avoid having students memorize a host of myriad detail; instead have them structure generalizations from subject matter detail. Intellectual capacity, we are told, is developed not from memorizing details but from abstract understandings and reasoning through a series of hypotheses and generalizations; at the college level, at least, the latter is considered the more important of the two approaches.

Uncertainty has been described as the most difficult condition for human beings. The instructor has the opportunity to introduce or to allay student uncertainties. College teaching should not be a game wherein the student and teacher try to outguess each other. They have or should have a common cause—learning. Accepting this premise means that they work together to achieve that goal. Their paths toward learning can be made less steep and less tortuous by the use of these six R's of learning—receptivity, reinforcement, respite, relevance, romance, and retention.

Some Methods and Techniques

Planning the course carefully can raise the probability of your achieving your goals for the semester. The real test, however, lies in translating your plan into the reality of the classroom. In essence, how do you "teach" someone? The answer is a deceptive mixture of simplicity and complexity. All of us have been teaching for years outside the classroom. In an informal manner, usually without a scientific or artistic plan, we may teach a relative or friend to drive a car. We may teach a child to catch a ball or a dog to fetch a stick. Teaching by explanation, demonstration, and practice must predate recorded history. Both informal and formal teaching offer a variety of teaching methods and techniques, varying in effectiveness.

In selecting these methods and techniques, we are guided by some general assumptions and research findings. One major point is that any teaching method has both advantages and disadvantages. Trabue reports some additional points that need consideration here at the outset (371).

1. Class size is not as big a factor as has been thought, if the prime objective is the transmission of information.

2. Relatively little is known about the "best" plan for organizing learning material.

3. Textbook teaching remains prevalent—and unsatisfactory.

4. Every phase of learning (including tests) can be improved.

5. The teacher's personality will determine choice of method.

Guilford implies another preliminary point, that the whole process of effective learning requires creativity, both from teachers and students. The author supplies several techniques for encouraging creativity (149). Creativity in method is also found in another article which states that teachers should be unprepared (246). This shocking revelation leads to a valid argument, that teachers might teach better by allowing the students to formulate the course as they see and need it, rather than to follow the rigid prescriptive format prepared in advance by the teacher. Parnes presents a useful survey of research on creativity (282).

Many authors provide discussion of the art of teaching and its application. For additional reading, see the bibliography, for instance, Morton (264), Mayer (234), Garrison (129), O'Neill (278), Eels (95), Chapman (56), Rapp (304), and Horton (178).

There are some who may quibble about the difference between *method* and *technique*. While these terms are frequently used interchangeably as synonyms, we choose to make the following distinction. A *method* is a systemic arrangement, an orderly procedure, a mode of handling intellectual problems; a *technique* is a skill or device in the specialized details of a method. Method is a broader term, a unified plan composed of various techniques. The following illustrate some of the standard methods and desirable techniques.

Lecture

The most common college teaching method is the lecture. The general concession is that it may be *most* useful for transmitting information (240:15). As you know from experience, this method can enthrall or bore certain students or even a whole class. During his presentation, even the best teacher is likely to "lose a few" at either end of the ability scale. Nevertheless, a strong case can be made for the lecture (225).

A lecture should present new and additional material not covered in the textbook if it is to be beneficial. Furthermore, the material should have excellent organization and language clarity if it is to be readily understood. A study of outstanding lecturers at Ohio State showed that their plans were simple and the examples abundant (86:150). All significant generalizations should be well developed with various kinds of interesting examples and research, all of which should be carefully documented. Fact and opinion should be clearly distinguished. Clearly visible logic must be employed in areas requiring reason.

In contrast to the small class lecture, the formal lecture has also become, thanks to the vast crowded lecture halls of some of the large universities, a symbol for impersonal and ineffective instruction. However impersonal such classes may be, contrary to the myth that large classes mean decreased learning, there is ". . . no statistically significant difference in post test performance of groups subjected to the two methods of teaching . . ." (132:384).

Large classes can be as effective as small classes when the proper techniques are used. According to Woodworth, there are several substantial advantages. The likelihood of careful preparation is increased; there is less tendency to digress; a larger number of stimulating students may be included (399). The techniques of teaching larger classes are discussed in some detail by Payne (283).

Most college teachers may have the ability to prepare a strong lecture, but far too many "spoil" their lectures in the delivery process. Reading a lecture from complete manuscript creates several problems, the most important of which is the lack of eye contact with the class audience. Working from an outline or checklist, the instructor can phrase his ideas with spontaneity, establish audience contact, and monitor the feedback of student reactions and questions.

The lecture method has advantages, despite the criticism directed at the stereotypes of professors mumbling and reading from brittle, yellowed notes to dozing students. The lecture allows the instructor to compress a large amount of supplementary material into a short space of time, to emphasize and dramatize the most important points of his subject. History, for example, can be brought to life by an imaginative instructor who combines his enthusiasm with exciting content and a flair for drama. Even English composition has been taught successfully with lectures on tape, heard outside class away from the lectures (309). A lecture can also be especially useful when several class sections are combined for an outstanding lecture, frequently followed by smaller discussion group meetings. The lecturer is selected for his unusual ability in both content and delivery so that he can be shared with all the students rather than with only a few students. Such a procedure also provides large audiences for those instructors who respond enthusiastically to large audiences. The group discussions allow the students to interact with an instructor and among themselves.

Oral Interpretation

The lecture is an original speech prepared and delivered by the lecturer himself, but oral interpretation is the analytical and interpretative reading of materials written by other people. Interpretative speech is an art that can be used effectively by people in many professions, including law, the ministry, government, politics, and teaching. Teachers of English, literature, acting, speech, and oral interpretation itself especially need to develop ability in this area, but all college teachers could make use of interpretative speech as a means of adding variety and interest to their art.

While "interpretative speech" is taught as a separate course among the other speech arts curricula, it is a significant teaching tool. At its minimum, it is effective reading; at its best, it is rich with feeling and interpretation through vocal and bodily responses to the printed word. Warm, sensitive, sympathetic, and responsive personalities are the best interpreters. Technical skills needed are those related to the analysis and understanding of literature, the proper selection and preparation of literary materials, and the kind of proficient delivery that will make the material come to life for the audience. The material lives if all the emotion, depth, and meaning of an author's work are properly communicated to the audience by the interpreter's mastery of these characteristics. Oral interpretation not only helps to instruct students or to persuade them, but it also has the advantage of a built-in entertainment value.

Socratic Method

Frequently used as a teaching method in higher education is the Socratic system, which employs the use of questions "to develop a latent idea, as in the mind of a pupil, or to elicit admissions, as from an opponent tending to establish or to confute some proposition." Socrates tended to use his method as his one and only approach to learning; it could be so used today in some cases, but more often it is used for variety at the conclusion of lectures, its purpose being to challenge students to think for themselves and, perhaps, reach their own conclusions. The Socratic method suggests that the teacher does the questioning and the student the answering; it also suggests that the teacher answer a student question with a question of his own. In essence, the student is supposed to find the answer to his own question by gaining insight into the facts through provocative questions supplied by the instructor.

Any question-answer period, whether Socratic or otherwise, is a necessary part of any instructor's methods of teaching. Students become frustrated if they do not have the opportunity to ask questions in a class. They have many problems arising out of the learning environment and these problems must be solved if the learning is to be effective. Student questions provide a change of pace, introducing a voice other than the instructor's. As a side effect, the questions allow the student to develop his ability to phrase inquiries and present them before a group. A question-answer period serves as a catalyst in soliciting both classroom participation and achievement. Students are apt to be better prepared in their reading and listening assignments if they know they may be challenged or called upon to speak. If their responses are evaluated or graded, they tend to display more interest and attention to the class work. "Effective learning requires mental self expression on the part of the individual student. The extent to which the students actively participate in the learning activities . . . will be considered a measure of effective learning" (230:2). Student participation is specifically recommended by the Maryland Standards for Community and Junior Colleges.

Various technical skills are needed in the Socratic or question-answer methods of learning. There are no sure answers as to the best place to include these methods in course instruction; the placement and timing relate to individual teaching styles. One effective technique is to base the lecture on a series of questions which are asked of the class, each one serving as a basis for their responses and your follow-up comments. Considered a "bad" technique by many instructors is the employment of purely factual questions, such as "In what year was the Norman Conquest of England?" Or "Which person was the first to sign our Declaration of Independence?" Thought questions requiring analysis or reason are considered best. Instead of the "what," "where," or "when" questions, try to get at the "why" or "how" aspects. For instance, "Why did the Normans invade England?" The "what" in "What caused our founding fathers to develop a Declaration of Independence?" is really a "why" question; "Why was the Declaration of Independence developed?" Here, we wish a student to reason out an answer through an analysis of cause and effect. The typical Socratic method would appear as follows: The student asks, "Is capital punishment a good law?" And the professor answers with a question of his own, "Does it deter crime?" The value of the question method of learning seems most valid when students are stimulated and challenged to establish their own propositions and support them.

Informal Group Discussion

Emphasis is upon questions in the Socratic method, but in informal group discussion the emphasis shifts to sharing ideas or comments in order to arrive at a mutually satisfying agreement among the members. If a class discussion turns into an argument between opposing factions, then it is no longer pure discussion but, in fact, a group debate. Classroom discussion is usually classified as informal because it follows no rigid construction or organization and it includes *no* outside audience. In essence, it is *free* discussion. It may or may not include a discussion leader. If the students are briefed, are told what subject they must discuss, are provided a leader serving as a guide and a secretary serving as a recorder, the discussion takes on characteristics of formal presentations. The informal type may produce as much learning as the more formal type of discussion. For classroom purposes, however, some form of control is necessary, at least in terms of course objectives and goals; even with controls, the lack of an outside audience characterizes class discussion as informal rather than formal.

Discussions offer a stimulating change from the lecture method. Current research indicates that discussion is more likely to change students (240:15). Once they begin to participate, students discover they enjoy participation and learn more as a consequence. Critics of discussion point out that students' time can be wasted, especially when the group is not held to the topic. Critics describe discussions as unorganized "bull sessions." They contrast the occasional noisy digressions with the organized lecture. They forget that the silence of the lecture audience may represent boredom as well as learning.

Discussion techniques have proved themselves in desirable learning effects (44), but success requires careful planning. By providing a challenging problem or topic area, the instructor, perhaps with student help, prepares the group to work toward predetermined goals. The instructor himself usually serves as a guide and resource authority. Once the discussion begins, it is wise that he interfere only upon necessity—for instance, when the discussion appears to stall or to disintegrate.

Size plays a role in success. The members of a six-man discussion group have adequate time to participate and react to others' comments. As the group expands, the time for each member contracts, until it is virtually impossible for everyone to participate appreciably in a large group confined to fifty minutes or less. The answer, of course, is to establish several small discussion groups and to circulate among them and sit in for a short time. Gnagey's experiments with small-group versus teacher-led discussions suggests an equally effective alternate to discussion sessions in the usual pattern. No significant difference was found in achievement, but teacher-led discussion, the students thought, was significantly more practical and understandable (139:30).

You may find worthwhile the method popularized by industry—*brainstorming*. The goal is the creation of fresh ideas; the atmosphere is permissive so that inhibitions are minimized. The results can be stimulating, for each idea triggers others, with the usual critical reactions eliminated. The class members may perceive their colleagues and themselves differently after participating in this process. The process is most useful when a course lends itself to creative ideas and when the instructor wishes to develop imagination and innovation among his students. The instructor's own ingenuity determines where brainstorming can be used with a likelihood of success.

As the name suggests, one teaching method involves dividing the students into small groups for the purpose of buzz group discussion. Doyle advocates small group buzz sessions and provides some useful information (90). An interesting experiment which suggests that student discussion group members can learn as much as they learn in conventional lectures, is reported by Beach (21). Buzz sessions allow the student to participate actively in the education process rather than to be a passive receptacle waiting for the instructor to pour out the information.

Hurst makes a strong case for the group decision method (181). The author reports that the method is an adaptation of a technique developed by Lewin in his wartime studies of changing food habits. "In brief the method outlines a problem to the group, gives them all the available information and describes its relation to the problem and then directs them to reach a group decision as to how they could handle or solve the problem" (181:148). Another name for the method may be problem-solution discussion.

Formal Discussion

Formal discussion is chiefly the type that is conducted before an audience. There are various types of formal discussions, but the most prevalent type is the *panel presentation*. Certain students are selected to sit on the panel. They may prepare speeches on a given subject or topic area, with a panel chairman serving the group. This form is more properly called a *symposium*. Or they may freely discuss a problem as the chairman guides and directs the questioning. A symposium-panel is a combination of prepared speeches, followed by free discussion. After the completion of the symposium or panel, the audience can be invited to question the group or to make comments of their own. Audience participation with the formal group is called a *forum*. The chairman, sometimes called the *moderator*, directs the whole process. When topics are potentially awkward, he may ask that questions be submitted in writing so that they can be edited or assorted for selection beforehand.

Techniques used in formal discussions such as the panel or symposium are numerous and relatively detailed. Much more organization and responsibility are needed here than are needed for informal discussions. The moderator, for instance, needs to limit the comments of discussants who try to take more than their share of time. He needs to keep the discussion on the track and make sure that it does not disintegrate into a debate, which is a quite different method. The moderator or chairman is usually responsible for the overall introduction and conclusion to the discussion. In short, he needs to exercise a number of skills in fulfilling his various responsibilities. Time usually restricts the number of participants to five or six.

When a panel or symposium group is reduced in number to two members, the classification is usually called *dialogue*. This form is perhaps most effective when the participants represent opposite sides of a question; for example, one guest representing management, the other the union. Once again, we must not confuse dialogue with debate, as normally defined. If dialogue is a true discussion, its aim is to reconcile differences and reach a mutually satisfying conclusion. A dialogue can be expanded to allow questions or comments from the audience. In the class situation, the instructor may follow up the dialogue (or symposium-dialogue) with questions of his own, a technique which can establish more dialogue and perhaps encourage student participation.

Debate

Debate places heavy emphasis on winning support for one point of view as opposed to another. If the teacher's purpose is to arrive at agreement, to emphasize unity of class purpose, he'll use discussion; if he wishes to introduce the enthusiasm and special interest that students develop when arguing and defending a position, he'll use debate. The class, too, can be much more interested when the drama of a contest livens their studies. Conflict of any kind arouses students to become more conscious of what they believe. They may continue to talk about a class debate conflict for many days after the debate is over. Probably it is this particular effect that makes debate such a valuable teaching tool.

Debate, like discussion, may take many forms and employ various techniques. The most popular form is that in which two-man teams compete against other two-man teams. One side establishes the debate proposition and supports the affirmative, while the other side argues the negative. Debate judges, sometimes total audiences, decide upon the winning team. For specific techniques of debate, you should consult any reliable debate manual or speech textbook.

Debate can be used in many college courses; most subject areas have certain controversies and, rather than the teacher's presenting the pros and cons, the students should become involved in all the aspects of research and thought necessary for good debate. Many teachers can stimulate their classes through the use of such a method.

Laboratory

Science has led the way toward the immersion of students in direct experience rather than having the instructor talk about the experience. Laboratories are standard accompaniment for science lectures, but lab sessions can also be held in most other subject fields. A project or study lab is the most common form adaptable to other areas. Labs are especially useful in business skills courses and foreign language instruction and in any area, in fact, where direct experience happens to be a significant goal in learning. The community, as well as the school, provides extensive laboratory facilities, many of them surprisingly convenient. Frequently business firms are delighted to have students participate directly in work-study programs, alternating paid employment with classroom theory. Sociology students often participate in community surveys, wherein they develop interview techniques and simultaneously provide the school and community with useful data. The values of the laboratory method are well established among both educators and the lay public.

The essence of the lab method is direct, carefully planned experience which replaces the vicarious experience of the lecture with first-hand learning. The instructor, in fact, must prepare the lab program as carefully as he would a lecture program. Many hours must go into the preparation. The lab session must be introduced properly and checked constantly while the students work. In the cases where many types of equipment and supplies are used, the instructor must select and order these materials and constantly supervise their use and management. The good lab teacher never lets the students work alone while he sits behind his desk; on the contrary, he moves freely from student to student to check their work and offer suggestions for improvement.

Guidelines and Handout Sheets

Perhaps more of a supplement than a special method of teaching is that of furnishing the student with printed reinforcement of the teacher's oral communication. There are occasions when you may wish to save valuable class time by providing a printed booklist, a course outline, a classroom policy, or perhaps a lecture outline. Especially valuable is a printed list of behavioral objectives. These materials are usually an expression of the instructor's determination to provide the student with a maximum of support for the lecture or other communicative methods of learning.

There are a few desirable techniques relating to guidelines and handout sheets. Obviously, they should be well organized and clearly structured in language. They should make some useful contribution to the course goals. They should be relatively brief. They should be presented to the students at the proper time during the course. In the matter of time, you should be aware of the potential distractions that printed materials can introduce. One desirable technique, which minimizes distraction, is to move down a guide or checklist with both instructor and students following each item in turn.

Student Reports

Occasionally you may want to vary your methods by allowing a student to be the focal point of class attention. Student reports include various advantages: they introduce a change of pace and voice; they provide the student with the experience of speaking to a group (a goal of general education); they allow each student to concentrate his study on one area of the course; they structure the class so that each student receives a series of other student reports in exchange for his own.

There are some potential disadvantages: The student who is poorly prepared wastes class time as well as his own; even if well prepared in content, the student's organization and expression may be so confusing or misleading that additional precious time must be spent by the teacher or students in seeking clarification; the student's vocal and physical delivery may bore or distract the class from the real values of the report; the student may not have been well briefed by the instructor in setting up the reports so that confusion and student resentment result; the reports may be only busy work, not contributing significantly to the course goals. In spite of these possible weaknesses, student participation by the report method is an excellent learning device which should be useful for almost any course in the curricula.

Student Papers

Student reports, normally delivered orally, can also be written and turned in to the instructor. Such a method is especially useful when there is a lack of class time for oral presentations. In the absence of oral delivery and corrective feedback, the student needs to be concerned primarily about his content and organization. Knowing how to write, as well as speak, is one of the fundamental goals of education. Regardless of the subject or course being taught, there is always a need for various types of student papers, for they help every instructor to evaluate the total student and his learning. In addition, papers can motivate learning by forcing the student to explore a given area and formulate conclusions of his own.

Should a teacher employing the student paper method be responsible for only the content and organization in a paper? We would have to say no. Most good teachers realize the need to read and respond carefully to comment on such elements as usage, spelling, punctuation, capitalization, and sentence structure. The responsibility demands, of course, that the teacher himself masters his language.

Independent Study

If one method had to be chosen as the subject of the focal point of community colleges during the late sixties, the choice would probably be independent study. The best known community college use of this method can be found at Oakland Community College in Michigan. Tirrell's report on the philosophy and program of the "audiotutorial method" describes the method and its origins (368). Tirrell's plan has at its heart the thoughtful, systematic analysis of objectives. Most methods can be enhanced by such an analysis. But equally or even more important, the student's achievement of the objectives is evaluated with unusual care at the conclusion of the process. Thus, the student is oriented thoroughly on the skills or knowledge he must be able to demonstrate. Indeed, his means of demonstration are also spelled out as clearly as possible.

These concepts are fused with the Oakland Community College campus. However, more conventional campuses across the nation have been experimenting with similar methods which individualize instruction through the employment of various electronic supplements to the instructor. For a study of the college and university practices which preceded the Oakland Campus, see Felder's study which presents a survey of the more traditional independent study practices (110).

One growing approach to independent study is the case method. Borrowed from various professional schools—law, medicine, social work, etc.—case method is being used in various applied fields and adapted to certain theoretical fields. Baur provides a general discussion of the techniques and criteria of this method (20).

Within the traditional framework of independent study there is some difference of opinion. Brown and Adams (40) claim the program supports the value of independent study. However, others, for example Hatch and Bennett (160), suggest that in the quality of learning there is no significant difference between the traditional class meetings and independent study programs. If the opportunity should arise, you may want to experiment with an independent study program, even though it may be very difficult to compare the results with those of the lecture method.

Honors Seminar

Another approach which is rising in popularity among junior colleges is the seminar (41). In a small class the honors seminar brings together students who show unusual academic potential. Presenting an understandably high cost of instruction ratio, such classes can be very stimulating to the instructor as well as the students. The opportunity to pursue ideas in a small group of especially able students can accelerate intellectual maturity through the analysis and articulation of ideas. Bogdan's experience is described with enthusiasm. "Perhaps the most rewarding experience of this class was the enthusiasm with which the student approached the study of history and the accuracy with which he followed through. This, in itself, is adequate justification for honors endeavors, even at the freshman level" (32:189).

Similar testimonials can be found in other disciplines. Dawson discusses a sophomore honors class in English (87). A social science honors seminar is described by James (184). Great success in terms of observations of students, teachers, visitors, test results, anecdotes, and case studies is evident in liberal arts honors seminars, according to Majella (224). However, a slightly different viewpoint is provided by Swets (352) who feels that admission criteria should be scrutinized rather carefully. Dannick and Carson (85), in describing an honors program at Cozenovia College, indicated supporting methods as (1) the establishment of a relaxed atmosphere in which all topics are discussed, (2) team teaching and drop-in teachers, (3) a common denominator in the fact all students had completed introduction to sociology and were currently in the social problems course, (4) the use of the *New York Times* as a common reading to relate theory to the real world, (5) field trips, and (6) no set content outlined. Added to this advocate position is the problem of determination of faculty load.

Team Approach

Just as the exchange of ideas can be stimulating to students, instructors often can be stimulated by teaching in a "team" relationship rather than in solo. The exchange can be particularly rewarding when the course is interdisciplinary. Young (402) suggests such values as interstimulation, intertesting of ideas, shared responsibility, larger classes, burdens shared, more careful preparation, better objectivity, and better motivation to learn. He adds, however, a list of pitfalls: possible clash of personalities, rigidity of ideas, feeling of being threatened by the other, refusal to accept differences, dominance of one by the other, disproportionate amount of labor, and students pitting instructors against one another.

If you are interested in learning more about team teaching, read Wetzler's comments (389). Even though his examples are drawn from the teaching of world literature, his description of the steps for team teaching may stimulate you to consider the method as an alternative to individual lecturing.

An answer to the apprehension that team teaching may be ineffective is provided by Fredenburgh: "No one method—whether lecture, small group discussion, the problem-oriented approach, the project-centered method, the case-study approach—is found to be superior to any other" (119:12). He also underscores an essential to successful team teaching: The instructor must have unusual depth and breadth in his preparation.

A type of team teaching is in the work-study plan, which is found in such junior colleges as Mohawk Valley Community College and the Loop Branch of Chicago City Junior College (180). The usual approach is a division of the student's time into regular course instruction and the kind of practical instruction provided by direct work experience supervised by those in the various occupational fields. Certainly the team of teacher and field supervisor is to be considered where possible.

Technological Methods

The choice of methods and techniques can be simplified by answering two questions: (1) Can audio-visual devices clarify information or motivate better learning in certain portions of the verbal presentation of subject matter? (2) What devices would do the job most effectively?

When it seems necessary to stimulate better listening and better understanding of the hearing sense, teachers can use supplementary all-audio devices—radios, telephones, tape recorders, and phonographs. But what about visual observational devices? Isn't it true that observation, the sense of sight, can reinforce the hearing process? Just watching a lecturer is not enough. The lecturer must be doing something as he speaks; for instance, he could be demonstrating. Here, the visual combines with the audio sense and demands more direct student participation through the involvement of both eyes and ears. Participation itself is considered the most direct aid to learning (230:2). Add to that a long list of techniques which include field trips for on-the-spot visual observations, various types of exhibits and school museums, motion pictures, still pictures (slides, film strips, photographs, and the like), and visual symbols (such as charts, graphs, and maps). Aids can be as simple as the common blackboard or as complex as the closed-circuit television operation.

Specific techniques within the various technological methods can only be learned and mastered with practice; many of these techniques will vary with each teacher. Currently popular with most teachers is the overhead projector, which enables the instructor to face the class, while his writing is projected behind him, visible to the class. In essence, the overhead projector approach is a substitute for the chalkboard. Overhead projectors come in various sizes and kinds, most of them portable. Sometimes they have the disadvantage of requiring a partially darkened room, although the new projection screens allow more room light than in the past. Recent processes enable the instructor to transfer book pages, newspaper illustrations, virtually any printed material onto a transparency for projection. Having the advantage of rapidity and versatility, they allow the instructor to present to his class a column or photograph from the morning paper on the day of publication.

Sometimes an instructor wishes to share class material that does not lend itself to transparent production. If he wants to project a student paper so that the class can examine it, he uses the opaque projector. Books, papers, flat objects can be projected by an optical system which bounces the light off the material rather than through it. Opaque projection is particularly compatible with photographic prints; a Polaroid snapshot can be shown on the screen a few minutes after the photograph has been taken.

Photographic transparencies, either the 35 mm or the less common 2 X 2, also provide a convenient means of supplementing words. Cameras, color slides, and projectors are extremely popular outside the classroom; they provide a potential source of teaching aids, when the coverage happens to be an area or country being studied by the class. In addition to slides made by the instructor himself are the many commercially produced transparencies in such fields as art and architecture; these enable a class to see a Van Dyke painting or a Frank Lloyd Wright building enlarged beyond the boundaries of printed word or picture. Transparencies are also produced in strip rather than mounted individually. The film strips are often accompanied by recordings which are synchronized, combining sight with sound.

The combination of sight and sound with movement is most familiar in the motion picture. The addition of movement increases the interest of the audience and adds a dimension which makes development and progression possible. Literally thousands of 16mm films are available to college instructors. Effective usage involves a systematic preparation of the class so that the students know what to watch for and what is to be emphasized. Follow-up student activities are also essential, if the experience is to be focused on the purposes.

Motion is also available through television. Within the past several years a growing number of schools have added television facilities to their technological resources. Perhaps the most common is that of the closed circuit, which is ordinarily confined to campus. This has been extremely useful in such activities as laboratory demonstrations where the television camera brings the demonstration to the last row in the lecture hall by means of the television screen. Large class lectures make similar use of television techniques.

Where scheduling makes it feasible, some classes use live television from off-campus, for example, documentary and news coverage which relate to class activities. A major difficulty has been that the coordination of class and program is difficult to arrange and is rarely coincident. Fortunately the cost of video tape facilities is decreasing and the availability is increasing. It is now possible to tape a live show from a home receiver and store the material for later presentation.

Video tape is considerably cheaper and more rapidly screened than its competitor, the motion picture film; because of these advantages video tape has enabled colleges to experiment with the recording of staff lectures and demonstrations for re-use. This technique, in combination with electronic equipment, has made it possible for students to dial a lecture for an individual showing. This procedure has added advantage of enabling a student to review a lecture without inconvenience to the instructor. The instructor, himself, is thus enabled to evaluate his own teaching at his convenience. Video tape is also considered one of the "greatest innovations" for performance courses, particularly in speech (320). The student speaker, like the teacher, is more apt to improve dramatically after seeing himself deliver his speech on video tape replay.

Appealing to sound alone are the magnetic tape recordings. Even without an appeal to sight, sound recordings have numerous applications to teaching. Taped recordings should find some use in all classes, but they become a central means of teaching effectiveness in such courses as speech and foreign language. Taped recordings can capture and release a student's performance for his own as well as the class's and instructor's analyses. A growing number of colleges centralize their taped learning resources and make them available to the whole campus through a dialing system. Foreign language laboratories, in particular, use tapes and tape decks extensively.

Also inexpensive are disc recordings, sometimes offering recorded material not available in tape form. Quite often commercial releases of stage plays and classical music are issued first on long-playing records. Every instructor should familiarize himself with the many listings of LP recordings. Such useful aids as poets reading their own poetry, the sounds of World War II, the songs of the Civil War, the astronauts' voices from the moon, are waiting to assist the instructor. Reproducing, as they do, the varied sounds and programs of life, disc recording companies often have a record that fulfills a special need for an instructor's class.

Although space limits our discussion of these and other technological aids, we cannot conclude this section without describing briefly what may well be the most revolutionary technological assistant to instruction—the computer.

A student sits at a console or station connected by a telephone line to a central computer. He "talks to" the computer by employing the console typewriter keyboard or a television screen that can display written messages, drawings, equations, and other graphic material. The student may use a light pen to select answers to the problems shown on the screen; he may even erase or change the images that appear. The student hears the computer talk to him through a pair of earphones or a loudspeaker; the verbal communication, especially when new concepts are presented, provides interaction.

The student and computer interact at three specific levels, each of which is a separate system of instruction: individualized *drill-and-practice system, tutorial system,* and *dialogue system.* (1) Drill-and-practice work is used for the skill subjects. The teacher introduces the concepts and ideas preliminary to ordinary drill and practice, and the computer provides the drill-and-practice exercises by presenting, evaluating, and scoring them without any effort on the part of the classroom teacher. The drill-and-practice system is individualized so that each student works at his own rate from his current level of ability. (2) The tutorial system helps the student understand a concept and develop skill in using it. The system is called tutorial because it approximates the interaction between a patient tutor and the individual student. The drill-and-practice and tutorial systems are already functioning on the experimental level (3). The dialogue system, because of many technical problems for present-day operation, is less advanced in use. The dialogue system requires that the student be able to conduct a genuine dialogue with the computer, very much like ordinary dialogue between teacher and student. The dialogue system enables students to ask questions and discuss a point with the computer.

Will the computer system of learning replace the teacher? No. It is now a supplement, an aid to learning. The teacher is still the necessary force in the classroom. Can computers individualize instruction? Yes. Present-day instructors cannot fully cope with the problems of differing abilities, rates of learning, and approaches to learning—not with so many students in their classrooms. But one means of providing individualized instruction is the computer system, which deals on an individual basis with many students simultaneously and thus lowers the cost per student of the computer.

What about the teacher's role? For one thing, he is saving himself the burden of preparing and correcting large numbers of drill-and-practice exercises. For another thing, he has greater opportunity for personal interaction with his students. Teacher-administrator relationships should be strengthened as skill is developed in interpreting and using the vast amount of computer information. Each area of the curriculum is improved by the findings. Students in computer-assisted programs will work at their consoles no more than a third of the time they are in classes; this time should be enough to demonstrate the value of the computer as a newer technological advancement helping students to learn more effectively.

The New Teaching

Programmed materials are growing rapidly in popularity. Whether classified as a method or a technique, automation or teaching machines, or computerized instruction, these methods enable the instructor to design a course of instruction for thousands of students to learn through a clearly intermediate means.

The initial fears and hostilities aroused by these methods have been somewhat allayed, although by no means eliminated. There is an increasing awareness that there can be advantages to using machines for routine work. When Roberts (317) suggests that CJC teachers abandon teaching facts, he does so with the suggestion that the instructor leave fact-teaching to a machine in order to liberate the instructor's time for discussing problems and concepts.

Of the comparative studies which have been made, an especially interesting and durable one is Collins' (66). His experiment compared the learning through lecture, self-tutoring with the use of programming and machines, and the two methods combined. The result was no significant difference in academic ability as measured by the Ohio State psychological test at the end of the semester: Additional implications are provided by Stolurow (345) whose predictions have been confirmed. Auto-instructional methods are here to stay because of their usefulness in increasing student knowledge.

Computerized instruction has also become commonplace, with growing sophistication in community college use of "software" as well as hardware. Methods of teaching are inexorably changed with the introduction of a growing number of applications of computers. Now the instructor is made available potentially to an infinite number of students, whereas previously the limits of his accessibility were clearly defined.

Closed-circuit television has become relatively commonplace in community colleges. The research seems to suggest that in effectiveness there is little difference between a television presentation and one which is live (241:92). Both methods are a mixture of advantages and disadvantages. The live lecture, for example, has the advantages of being flexible and interactive; but it is also slower than reading or television viewing.

Further discussion and additional methods and techniques are described in Johnson's survey of innovation techniques (190). Additional programs are discussed in some detail by Skaggs and others (334). A sample of the wide national variety is reported by Carlyon (50) who traveled with a 14-member faculty team, studying 64 institutions in 9 states. Their 147 recommendations were used to design the new Delta College.

"New" teaching, whatever else it may be, reflects an awareness of student demands for active learning experiences which seem relevant to the student's life. Student critics maintain that traditional designs and methods must be redesigned or even scrapped in order to introduce relevant experiences which result in useful learning. Disadvantaged students in particular have stimulated the colleges to expand the curriculum concept so that it reduces the passivity of the student role in traditional disciplinary approaches. Similarly the teaching methods and activities of the past are justifiable only as they contribute to structured, relevant experiences.

An infinite number and variety of student experiences can result from any one college course or teacher. Consequently, careful design of student experience is basic to success, and no one experience may fit all students. Also, the structured-experience approach must use by necessity one or more of the teaching tools indicated so far, for every learning experience requires some mode of intercommunication. Undoubtedly, the structured-experience approach is a different emphasis upon and use of existing methods, all of which are designed to help students reach a desired learning goal. Although the lecture method still remains popular in higher education, the CJC in particular is engaging in these various experiments and innovations, the results of which should improve upon the status of present teaching effectiveness.

Evaluation of the Student

Perhaps the most difficult step in teaching is that of student evaluation. The effect of our grading is clear when we find, according to Bard and others (15), that "for the nation as a whole 50 percent of those entering higher educational institutions fail to graduate." In theory the instructor is evaluating the effectiveness of his teaching and his students' learning, the two being inextricably entwined. The ultimate effect, nevertheless, is that of evaluating the student. Student evaluation may appear to be simple. Despite its appearance, the process is intricate; it brings to a focal point the relationships between the instructor, the student, and the subject matter—all of these immersed in relationships with the rest of the students and the faculty.

High standards are important. However, they are more than just severe grading. To enable teachers to raise standards, Collins makes eight suggestions: Prepare solidly for each class, use concrete examples in lectures, give the essence and avoid minutiae, get student feedback to check their understanding, show value and significance of what is learned, check student notes or provide outline, evaluate frequently, get them to read the text (65:23).

In this discussion area we concentrate on the "how" of this evaluation. The more mechanical aspects, such as grade accounting, have already been discussed elsewhere. In the following discussion, qualities or guidelines which seem to be outstanding reveal characteristics of effective student evaluation. While the list is incomplete, you may find it a useful beginning.

Early and Clearly Defined Evaluation

Students usually resent evaluation that is not explicated at the beginning of the course. Your first meeting and several subsequent reiterations should make the bases for evaluation unmistakably clear. In essence, you and the students are in a contract situation. If, from the beginning, you have spelled out the contract clearly to the student, his remaining in the class implies acceptance of the terms. You may find that the explication of the evaluation forces you to think through the course and perceive it more clearly as a result of the scrutiny. In any case, both you and your students are bound to the contract, and no changes should be made without some form of mutual consent.

Evaluation Related to Course Goals

Students are incensed understandably by evaluation which is not related to the objectives of the course. This lack of relationship may reflect a lack of clarity of objectives, which may be the fault of the student or instructor or even both. Thus, it is of major importance that the instructor define the objectives as clearly as possible, inasmuch as the evaluation is based on the achievement of these objectives. The more clearly the objectives are defined, the easier it is to decide what means of evaluation should be used.

Appropriate Selection of Evaluation Methods

There are, of course, various methods of evaluation. During your years as a student, you have probably encountered most of them. Tests, either subjective or objective in form, are the most familiar. As a teacher, you should try not to become completely dependent on either form of examination. Ideally, you want to give each student a variety of opportunities to demonstrate his achievement so that he can be seen in a favorable light. Both subjective and objective forms of evaluation represent a mixture of advantages and disadvantages, as will be seen in the following discussion. You may even want to use a technique that predates written examinations. Hartnett (159) refines the traditional oral examination by enabling the students to conduct it.

The subjective examination, sometimes referred to as essay, has the advantage of being relatively easy to construct. It also furnishes the student with opportunities to organize and synthesize what he has learned. Essays allow the student who is well prepared to display how much he knows. One major disadvantage is the difficulty of correction or grading. Other drawbacks are lack of objectivity and emphasis on verbal skills.

Numerous experiments have been conducted to demonstrate the wide range of grading of essays. Even handwriting can influence the reader, just as verbal facility can often conceal or offset lack of preparation. Essays tend to favor the glib student. There is the instructor's time problem, too. Reading several pages carefully can consume as much as a half hour. Multiply that amount of time by the members in the class, and again by the number of classes; the result is many hours of reading. Because of the time element, essay examinations represent a real stumbling block at the end of a course when grades must be quickly compiled and turned in.

Objective examinations have their own shortcomings. Many hours have to be invested in their construction. This time, however, comes back to the instructor in a variety of dividends. There is first the relative speed and ease of correction. Today, many junior colleges furnish the instructor with data-processing equipment. Consequently, you may find that your objective examinations can be machine scored in a matter of minutes. If the equipment is sufficiently sophisticated, it can provide you with scores, grades, and an analysis of your examination. However, a built-in defect of objective examinations is that they do less to acquaint you with the student's personality or style of expression.

The construction of examinations is an art in itself. Every instructor has the experience of writing an occasional essay question which elicits a response far different from that in the instructor's mind. As a teacher you will need to develop a skill in anticipating student responses. Be sure that you allow some feedback at the time of the test; often a student's question may enable you to steer the group away from a misunderstanding. Essay questions should be limited in their scope, and they should avoid vagueness. You may want to limit the response to a set number of sentences. This has the fringe benefit of forcing the student to polish his response and develop his verbal ingenuity. Of substantial value to you is keeping the length to manageable proportions.

Objective tests take various forms; they may include some brief writing, as in a fill-in response. This type has to be reviewed rather carefully to avoid tangential responses even though logical. Nevertheless, the fill-in does emphasize recall rather than recognition. True-false items are relatively easy to write. The chief danger lies in the instructor's leaning too heavily on the text as a source of true-false statements. There is also the drawback of chance; guessing has a fifty-fifty chance of being right. And then there are give-away phrases such as "always" and "never" which signal the answer to the student.

Multiple-choice objective tests are popular for many reasons. They reduce the element of chance, although a poorly constructed question may eliminate all but two possible responses. Although more difficult and time-consuming to construct, they can be relatively sophisticated in their evaluation of the students' knowledge and abilities to think. You will want to be sure that your answers are parallel, so that the right one is not inadvertently tagged for the student. Matching-type objective examinations use a novel objective technique different from true-false or multiple choice. Machine-scored tests have a disadvantage in that the list has to be limited to five or six items. Nevertheless, they do allow the instructor to investigate the student's ability to relate such knowledge as events and dates.

Objective examinations lend themselves to objective analysis. A good teacher wants to know how efficiently his test evaluates. The most common means is an item analysis, whereby each question and response is examined. If, for example, all of the students get a question right, the question is too easy. More importantly, it does not discriminate between the average and better-than-average student. Conversely, if all the students, including your brightest ones, miss a question, you know that the item does not discriminate. And when the students with the highest scores consistently miss one question, that, too, should make you suspicious of the question's quality. Similarly, in multiple-choice tests you will find choices which are wasted or misleading for the wrong reasons. What you want to know is whether your test is valid—is it testing what it purports to test, and is it reliable? Does it give consistent results when used several times? Item analysis is a chief means of answering these questions. The whole process is time-consuming, but any teacher concerned with teaching effectiveness should examine his tests through such a process.

Tests are only one form of evaluation. The student should have other ways to demonstrate his achievement of course objectives. Short papers, book reactions, class reports, term papers, special projects—the list is limited only by your imagination. You will note that there are also learning activities which simultaneously allow you to evaluate the student. These activities may allow the student to evaluate his own achievement, a means which is considered ideal. Even tape recordings are being used as a means of student evaluation. Wotherspoon (400) uses recordings to build rapport and better student learning. By taping his reactions to students' blue books, he enables himself to respond in greater depth. At the same time the students have his comments available at their convenience in the language laboratory.

Fair Application of Evaluation

Beyond the means of evaluation is the question of its application. In other words, how is the ultimate course grade derived? This question confronts both the instructor and the student and is of critical importance to the latter. Again the answer relates to the contract relationship. Not only the means but the relative weights have to be made lucid to the student. How much do outside assignments count? What weight is given to the midterm, the final examination? Will you evaluate student achievement only, or will you give some weight to effort?

One method of determining fair application is to assign numerical values to each means of evaluation. For instance, the term paper is worth one-fourth of the grade, the quizzes are worth one-fourth, and so on. Thus, the criteria become relative, and the student who can log his own scores has a reasonably clear perception of his rank in the class. Most of the mystery of grades is dispelled when the students and instructor have the same data for evaluation. The whole problem of being fair probably relates to these factors: Treating all students the same in an objective manner, giving each means of evaluation a reasonable amount of weight. Related to this last factor, for instance, is the question of how much weight to give to the final examination. This is sometimes answered by the department or the institution. Some junior colleges explicitly limit the weight that can be assigned to the final; they may say that no more than a third of the semester grade may be derived from the final. In the absence of formal guidelines, the instructor must depend upon his own experience and empathy.

Consistency of Standard

As indicated in the above paragraph, consistency as well as relative weight is a factor in effective evaluation. Departments try to maintain standards of evaluation which will protect the student from glaringly inconsistent standards. This principle is of vital importance to the individual instructor, who must keep himself in a position to document his evaluation of each student, even after several semesters. Consistency demands that standards be the same for all students; it allows no teacher to depart from his class standards to reward or punish a particular student.

Evaluation is the ultimate step in teaching. It can send the student away frustrated, seething with the attitude that the instructor has little notion of what the student has achieved during the semester. Worse yet, poor evaluation may assign the greatest rewards to those students whose achievement was largely peripheral to the course objectives. Ideally, evaluation should provide a satisfying conclusion to the semester's voyage with the instructor. It should at once allow the teacher to know the student and his performance. But more important, evaluation should hold up the mirror to the student so that he can see himself and his colleagues with increased perspective. And the evaluation—like the objectives—must be made crystal clear at the outset of the semester.

Evaluation of the Instructor

Evaluation of the student, in a sense, is evalution of the instructor, who must share the credit or blame for every student's performance. Some junior colleges analyze carefully and systematically the records of students in relation to individual instructors. No institution will evaluate an instructor entirely on the basis of one student's achievement. However, when high-ability students fail in a consistent pattern with an instructor, the institution owes future students a serious evaluation of the instructor. In a similar fashion transfer records are studied with care. Follow-up studies can enhance an instructor's reputation, or they may cause him to re-evaluate his teaching methods. The institution has, to the instructor and student, a responsibility to see that they both achieve their potentials.

Although student failure and achievement also reflect teacher failure and achievement, there are other criteria designed to measure teaching proficiency and success. Department members and the college administrators frequently evaluate instructors through classroom visitations. During your early years as an instructor, you are likely to be visited and evaluated several times. Once or twice each year you will probably confer with the department head and/or the head of instruction. They may use an evaluation form which you may sign after it has been discussed. Ordinarily your formal evaluation will be a distillation of the facts and principles discussed in this text. Since each CJC has its own special style, you should be thoroughly briefed at your own institution.

You may wish to supplement the institutional evaluation with the more informal students' evaluation. Most instructors are concerned with student perceptions of their courses and their teaching. In many colleges these instructors are given instructor evaluation forms for students to check and return; some instructors design their own forms. All these forms are similar in their attempts to get students to comment on teacher and course weaknesses and strengths. The major aim is to help the instructor improve. CJC teachers must grow, even though not required to publish. Proper growth may also help to acclimate their "iceberg" images (223:12).

Student perceptions of other instructors may be useful to you for the purpose of personal comparison. Hoffman's study ascribes five major attributes of the excellent teacher. By percentage response, there were: 21%—teachers' attitude toward students, 20.5%—presentation, 18%—personal characteristics and worth, 12%—knowledge of subject, 11%—stimulation of thought and interest (174:21). Quick and Wolfe found six most frequent responses for the "ideal" professor: 19%—encourages independent thinking, 16.7%—well organized, 15.4%—enthusiastic, 12.4%—explains clearly, 12.1%—welcomes questions, 10%—careful evaluator (300:133).

Several problems can exist when the students evaluate the instructor at his request. The test may be easier to construct than to administer in an anonymous manner. By the end of the semester, the teacher may know student handwriting and therefore eliminate anonymity. If he is not careful, he may allow a destructive criticism to affect his relationship with and teaching of that student. Conversely, he may look with great favor, particularly at grade time, upon a student who offers glowing praise of the instruction. The instructor's problems of fear and insecurity relate directly to his students' evaluation of himself. There is also the problem of timing. If the evaluation is to cover the whole course, it should include the final examination, which may not allow time to fill out the evaluation with care.

These and other problems can be solved in various ways. Consider the following:

1. Look at yourself honestly.

2. Be willing to listen to constructive criticism.

3. Be able to face the facts of your possible weaknesses.

4. Be ready to follow up evaluation with positive changes.

5. Shorten your final examination to allow time for students to evaluate you.

6. Have evaluation forms requiring check marks rather than written material so that no handwriting can be detected.

7. Have forms which cover all aspects, such as teacher's personality,

his dress, his manner of speech, his knowledge of subject matter, his methods, etc.

8. Make the form relatively brief so that it can be completed in about fifteen or twenty minutes.

9. Prepare your students by expressing your sincerity in seeking their appraisal and in soliciting their fair and unbiased opinion along constructive lines.

10. Do not ask them to sign their names; keep the evaluations anonymous.

11. Consider having a student collect the forms and deliver them to you after the final grades have been turned in; or have the forms sealed in an envelope and given to the office for delivery to you upon your turning in your grades.

12. If objectivity can be maintained by all parties, ask for improvement suggestions from students once or twice *during* a semester.

Student-administered evaluations of instructors and courses are growing in popularity. Some of them are brutal; others are rather saccharine. They do represent, however, an increasing student determination to have a voice in the evaluation of instruction. When the evaluations are studiously fair and are not satiric or vicious, they can have a salutary effect. Outstanding instructors should be recognized and rewarded (223.12), and those who are not effective teachers should be concerned with improvement. It should be noted, too, that improvement and mastery normally come with increased age and experience; masterful first-year teachers, we think, are very rare. If the end result of teacher valuations is a campus-wide concern for good teaching and if students become more appreciative of the talent, imagination, training, and effort that circulate and culminate inside the classroom, then all those on campus can benefit from that change.

Evaluation of the Course

Although it may be impossible to evaluate a course completely apart from the instructor and the student, it is possible and worthwhile to allot some separate attention to the evaluation of the course itself. As a retrospective student you may have thought only rarely of a course apart from the instructor. There is an understandable tendency after taking a course to think of the subject matter as an extension or at least a partial reflection of the instructor. Similarly the instructor is likely to evaluate the educational process by your performance on examination rather than by an analysis of the course itself. And in earlier days you were no doubt much more concerned with an A for yourself rather than an A for the course.

Most significant as a method of course evaluation is the determination of the course's usefulness in preparing students for their needs in life. Because surveys, statistical reports, and other techniques were used initially to establish the validity of need, the course was added to the curricula of the college; however, we must remember that needs do change. A course may eventually lose its value to students. Instructors are apt to place a higher value upon their course subjects than are students. Especially in the area of required courses, students sometimes see few values. In these cases instructors have a problem of proper motivation. More important than what instructors and students feel, however, is the realistic status and trend in society. In view of societal changes, no college should consider any course completely permanent in the curricula. In the broad sense, instructors and students are incidental in the evaluation of need for courses. The greatest responsibilities lie with society and its institutions.

Related to the general evaluation of the need for the course is the method of testing the specific course goals. A course may be needed, but the goals may be misguided, poorly conceived and worded. The instructor himself assumes the major responsibility for this testing. He can compare his goals with standard guides such as Bloom's *Taxonomy of Educational Objectives* (31), he can compare them with goals set by other instructors teaching the same course in other schools, and he can solicit student, faculty, administrative, and community consensus. Along with goals, of course, he must evaluate his entire approach to the subject and to his students. Study and research should help him to evaluate properly and reach valid conclusions.

Student achievement after transfer is another common method used in evaluating courses, although this system places too much responsibility on the course. The belief is that the CJC course prepared the students very well when these students achieved well in their senior colleges and universities. Perhaps it is more accurate to say the junior college students learned well or the instructors taught well. When we collect the data of student achievement after transfer, such data supplied by these higher institutions, we find in most cases that CJC courses, instructors, and students are doing an effective job.

An example of student success after transfer is offered by Knoell, reporting on a national study of nearly 8,500 students from more than 300 two-year colleges in 43 states. These students transferred in 1960 to some 41 four-year colleges and universities located in a group of 10 states. Approximately 3,500 native students in these same senior institutions were also involved in the study for the purpose of comparison. The grade point differentials were small (0.3 lower) between the CJC grade and the first semester grade after transfer. In general the grades dropped slightly after transfer and then improved to about the same level of their junior college grades. The junior college transfer students compared favorably with the native senior college students in many cases (206).

A better test of a junior college course, insofar as the senior institutions are concerned, is whether the course parallels its counterpart at the senior institutions. Indeed, the course credit should be transferable if it is parallel. We have found many students and parents complaining of the fact that they cannot transfer all their CJC credits, but this fault may be due to inadequate counseling and program scheduling rather than to inadequate courses (206). Students having more credits than needed for transfer may naturally suffer loss of some of these credits. In most states courses may be transferred as electives if not as requirements.

A method of course evaluation which is growing rapidly in popularity is that of eliciting student response by means of a course, and/or instruction evaluation form. There is still considerable debate over the effectiveness of such forms. Nevertheless, they are being used with increasing frequency, despite claims that students are not qualified as evaluators. On the campuses of senior institutions the course ratings are sometimes an analysis of the total undergraduate program, course by course.

If you should decide to use the students for course evaluation, you may want to use one of the numerous forms already available. Most junior and senior colleges are willing to share their questionnaires. You may want to design a form of your own. There are several commonly used questions and techniques. The form which follows is a composite of numerous different evaluation forms. Space for comments may be added after each item. If all handwriting is to be eliminated, the heading information and comments can be eliminated.

Student's Evaluation of Course and Instruction

Date _____ Student's Major _____

Course _____ Student's Minor _____

Instructor _____ Expected Grade _____

You can be of considerable assistance to the instructor by helping him improve this course. Whether critical or complimentary, your answers should be thoughtful and honest, if they are to be helpful. Do not sign your name; leave out all heading information and comments if you desire, but check one response for each item.

I. THE COURSE CONTENT

	Outstanding	Excellent	Adequate	Weak	No basis for judgment
A. Value of the course to me personally	☐	☐	☐	☐	☐
B. Value of the course to majors in the field	☐	☐	☐	☐	☐
C. Value of the course to non-majors	☐	☐	☐	☐	☐
D. Value of the course to society in general	☐	☐	☐	☐	☐

	Outstanding	Excellent	Adequate	Weak	No basis for judgment

II. THE COURSE ORGANIZATION

	Outstanding	Excellent	Adequate	Weak	No basis for judgment
A. Clarity of course objectives	☐	☐	☐	☐	☐
B. Clarity of bases for evaluation	☐	☐	☐	☐	☐
C. Clarity of learning experiences	☐	☐	☐	☐	☐
D. Clarity of lectures and presentations	☐	☐	☐	☐	☐
E. Clarity of course organization as a whole	☐	☐	☐	☐	☐

III. THE COURSE AIDS

	Outstanding	Excellent	Adequate	Weak	No basis for judgment
A. Quality of the textbook	☐	☐	☐	☐	☐
B. Quality of the materials supplementing the text	☐	☐	☐	☐	☐
C. Quality of outside readings	☐	☐	☐	☐	☐
D. Quality of examinations	☐	☐	☐	☐	☐
E. Quality of assignments	☐	☐	☐	☐	☐
F. Quality of class discussions	☐	☐	☐	☐	☐
G. Quality of learning activities in general	☐	☐	☐	☐	☐

IV. THE INSTRUCTOR'S PRESENTATION AND APPEARANCE

	Outstanding	Excellent	Adequate	Weak	No basis for judgment
A. Effect of the language usage	☐	☐	☐	☐	☐
B. Effect of the vocal quality	☐	☐	☐	☐	☐
C. Effect of the volume	☐	☐	☐	☐	☐
D. Effect of the voice rate and pitch	☐	☐	☐	☐	☐
E. Effect of articulation and enunciation	☐	☐	☐	☐	☐
F. Effect of enthusiasm and interest in delivery of speech	☐	☐	☐	☐	☐
G. Effect of the mannerisms	☐	☐	☐	☐	☐
H. Effect of dress and appearance	☐	☐	☐	☐	☐

V. THE INSTRUCTOR'S ATTITUDE AND BEHAVIOR

	Outstanding	Excellent	Adequate	Weak	No basis for judgment
A. Availability for individual conferences	☐	☐	☐	☐	☐
B. Objectivity in handling controversial issues	☐	☐	☐	☐	☐
C. Kindness when responding to students	☐	☐	☐	☐	☐
D. Fairness in dealing with students	☐	☐	☐	☐	☐
E. Dedication to and interest in the subject	☐	☐	☐	☐	☐
F. General knowledge of the subject	☐	☐	☐	☐	☐

Part III   The Assessment

Chapter 9

Faculty Attitudes and Opinions

Teacher trainees and new teachers can benefit from knowing what experienced CJC teachers think about their work and their institutions. Faculty attitudes and opinions provide some guidance in understanding the nature of the profession and serve as a basis for developing one's own attitudes and opinions. In our college-faculty survey we asked our specialists certain questions which form the basic content of this chapter. Received in time for this analysis were 118 survey forms. The important categories were How Faculty Like Teaching, What Faculty Like Best, What Faculty Like Least, and How Faculty Evaluate Their Institutions. These areas are discussed in terms of findings, conclusions, and recommendations. The next and final chapter provides some resulting issues, problems, and solutions from the standpoint of faculty interests. We set the stage for these areas by revealing some administrative views as they relate to directing instructors and instruction.

Administrative and Supervisory Views and Policies

In discussing the CJC setting and faculty assignments, we purposely avoided an exposition of detailed criteria governing instructors and instruction. Such criteria are imposed usually by administrators and supervisors, particularly vice-presidents or deans in charge of instruction. While faculty voices and votes in governance are increasing, still existing are criteria that are frustrating, confusing, and even demoralizing. Teachers in the CJC resent too much supervision, and they make mistakes inadvertently when there is too little. Administrative and supervisory views and policies are often the heart of faculty discontent, and therefore supervision itself has not been greatly emphasized, either in the CJC or in the literature.

At least five reasons exist for the present status of CJC supervision of instruction. (1) Historically, goals for the improvement of instruction in the CJC have been stated only vaguely (403:33); (2) The belief is strong that instruction is basically the same at all levels (335:542); (3) The CJC is relatively new when compared to other educational institutions and therefore is still pioneering, experimenting, trying to find the right answers and directions (33:330); (4) In some states the CJC still is considered by some as an extension of secondary education insofar as the teaching emphasis is concerned (172:66); (5) There is hostility toward attempts to supervise teaching at the CJC level (7:645-47).

A survey study sponsored by the American Council on Education showed that, for 128 junior colleges, the percentages of colleges applying various supervisory job factors for promotion, salary, and tenure were classroom teaching 98.2%, personal attributes 69.2%, length of service in rank 63.3%, student advising 42.5%, campus committee work 41.5%, activity in professional societies 18.3%, public service 15.7%, supervision of honors program 4.3%, outside consulting 4.0%, competing job offers 3.1%, research and publication 1.0% each (13:361-75, 216:11-13).

In determining the frequency with which the various sources of evaluative information were used in the junior colleges, the following percentages were found: dean evaluation (82.7%), chairman evaluation (65.8%), class visits (42.2%), course syllabi and exams (37.0%), informal student opinions (29.2%), grade distributions (30.6%), colleagues' opinions (29.2%), long-term, follow-up of students (26.1%), self-evaluation or report (22.3%), student examination performance (21.6%), systematic students ratings (16.1%), committee evaluation (15.7%), alumni opinions (8.2%), enrollment in elective courses (6.8%), scholarly research and publication (4.2%).

Kelley's study revealed administrative and supervisory views and policies in three areas: the conditions of instruction, the evaluation of instruction, and the improvement of instruction. Criteria were selected for survey purposes only after they passed the test of consensus in literature written by authorities across the nation. The survey to determine status and use of the criteria covered virtually all of the California junior colleges (201).

Prevalent conditions favorable for instruction existed only partially in some institutions; those criteria which were agreeable to the chief administrators and deans of instruction in at least 50 percent of the colleges were these:

All instructors teaching subjects they like

All instructors teaching less than 25 class hours per week

An equated class load satisfying to both faculty and administration

Democratic formulation of policies affecting the roles of instructors and administrators

Group and personal orientation given at least annually to all instructors

Faculty handbooks and other printed aids given to all instructors

Salaries competitive with other nearby colleges

Sabbatical leaves for all qualified instructors

Open and direct communication lines between teachers and administrators

Recognition and existence of academic freedom

Off-campus faculty freedom without fear of college punishment or dismissal

Permission and encouragement in classroom experimentation

Faculty promotion within the college when members are equal to or better than outside candidates

Sanitary, safe, and satisfying building facilities

Committee and extra assignments unburdensome

Faculty choice of committees or extra assignments

Faculty commended for their accomplishments

Textbooks and other aids selected by instructors

Convenient and adequate audio-visual aids

Ample budgets for instructors' needs

Duplicating services and clerical assistance for instructors

Counseling support for faculty in scheduling and counseling

Instructors' choices in outlines, methods, and teaching philosophies

Faculty welfare (sick leave, etc.) as a goal of the college

Respect of instructors' options in attending school activities

Social functions for faculty enjoyment

Administration's objectivity and fairness in helping solve faculty problems

Cooperative and agreeable supervisory policies

Administrative attitude of equality with rather than superiority over teachers

Reasonable notice to and time for an instructor to improve himself before threat of dismissal

Joint administrative-faculty committee for hiring and firing

Valid methods of evaluation of instruction proved to be administrative rating scales, student ratings, alumni ratings, and self-ratings. The administrators also believed that rating devices should be cooperatively written and approved, that more than one person should determine evaluation results, that those who rate teachers should see the teacher in classroom supervisory visits, that all instructors should be visited at least once a year, that teacher-supervisor conferences should be held after each visit, that observation reports should be signed by the teacher and filed, that instructors should also be evaluated for their school activity outside the classroom, that instructors' personal traits should be considered in evaluation, that teacher-made examinations and course materials should be studied as a means of evaluation, and that an analysis of student grades should be made as an evaluation technique.

To assist the instructor's self-improvement, the administrators generally believed in providing the following: professional literature, a professional section in the library, primary recognition of teaching skill rather than research and publication, a list of characteristics of good teaching, faculty meetings to inspire better teaching, demonstrations of teaching materials, teacher workshops, talented speakers for teacher improvement, advisers for probationary teachers, team teaching, attendance at professional conferences, incentives in salary schedules, material or financial aid for those taking graduate training, local extension courses, leaves of absence for improvement, encouragement of communication skills, preservation of class standards, student testing information for teacher perusal, easily accessible follow-up studies to teachers, and corrective help and guidance to teachers.

Kelley also found that more than 80 percent of his respondents believed in and used a moderate form of teacher supervision in contrast to a slight or strong form, that teaching improved considerably in most colleges after the addition of a dean of instruction and a program of supervision, that several administrators believed in some of the above criteria even though not practiced in their institutions, and that there were no significant differences between the views of the college presidents and their deans.

How Faculty Like Teaching

Students planning to enter junior college teaching should know how well faculties like working in the two-year college. Although realizing the results would be far from conclusive, we asked this question of our respondents. Their candid answers are merely a sample. The question was divided into two areas: in terms of the instructional areas themselves, and in terms of how the respondents felt the general individual faculties felt about CJC teaching.

Vocational-technical teachers tended to have greater enjoyment in their teaching at the CJC level than did those in other teaching areas; speech and drama specialists tended to enjoy their work least. Of the total of 118 faculty, only 4 persons marked "moderately," 45 marked "very well," and 66 marked "extremely well." No person said that he enjoyed his teaching "not at all." Three persons did not answer the question.

While 66 liked junior college teaching "extremely well," only 33 felt their general faculties liked the level to the same extent. While 45 liked the level of teaching "very well," 74 felt their faculties liked the level to the same extent. Five persons marked "moderately" and 6 did not answer. Once again no one marked the "not at all" column.

It was clearly evident that the overwhelming majority of our respondents (94 percent) enjoyed junior college teaching very well or extremely well. The remaining 6 percent either liked this level of teaching moderately or they did not answer. Undoubtedly the profession has some unhappy, disgruntled teachers, some of whom may be searching for other fields of activity, but they seem to be in the distinct minority, regardless of the sample taken. Many of the factors keeping teachers happy at the CJC level are expressed by the respondents themselves in the following section.

What Faculty Like Best

This question and the next "what faculty like least" were open-ended. It was felt that free response would be better than a checklist because of the fact that planting the seeds of response is apt to limit responses rather than foster creative ones. Weighing and categorizing these responses, we found certain aspects to be mentioned frequently. In the following 10 prominent areas, listed according to frequency of response, selected respondent comments are included as illustrations:

1. *Academic and Personal Freedom:* 62 responses.
"As far as I'm concerned, two-year colleges have greater freedom for teachers than do high schools and senior colleges and universities; high school people are plagued by multitudes of nonsense duties and the higher institutions by pressure to publish or perish." "There are fewer pressures here than in other levels." "In most aspects I'm my own boss." "No one bothers me; I can teach as I wish."

2. *Emphasis upon Teaching:* 56 responses.
"The J.C. is a happy choice for a person primarily interested in the art of teaching." "Much depends upon the teacher for the quality of teaching." "I like the informal teaching situation." "Learning at the grass roots level, the emphasis upon teaching." "I like teaching at any level, but particularly at the junior college." "I'm most pleased about the opportunity to teach rather than to combine it with publication."

3. *Challenge of Students:* 51 responses.
"My students challenge me to teach to the best of my ability." "We get all kinds of students, and this is most stimulating to dedicated teachers." "I enjoy most the opportunity to help students in areas not offered by many

high schools." "Challenge of taking students with poor backgrounds as far as possible." "The challenge is great in teaching at this level." "Satisfaction in helping the junior college type of student." "Helping students at a critical time to find a better way of life."

4. *Close Relationships with Students:* 43 responses.
"Intimate contact or association with students." "Close rapport and working relations with students." "More attention to students in smaller colleges." "Friendliness between students and teachers." "Mutual respect between faculty and students." "Working with students who want to learn and who show appreciation." "Continuously refreshing contact with students."

5. *Close Relationships with Faculty:* 37 responses.
"Close relationship that is possible with fellow teachers in other departments." "Friendly relations with staff members." "The faculty tends to be more friendly." "No intra-department frictions." "There is a sense of fine cooperation among our staff members." "I number junior college teachers high among my best friends." "Except for rare exceptions, we get along well together."

6. *Higher Level of Students* (compared to high school): 35 responses.
"Junior college students have better attitudes than those at the high school level." "Because of higher level of students, we have few discipline problems." "Students are dedicated and hungry for education in vocational-technical programs." "Our students appear to be better motivated than the general example in the high school."

7. *Responsive Administration:* 31 responses.
"Our open door extends right to the president's office." "Our administrators listen to us and endeavor to follow our recommendations when possible." "With few exceptions we have excellent relationships with our administration." "We appreciate the quality of the administration."

8. *Feeling of Service:* 25 responses.
"I like best the feeling of being of real service to my students." "Pride in the work I am doing." "My students depend upon me, and I enjoy helping them achieve." "There are higher levels, but not for many technical-vocational students. I'm their last port of call, and it is a great obligation and a marvelous opportunity for me to send them on well prepared for the world of work."

9. *Work Conditions:* 22 responses.
"Small school." "Small classes." "Good working conditions." "Lack of rank." "Lack of political pressures." "Lack of bickering for promotion." "Salary." "Less complicated bureaucracy." "More time to prepare in the junior college." "Better hours than the high school." "Promotion rapid." "Opportunities plentiful." "Opportunities for professional growth."

10. *Junior College Philosophy and Characteristics:* 15 responses.
"The 'missionary spirit' growing from opening 'cultural' doors for the first time . . . a student said, 'If I had known how much I would like that symphony concert, I would not have taken 21 years to get up courage to go to one.' " "The junior college philosophy gives impetus to career education for the world of work." "New, young creative movement." "Continual challenge of new development—never a dull moment." "We are not bound by traditions in our state, as it is a new idea." "Basic philosophy of the junior college." "The junior college can experiment and innovate more than most levels." "Pioneer spirit of the current junior college movement."

Our attempt above was to categorize answers into appropriate general headings; these 10 had the most frequent responses. All other answers seemed to categorize into areas having fewer than 5 responses. For instance, college-community relations was mentioned 3 times with answers like "excellent feeling of the community toward the school." Many respondents listed more than one thing that they liked best about junior college teaching, a fact which accounts for the total responses being more than the total of respondents.

It seems to us that the respondents as a group felt keenly appreciative of their teaching responsibilities and the free atmosphere under which these duties could be fulfilled. Over half of the respondents expressed an intense liking for academic freedom as existing on their campuses. Should it be surprising that the next three items by frequency of response were emphasis upon teaching, challenge of students, and relationships with students? It is expected that these items should be prized highly and should, in essence, be a part of the status quo in the CJC. If they had not been, 94 percent of these respondents would not have answered that they liked junior college teaching very well or extremely well. In contrast, the next section delves into their dislikes about junior college teaching.

What Faculty Like Least

Ten of our respondents had no complaints about their work or the two-year college institution. "There is no *least.* Community college teaching serves a specific purpose, a bridge between high school and senior college, a transition from adolescence toward relative maturity." "No comment." "Nothing." "If I didn't like it, I wouldn't be teaching in a junior college." So went some of the comments of those who found no fault with the junior college. Five others did not answer the question at all, but 103 did. Once again categorized into groupings according to frequency of responses, the following list includes representative answers in quotations. Although there were a few isolated categories, at least 10 were prevalent.

1. *Inadequate Working Loads, Compensations, and Aids:* 52 responses. Salary was mentioned most frequently as an item, 26 times; items relating to working loads were mentioned 22 times, while aspects of facilities and equipment were mentioned 18 times. "The teaching load discourages independent study, professional development, and publication." "Too many clock hours with students." "Salaries are much too low compared to others with less education." "Demands upon time, leaving little time for personal study or family." "Too many committees." "Too many meetings for too few problems." "Too many club activities." "Facilities inadequate for P.E. and intramurals." "Lack of supplies and equipment." "Monotonous, uninteresting duties apart from teaching." "I have too many students and too many classes to do the best job of which I'm capable."

2. *Too Much Diversity and Poor Quality of Students:* 40 responses. "Frustration of handling lower ability students." "Failure to 'get through' to many students." "Poor quality of majority of students." "We are expected to teach the unteachable in many instances." "Need for working with more talented students." "Students often too immature scholastically." "Too high a percentage of students . . . louse up college transfer curriculum." "Tragically poor preparation students get in high school." "Indifference of students toward aims and goals—their satisfaction in just getting by." "Juvenile attitudes of some students." "Students not taking their work seriously enough." "How to maintain standards with so many poor caliber of students." "Reluctance of some students to accept two-year or terminal programs; many want four years because of draft and unemployment."

3. *Loss of Students—Limitations of Two-Year College:* 34 responses. "Lack of graduate students—most frustrating." "Cannot keep students long enough to watch and help them grow." "Impermanence of the student body." "In such as band or choir, we have students only a semester or two, two years at most, and each year we must almost start from scratch." "Losing students so fast." "Students leave just when we get to know them." "Students miss influence of juniors and seniors to set standards of excellence." "Allowing the four-year college to reap benefits of our work—limitations of the two-year college." "I miss my team of last year."

4. *Poor Status, Prestige, and Influence of the Junior College:* 29 responses. "Attitudes of some four-year college people to which our students transfer." "The idea that one is less able or competent in his subject than his colleagues at the four-year college or university." "Does not have the university image." "The reactionary community (rural area) has too much influence over the school (low status)." "No rank among our faculty, while university people enjoy this extra status symbol." "External factors —lack of recognition of the roll of our school in higher education."

5. *Administrative faults (personnel, policies, attitudes):* 24 responses.
"High school attitudes of the administration." "Prescriptive at time with trivialities, but does not apply at this institution." "Administrative failures, such as in registration policies." "Poor communication with the administration, who know little of the junior college." "Lack of voice in policy making." "Weak, untrained administrators." "Administrators who reward mediocrity and ignore merit in teaching."

6. *Lack of Subject-Matter Challenges:* 16 responses.
"Lack of academic stimulation that comes with conversation and working with active researchers and graduate students; hard to stay up-to-date without stimulation." "Not challenging in respect to exploring subject area in depth with the students." "Getting into a rut after being in a junior college for 23 years." "Limited scope of subject matter." "No opportunities to teach higher levels in special fields of interest." "Limitation of course offerings."

7. *Improper Emphasis in Curriculum:* 12 responses.
"Providing general education of enough substance to be of value to those students whose education will at least formally terminate upon graduation." "Heavy emphasis on liberal arts and academic phases and decreasing emphasis for career education and occupational programs." "Terminal program does not fit into the junior college; the emphasis should be entirely on transfer education." "Remedial programs should be left to the high schools or adult education at the high schools."

8. *Creeping High School Philosophy:* 9 responses.
"Danger of becoming another high school or vocational school." "Certain carry-overs from the days when we were on the third floor of a high school building." "We have too many influences from secondary education." "We are a college, not a high school, and we should act like a college."

9. *Lack of Quality Among Faculty:* 7 responses.
"Lack of professional attitudes among our faculty." "Faculty not uniformly of good quality." "Too many staff members are lazy." "We have some excellent teachers, but some others should not have been hired; there is no excuse for hiring and keeping people who lack the professional attitude and dedication to excellent teaching."

10. *Junior Colleges—New and Innovative:* 5 responses.
"Frustrations of being a new college trying to find itself." "Lack of innovations within junior colleges." "Our problems are found in every area, but we are new; in time we should solve them, but it is frustrating in the meantime." "I like least of all the rut we've gotten into. We need the excitement of new developments and innovations."

   In the above list we see that certain types of working conditions seem to be liked least of all by the respondents; about half of those who had complaints (52 out of 103) mentioned this item. The great diversity and quality of student bodies bothered the respondents next; 40 people mentioned this aspect. The remaining 8 items descended rapidly in terms of the number of people who responded in these areas.

The two lists, what the teachers liked best and what they liked least, revealed more frequent responses in likes than in dislikes. It seems an obvious conclusion that teachers can be generally happy in their junior college positions and yet find some areas which "bug" them. Many of these areas are involved in issues and problems discussed by the respondents in Chapter Ten.

How Faculty Evaluate Their Institutions

The 118 respondents evaluated selected aspects of their 22 two-year colleges by marking each with a grade of A, B, C, D, or F. These grades meant what they normally mean in the grading of students: excellent, very good, average, needs improvement, very poor. Many marked the "unknown" column which signified that they did not know what general grade to apply. Several others indicated that the item did not exist as an aspect of their institutions. A few gave two grades. An A-B grade, for instance, was counted as two separate grades in order to arrive at an accurate average for the total frequency of grades.

The data show that all respondents gave all 21 selected aspects a total average grade of approximately 2.8, slightly below a B grade. Academic freedom was rated highest at 3.4, followed by instructors (and instruction) at 3.12, faculty relations at 3.1, transfer education at 3.1, and faculty-administrative relations, terminal education (technical-vocational), and administrators (and administration) at 3.0. Receiving below 3.0 were all the others: college-community relations, general education, and counselors (and counseling) at 2.9; faculty orientation, adult education at 2.8; general work conditions, committees, guidance programs and community service at 2.7; teaching loads at 2.6; salaries, faculty senate, remedial programs, and student personnel programs at 2.5. The lowest ranked items, then, were graded midway between a B and C, between "very good" and "average." The highest ranked item fell approximately midway between A and B. Although the overwhelming responses were in the C or better columns, 177 checks were in the "needs improvement" area, and 19 were in the "very poor" area.

These findings indicate that faculty within a given college may differ extensively in their assessment of various aspects of their institutions. Out of 462 possibilities of agreement (21 institutional aspects times 22 colleges in the sample), agreement was found in only 12 cases where two or more respondents came from the same college; there was no perfect consensus on all 21 aspects in any case. Faculties tend to be freely independent in their attitudes and opinions; their choices are not handicapped by indoc-trination or restriction. As professionals at the heart of the educational system—the teaching of students—they should be able to assess with ac-curacy the possible values of their institution. All the selected aspects were graded as slightly above average or better, and so we conclude that the 22 institutions were functioning very well in almost all of the major areas where evaluation should be made. On the other hand, because of the rather large numbers who marked the D and F columns, we feel that some improvements may be in order.

Related Studies

Many other studies exist in respect to faculty attitudes and opinions. Some are on the local level, such as those at American River Junior Col-lege (5). When asked what type of school they would prefer for their children if they had graduated with a B average from high school, the men at this college gave their preferences in this order: junior college (44 percent), private college (30 percent), state university (22 percent), and state college (4 percent); the women selected private college (33 percent), state university (26 percent), junior college (24 percent), and state college (17 percent). According to the study, these differences between the men and women faculty could be owing to the fact that fewer of the women faculty had attended the CJC or that more women than men were recruited from four-year college teaching. Almost two-thirds of the faculty were satisfied that the public generally accords pres-tige to junior college teaching, 66 percent of the men and 54 percent of the women checking "high status." The males were confident that the quality of ARJC instruction was superior to that of both the university and the state colleges; women tended to rate the quality as "about the same."

Clark's study at San Jose Junior College showed disagreement on all 15 question responses dealing with the CJC (60:107). Academic teachers and applied teachers showed disagreements in all 15 areas. The widest difference was 61 percent on the statement that the main emphasis in the junior college should be on vocational education; 70 percent of adminis-tration and only 9 percent of the academic faculty accepted the state-ment. The area of closest agreement was the statement that faculty rela-tions in the junior college are apt to be more congenial than that found at four-year colleges or universities; 80 percent of the administration and 60 percent of the academic faculty accepted the statement.

An example of a wider sampling was Kimball's study of Michigan community colleges (204). This study showed significant contrasts be-tween faculty and administrative opinion regarding the community col-lege. Weaknesses, according to findings, were found in various areas, such as admission standards and the guidance program.

A study by Blocker and Richardson (27) covered morale in six public colleges and found wide variation. Morale in several categories was consistently low: lack of opportunities for professional advancement, poor salaries, heavy work loads, poor work environment, difficult relations with students.

Eckert and Stecklein found that 31 percent of those teaching in the junior colleges said they were very satisfied with their careers (92). Nearly 79 percent of those polled, however, said they were completely or well satisfied with their present positions in the junior college.

In a survey of views of teachers, counselors, and administrators on selected issues in the open-door colleges, Muck (267) found strong feeling that adult education was relatively unimportant and that remedial education was accepted, but that it should be the job of the high school. There was strong support for the open-door admission policies. Tuition was an issue, as respondents' disagreements were significant at the 1 percent level. Opinions were in general agreement on probation policies; it was felt that they should be the same for both transfer and non-transfer; standards should be equal to those in four-year colleges, it was strongly felt. The prevailing opinion was that all students meeting graduation requirements should be given an A.A. degree; the idea of an A.A. for transfer people and other diploma or degrees for terminal students was rejected by most respondents. In general, administrators and counselors tended to agree on most of the items within 18 sections of the survey, while teachers and administrators disagreed on 11 of these sections, significate at the 1 percent level or better.

What about the opinions of junior college teachers by university and senior college staffs? According to Rainey (302) who surveyed all Oklahoma colleges, these criticisms of junior and community college faculties were prevalent: research inadequate, insufficient professional writing, lack of training in their fields, little practical experience in their fields, not enough participation in professional groups, lack of background for college teaching, insufficient depth of experience in college teaching, poor maintenance of high standards, insufficient professional growth. These were not indictments against *all* CJC teachers, of course, but tended to be areas where the professors felt general improvement was needed.

We have seen some specific examples of faculty opinions and attitudes within our own study and a few others. These views lead directly into the clash on issues, problems, and solutions, which round out Chapter Ten and complete the general survey of the assessment.

Chapter 10

Issues, Problems, and Solutions

Those in the college-faculty survey were asked to provide uninhibited comment on currently perplexing issues and problems in the CJC and to offer what they consider to be possible solutions. A total of 309 comments listed by type were received. Eight people made no comments, while many people listed several items, 6 being the largest number from any one person. Some people who commented on issues and problems could offer no solutions; 101 respondents offered comments on both problems and solutions, however. Altogether there were 25 pages of comments from the respondents when these comments were re-typed on standard typing sheets and double-spaced. Sample comments comprise the bulk of this concluding chapter on the assessment of the CJC and teaching within these institutions.

Most comments categorized into ten areas: according to frequency they were teaching procedures, standards, and attitudes: 52 responses; personnel relations, organization, and communication: 45 responses; general working conditions: 41 responses; curriculum: 36 responses; status, identification, and image: 32 responses; staff abilities and growth: 24 responses; two-year college philosophy and level: 22 responses; students: 20 responses; counseling and advisement: 16 responses; staffing the two-year college: 12 responses. We follow these discussions with other comments and studies and a final conclusion to the book.

Teaching Procedures, Standards, and Attitudes

Dressel says, "Good teaching . . . requires not only competence in one's discipline but also insight into the effect of one's instructional practices in promoting both the quantity and quality of student learning. . . . Only by systematic study of student learning—by evaluation—can the teacher know his effectiveness and make such judgments as promise to increase it" (91:11). If our respondents are any indication, good teaching *is* a problem, even for experienced persons. What are some of these problems? Following are comments showing key areas.

"Motivating the masses who couldn't care less about making the most of their opportunity for educational excellence; many come only to say they attended college."

"Standards; how do you maintain them when there are so many poor students?"

"Keeping courses and labs timely, interesting, and valid."

"Output we'll have—*quality* is the problem."

"How do we *really* meet the needs of all the students available?"

"There is a difficulty in offering night classes without watering down established objectives."

"How to prepare average students for the years ahead."

"Level of instruction—what it should be, how hard the teacher should be, and what he should require."

"There's too much tendency to coddle the student and to protect him from the disciplines and demands of higher education."

"Lofty goals announced from the commencement platform are frequently difficult if not impossible to achieve in the classroom."

"Teaching students the values of study and how to study."

"How to incorporate new methods of teaching in lab and lecture—or is there a better way than lecture or lab?"

"How do you foster good attitudes in both teaching and learning if certain teachers and students won't accept them?"

Solutions to these problems were more general than specific; they included such as expert teaching, small classes for more individual help, keep standards high, simpler grading systems, better system of academic motivation, homogeneous groupings, weed out some probationary students, conferences on good teaching, research that puts more science into the art of teaching. Some sample comments follow:

"Departing from the traditional methods, taxing the imagination as well as the pocketbook."

"Concentrate on valid beginnings and allow more advanced students to work ahead of others; go as far as possible without ignoring the basics."

"Poor achievers need extensive developmental center with psychiatrist, psychomotrist, etc."

"Better grouping of students would help solve the lack of motivation and success to help them succeed and find interest in an education."

"Highly qualified faculty is the key."

"Crack down on faculty; instill in them proper attitudes for excellent teaching."

Personnel Relations, Organization, and Communication

The second most prominent problem dealt with staff relationships, the organization of and communication between teachers and other staff members. Items: domination of one group over another; tendency of administration to distrust faculty integrity; some people bothered by the continual need for change, dogmatic attitudes of administrators; faculty evaluation; lack of leadership; strained faculty-administrative relations; unclear division of responsibilities; lack of faculty voice in policy-making; finding faculty agreement on certain issues; cohesive working of four major units—board, administration, teachers, and students; proper organization and channels of communication.

"By nature, the junior college curriculum is general or liberal arts. This calls for a great degree of cooperative planning and working together to coordinate the efforts of the many departments and teachers. Misunderstandings occur and mistakes happen which result in difficulties and hurt feelings among teachers, students, and administrators. In our college this problem seems to be most prevalent."

"The organization at our school does not allow for faculty voice in policy-making; this situation creates poor morale and difficulties in communication and proper relationships among both faculty and administration."

"We have an infrequent change of division heads. Administrators are frequently absent from campus. There is insufficient staff-administrative communication. There is insufficient supervision of faculty. Many goof off. Being on their honor, many take advantage of trust."

Some of the solutions offered by respondents are the following:

"Simple meeting of minds to agree on basic principles, goals, roles to be played by faculty."

"Explanations of specific duties and responsibilities of personnel."

"Need for cooperation, loyalty to the administration, to work with those who are better trained, to follow leadership of the 'quarterback,' for without this cooperation wrong goals will be reached. To have a successful operation, everyone must pull together."

"Improve communication and foster the feeling that career faculty are professionals."

"Start a faculty senate to give faculty voice in policy-making."

"Train and select administrators to make themselves available to faculty and students."

"Administrators must communicate trust in faculty and instill pride; decisions must be openly determined."

"Secure a good workable faculty evaluation system incorporating the better means of communication."

"Get the administration out of the faculty association so that faculty who fear administrators can express themselves; this should help solve problems of communication and poor relationships with administrators."

"Maintain equality to avoid domination of one group over another."

"To have faculty agreement on issues, we must utilize the findings of research; in some cases faculty must be persuaded to accept consensus and the democratic way."

General Working Conditions

Problems in this third ranking category dealt with such items as salaries, tenure, teaching load, hiring-firing policy, size of classes, capital improvements, equipment and supplies, rank, promotion, sabbatical leaves, retirement. Lack of time to do an effective job along with lack of adequate salary were mentioned most often; nearly one fourth of the total respondents commented on these two items. Specific comments follow:

"Committee work absorbs time that could be used for better teaching."

"Money is the most urgent problem, especially for private, church-related schools."

"The absence of a salary scale, and the secrecy of it all."

"Teaching is the only profession which gives less than regular pay for overtime."

"Too many hours on campus—the 'punch clock tendency.'"

"How can we reduce the excessive load of our teachers?"

"Lack of policy (from the administration, the board, or state) on such matters as tenure, school year length, clear method of rank and promotion, sabbatical leave, etc."

"Limited library facilities—the librarian's refusal to comply with instructor's requests for new books until she had read 'at least three favorable reviews.'"

"We need a better retirement system."

"Keeping the learning labs open 14 hours a day to serve the community is a drain on faculty because utilization of the learning areas is very light during much of the time."

"How can we improve our facilities and purchase better equipment and more supplies?"

"Time and money—money and time."

According to the general consensus, the problems of working conditions could be solved by reducing the work loads of teachers, by providing better salaries and other benefits common to the profession, and by allowing faculties greater voices in determining the policies of work conditions. The last solution involves the need for a simple, democratic operation, while the first two solutions require additional monies. Few had solutions for the money problem, but some said that some budget items could be reduced to allow greater amounts for teachers and instruction. Others spoke of tax increases, student tuition fees, greater state and federal support, and campaigns to secure voluntary contributions. Sample quotations follow.

"To improve work conditions, there should be more realism and honesty on the part of those who make policy. But here again, politics and dependence on the public treasury probably make realism and honesty impractical."

"Greater concentration of effort is needed by the staff, board, and administration in having set policies in tenure, sabbatical leave, rank and promotion, etc." "The administration and accrediting associations should solve problems of work conditions."

To help solve problem of overloading of teachers: "Addition of more teachers in needed areas." "Secure more financing to relieve student-teacher loads." "Find new avenues of financial support." "Seek more denominational support for financing private church schools." "Have part-time teachers teach night classes." "Hire clerks for non-teaching duties." "More even distribution of work loads."

To have better teacher salaries: "General public should be shown the need for better teacher salaries; they may agree separately on the need but not as a total group." "Establish an 11-months contract plan so that teachers can earn more and have more time for professional reading and preparation." "Let students bear more of the cost by starting or increasing tuition fees." "Secure tax base derived from ad valorum taxes."

Curriculum

If educational institutions exist for the purpose of promulgating and presenting knowledge, then curriculum may be singled out as the heart of these institutions, with teachers being the chief designers and students being the chief participants in learning. Ranked as the fourth leading problem in the survey results, curriculum centers around the problem of "what should be taught." Almost all of the comments of the respondents dealt with this question. Only two people mentioned the "how" aspects of curriculum constructions. Let's sample a few direct quotations:

"The problem is where a two-year college education should begin and end."

"Trying to offer both terminal and transfer programs simultaneously is like serving two masters."

"In the junior college there is a procedure of repetitiousness of high school subjects; there's a need for more varied subjects."

"What subjects best prepare students for transfer?"

"With so many things to be taught, what should be selected?"

"In establishing curriculum, how can we remain a college and yet help people become adults?"

"How do you develop a comprehensive college, one that offers subjects that meet the needs of all the students who wish to enroll?"

"The problem of emphasis on programs—what should it be?"

"How can the junior college programs bridge the gap between high school and senior colleges or universities?"

"Presentation of a curriculum geared to all aspects of the modern world and present-day society with the future in mind but not forgetting the past."

"Finding curriculum and study designed for terminal students, the non-major, and majors in a given field."

"Reconciliation of differences between various disciplines as to their relative importance and emphasis in the curriculum."

Samples of solutions offered are the following:

"To protect the integrity of the established curricula, some form of remedial education should be essential for the non-performing students."

"We need a transitional program for marginal students."

"To solve the problem of development of a comprehensive college, a course in curriculum development and an appreciation of comprehensive college curriculum would be in order."

"Have a more powerful curriculum committee."

"Study the needs of students and the community; if there is enough demand, offer the additional courses."

"Develop and establish uniformity in community colleges insofar as curriculum and objectives are concerned, yet allow certain autonomous features based on traditions of the local college."

"Enlarge scope of subjects to be required or selected."

"The policy should be changed so that branch campuses can have their own courses, not necessarily those required at the main campus."

"Constant reevaluation of course offerings."

"Experiment with new offerings."

"Some system of uniformity of course offerings and requirements for the various fields of study in the state."

"Curriculum problems are resolvable only within the framework of dialectic, the give and take of discussion."

Status, Identification, and Image

Probably because of historical factors and an abundance of literature on the problem, many respondents were concerned about the status, identification, and image of the two-year colleges and of the faculty. Is the CJC secondary or higher education? Is it a genuinely academic institution or an extension of the "social activities oriented high schools which abound?"

One person charged the CJC with the tendency to imitate the four-year college. Another felt there was a problem of prestige for terminal-vocational programs. Respondents felt keenly aware of problems in the general subject area, as noted below:

"Are we academic (freshmen-sophomore) or are we retarding intellectual growth (13-15th grades)?"

"We have a bad image because too many poor teachers who cannot teach college level have rooted themselves in the junior colleges."

"The junior colleges tend to become intellectual garbage cans."

"Are we an easier form of college—or the *first two years* of college?"

"STATUS—secondary or college?"

"Absence of college atmosphere and common student involvement."

"Maintaining public relations to build better understanding and image."

"The general assumption that the two-year college is inferior or secondary to the two primary years in a senior college does not correspond to reality."

"An identification with high school curriculum, methodology, and atmosphere is *bad*."

"Defining the role of the junior college movement in education is a problem."

Solutions to the problem of status, identification, and image seemed to crystalize into these steps: (1) Establish in each state a legal description which identifies the two-year college as a part of higher education, (2) Secure agreement and provide on each campus a true college atmosphere which involves faculty, curriculum programs, student activity, etc., (3) Eliminate educational programs which are non-college in nature by giving such programs over to the authority of high schools (adult education or non-college vocational education), (4) Conduct extensive campaigns in public relations, (5) Create better understandings and relationships with other levels of higher education, (6) Coordinate and articulate as much as possible with lower division programs in senior colleges and universities, and (7) Evaluate and improve continually the nature and aspects of the two-year college.

Examples of comments are as follows:

"We need to have recognition by the state department of education, the university board, and we need a general progressive attitude toward West Coast originated junior college movements by East Coast states."

"Many of the problems are inherent within the junior colleges. Morale and lack of identification will remain in the junior college. The staff must adapt to this less than ideal condition."

"Improve the junior college image through a massive public relations program: concentrate upon the general public but also our critics at the university level."

"We can eliminate our intellectual 'garbage can' image by eliminating the 'garbage cans.' We don't have to keep students simply because they enter our 'open doors.'"

"Have quality programs and faculties strictly on the college level; cut away people and programs that do not add to this quality. Many of our programs and people should be handled at the high school level or adult education level."

"A high school is not inferior to a junior college; it is merely a lower level of age group instruction, just as the junior college is a lower training level than the upper division or graduate level. We must maintain the status of lower division instruction and, at the same time, educate society as to our many assets and contributions to the general public."

"Closer associations with higher education needed. We can do this legally through state laws and extra-legally through many coordinated activities within and between levels and types of higher institutions."

Staff Abilities and Growth

Those who selected this area as a pressing problem spoke of educating the faculty on the nature of the junior college, how to choose membership in professional organizations when there are so many from which to select, lack of faculty understanding as to basic philosophy involving ethics and duties to students, whether or not it is worth the investment to go on for the "union card" (i.e., the doctorate), lack of sufficient academic background of faculty, the use of faculty misfits who are "promoted" from high school or "deserted" from colleges, the difficulty of faculty to really understand students, the need for financial help from the institution in helping faculty obtain higher degrees and greater professional growth, trying to stay up to date amidst the often insufficient intellectual stimulation in the junior college, poor teaching abilities among staff members, and the general problem of continuing professional refreshment and academic upgrading of faculty.

Most of the solutions offered by respondents centered around the common, well known remedies for improving staff abilities and increasing their growth. Mentioned often was the thought that the hiring of good teachers would, in the first place, improve the measure of general staff ability. More careful screening of applicants, involving faculty in the hiring-firing process, and the use of better supervision methods were mentioned by several people. Certain carefully taught education courses should help CJC teachers understand and improve their methods, procedures, and general abilities, it was felt by some. On the job, the colleges must do more to provide better orientation, to provide newer equipment and curriculum, to encourage innovation in methods as well as better use of old methods, to stimulate through workshops and institutes, to provide seminars and conferences, to keep teachers up to date by passing current journals across the desk instead of filing them in the library, to adopt a system of teacher visitation of classes, and to provide extra money or time off for the professional growth and improvement of teachers. These are the solutions offered in terms of two or more responses of teachers in each specific area.

Many answers seemed especially significant. For instance, "Seek to attract and develop faculty who are needed, professional educators and competent scholars, who both respect and command respect from the professional and academic life. If teachers are only mildly committed to scholarship, the student can hardly get very exicted about it. The administration can do much to develop the proper attitude in this respect and arrange opportunities for faculty to have seminars with outstanding people, as well as to do some extra study and research now and then." And another, "The college should hire teachers who are qualified and enjoy teaching particular courses when that is possible. It should hire the person who majored in sociology, for instance, or at least took several courses in that subject to teach that and only that. Again, this is not always possible, but the attempt should be made whenever it *is* possible."

Two-Year College Philosophy and Level

Ranked seventh as a category of responses was the problem area of the philosophy and level of two-year colleges. Although the problems here overlapped those in other ranked areas, the emphasis seemed to be placed upon the type of institution and basic philosophy. The open-door policy and admission standards were mentioned frequently. "The open-door policy creates too wide a variety of scholastic ability" and "the tendency of the two-year college to be all things to all people results in lack of direction and ignorance of administrative intent" are typical examples of comments. Seven people felt the open door philosophy is an issue, i.e., whether it should be retained or not, while others treated it as a system that needed clarifying direction and improvement. Several others found that the junior college level itself fostered problems such as "the lack of continuity in getting to know students," "the rapid turnover of student bodies and lack of students stability," and "difficulties in helping students grow when they are here so short a time."

No serious solution was offered for the problem of the CJC level, for obviously the level (type) of institution cannot be changed without becoming something quite different. A few people said that the two-year college might convert to a four-year college as a resolution of certain problems of college "level"; these comments might have been facetious in some cases. Critics of the open-door philosophy would resolve problems in this area simply by eliminating it in favor of selective admissions; those who support the philosophy would resolve problems by finding better means of administering it, by securing more careful placement of students, by providing different levels of courses for different levels of students, and by fostering better faculty understanding, acceptance, and teaching applicable to open-door philosophies.

Students

"Junior college problems with students" is a category that also relates to such others as curriculum, teaching, and junior college philosophy; however, this area was separated from the others when comments centered on the nature and characteristics of students. For example, respondents spoke of "the student apathy toward extra-curricular activities," "students coming to the junior college in order to escape the draft," "terminal students switching to transfer programs, and the resulting loss of credit," "difficulty in keeping students a second year," "grade consciousness of students," "lack of student direction and purpose," "students not adjusting to study and the college environment," "immaturity of students," "lack of quality among students," "hopeless attempt by some students to compete with better students and remain in college," "lack of drive and ambition among students," and so on.

Solutions were varied. Some examples follow:

To eliminate the "draft dodgers," there must be "cessation of the war."

"Keep standards high and strive for excellence so that the 'easy' image is erased; then the 'playboys' and the 'husband seekers' and the lazy will know that they are not coming to a 'party' school to waste the teachers' time and theirs."

"Better counseling needed to help the students find themselves."

"Club advisers should devise means to increase student participation in school activities."

"All students should be required to take an orientation course or workshop so that their attitudes, understandings, appreciations, and actions are improved."

"Drop those students who are not serious about their education, who do not achieve; this should keep the general quality at a higher level."

"Careful selection of incoming freshmen should cause students to have more respect for the junior college and more seriousness of purpose."

"Certain problems of student attitudes and characteristics can only be solved by their maturity—and expert teaching."

Counseling and Advisement

Classified in this area were those responses indicating criticisms of counselors and counseling programs and procedures. The teachers felt, individually or with others, that students were frequently counseled into programs or courses in which they did not belong, that students were registered into programs or courses without the sometimes required permission of instructors, that there was a serious lack of proper student advisement in many cases, that there is some difficulty in counseling students as to specific college requirements for senior four-year institutions, that problems of time and patience develop in helping to plan elaborately a program for a student and then having him change his mind when all the work is done, that there is a lack of time to counsel students adequately, and that efficient and profitable counseling and advisement are difficult matters even for the best counselors.

No teacher proposed the elimination of the counseling function at the CJC level; on the contrary respondents would hire better counselors where needed, provide counselors with full-time counseling positions (no teaching), give counselors time to counsel by providing them with smaller counselor loads, have more accurate testing and measurement for placement purposes, have a special developmental center with one or more specialists such as a psychiatrist, have counselors follow such required policies as having students secure teacher permission for "permission only" courses, have counselors leave subject matter advisements to the teachers themselves, have counselors confer frequently with faculties on matters of common concern, and have counselors on an equal rather than superior status in relationship to instructors.

Worth noting is the comment of one respondent speaking of the role of the counselor as an evaluator of the instructor. "Counselors are in a kind of unique position in respect to teacher competence. Students tend to go to their counselors when conflicts develop between students and teachers. I would guess that in the counseling office, complainers outnumber praisers ten to one, since a 'beef' or 'gripe' is more naturally motivating than the lack of same. If swayed by the one-sidedness of complaints and nothing else, the counselor can do a teacher great harm, especially the counseling dean who, by one policy, has a vote on the teacher's tenure or re-hiring. I am against any counselor using negatively biased student opinion as a basis of voting against a teacher or even using this one-sidedness to sway others to vote against the teacher. If anything serious develops in the mind of the counselor, he or she should always consult the teacher about the matter. In any case he or she should not be in an equal voting position with those supervisors who visit classrooms and know more accurately the strengths and weaknesses of the instructors."

Staffing the Two-Year College

Ranked tenth among the responses were those speaking of the problems and solutions of staffing two-year colleges. Although the wording differed in each case, the statement of the problem was simply the need to find qualified and motivated staff members. As other studies indicate year by year, CJC growth over the last decade has been increasing to the rate of fifty or more new institutions each year. Student populations among the older colleges increase steadily on the average. New staff members are needed continuously, not only to staff the new colleges and expand older colleges but also to fill vacancies caused by death, retirement, or transfer of teachers. Some of our respondents were very much aware of the acute nature of the problem.

According to a few respondents, one approach to the problem is to have "better salaries to attract well qualified people"; in general, to have more benefits and better working conditions. "Source of faculty" seemed to be the predominating theme of the solutions offered. In the past most of our CJC teachers were drawn from the high schools, but this source, as well as other educational sources, only creates shortages elsewhere. Some respondents said we should try to secure qualified people from retirement, from other professions and occupations, and from the home-makers—wives and mothers. Sample comments follow:

"To attract teachers, industry should be approached to release their personnel, ages 50 and up, to serve as adjunct professors in junior colleges. This group is *very* large. I believe that American industry is far-sighted enough that this proposition can be sold to them. An arrangement of this sort will make the junior college the greatest institution this country has ever developed."

"The United States Office of Education might prepare and publish a list of retired servicemen and government employees who are qualified and would accept teacher appointments in junior colleges. Employing officers could contact them more easily through the list, which would also state qualifications and other needed information."

"What is wrong with hiring housewives and mothers who have the degrees, training, and time but need the specific interest of and contact by a local community college?"

"We can help solve staff shortages by putting more emphasis upon new methods of instruction such as large group instruction with independent study, television instruction over wide educational networks and feeding into the colleges, and programmed learning methods."

Other Comments and Additional Studies

In addition to the ten ranked categories just discussed were miscellaneous areas having anywhere from one to five responses. Problems of articulation and coordination with other levels of education headed these other comments. The feeling was that better working relations should be established between the community colleges and the higher levels, that universities in particular tend to dictate to the lower levels, that liaison is not effective in some cases. One respondent mentioned "the failure of the state university to recognize (and coordinate with) the network of junior colleges (as in California and Michigan) so that the first two years can be taken in these community colleges. The university recently opened a branch campus within one mile of our campus." Articulation of curriculum was mentioned. Some felt that outside pressures from the community and other groups were problems. Solutions to these and other miscellaneous problems were quite general, i.e., the local colleges should apply pressures of their own, establish proper solutions and "fight" to uphold them, and rely upon themselves to evaluate and improve according to their goals. Other respondents, while writing of problems, could offer no solutions or were skeptical of the value of their answers or this survey.

A thorough report of issues and problems facing junior college faculty is that written by Roger H. Garrison (126). In a study of opinion in twenty colleges across the nation, this report found problems and issues in the following areas, among others: (1) time to do an adequate teaching job, (2) need for professional refreshment, (3) proper faculty roles in college government, (4) concern for professional affiliations, (5) teaching in the junior college as a permanent career, (6) faculty relationships to guidance and counseling, (7) preparation for college teaching, (8) orientation of new faculty, (9) communication with department or division heads, (10) faculty rank problems and issues. These problems and issues were all identified by those participating in our own survey; thus, it seems that these aspects are widespread.

In a separate report highlighting the 1965–66 study, Garrison organized key issues and problems into four big areas (130): (1) Administration and the administrative context in which the teacher works: Teachers share in forming this context, including salaries, fringe benefits, facilities, equipment, teaching loads, chances for professional growth, flexible administrative set-up, etc. Predicted is more faculty militancy, strikes, bruising confrontations revealing an administrative inadequacy. (2) Professional refreshment: job satisfaction, meaningful opportunities for faculty dialogue, specialized study, continued growth and intellectual stimulation on the job. All the faculty said over and over again that TIME was a problem. (3) Problems of being new and big: huge enrollments, growth problems, speed, lack of clear goals and how to reach them, aims and goals of instruction, how to increase efficiency, the teacher's part in filling college goals. (4) The teacher-administrator—a new breed? Promoting teachers to department heads and to deans, fast, before they've been oriented properly, the need for better training and orientation, communication a big problem growing from all this.

In a conference report sponsored by Lilly Endowment with the Center for Study of Higher Education, certain critical issues facing America's junior colleges were determined (218). Unique facets included the extension of higher education opportunity, localization, community centered programs, broad curriculum, identification of transfer potential, opportunity for *all*, remedial functions, and the teaching faculty. Issues already resolved were the acceptance of the junior college as higher education, nationwide development of private and public junior colleges with comprehensive and part-time programs, acceptance of the junior college as a teaching institution, and the concept of the public CJC as a local development.

The report listed critical issues and problems as (1) who should go? Should there be equal opportunity for all or selective admission? (2) Expansion of two-year junior colleges or decentralized extensions of four-year schools? (3) Is the vocabulary "junior, terminal, transfer" outworn? (4) Will attempts to define be broadening or stultifying? (5) How can variety be provided without seeming weak? (6) Can junior college be oriented to students of very different abilities? (7) How can appreciation and understanding of academic and vocational staffs be assimilated and developed? (8) How can private junior colleges be strengthened and kept strong? (9) To what extent should there be *free* public junior college education? (10) Should there be state or local control systems?

Solutions for staffing junior colleges are presented by Eurich (107). At least seven can be noted: (1) pay higher salaries or have flexible salary scales with merit properly rewarded, (2) build the prestige of the junior college, (3) have close relationship with a university (such as a cooperative internship program or cooperation in hiring university teachers on a part-time basis), (4) secure university programs for the training of junior college teachers, (5) organize cooperative curricular programs among groups of junior colleges, (6) recruit retired faculty members, (7) utilize part-time people to fill the staffing needs.

Year-round operation seems to be an issue in many states. California, for instance, started in the late 60's a conversion from the semester to the quarter system for its state colleges and state university. Although many faculties are divided on the conversion plan, the general feeling is that the quarter system may solve more problems than it creates. Junior colleges in the state have been somewhat reluctant to follow the trend. Nevertheless, they are moving slowly in that direction.

A study by Cope provides some information on year-round operation (77). He wrote that this operation is relatively new, although the University of Chicago had a four-term plan from its beginning, and George Peabody College since 1912. He described the year-round plan at Chicago City Junior College and provided comparisons of systems. Seventy junior colleges in the country were reported to have operated under year-round plans in 1963–64. (At least 7 of our 22 survey colleges were on the quarter plan in 1967–68.) Reasons for year-round operations, said Cope, were pressure of mounting enrollments, the need to make best use of existing facilities, the need to make better use of scarce faculty, pressures from state legislators to get the most out of tax dollars.

A two-year study by the National Committee for Appraisal and Development of Junior College Student Personnel Programs, an A.A.J.C. project funded by a Carnegie Corporation grant, was reported in an article in 1966 (301). Involved were 150 junior colleges and 600 staff members. It was found that three-fourths of the junior colleges in the country have not developed adequate student personnel programs. Counseling and guidance were inadequate in more than half the colleges. Student personnel programs were defined as including related functions designed to support the instructional program, respond to student needs, and foster institutional development. The program should provide orientation of students, appraisal of students, consultation with students, regulation of students, services for students, and an organizational plan for articulation, evaluation, and improvement. The study showed needed areas to be admissions, registration, and records; placement and financial aids, student activities, guidance and counseling; and a central administrative unit. Critical needs and problem areas included staffing standards, program interpretation, leadership development, counselor preparation, criteria development, field consultants, career information, community service, and centralized coordination.

Conclusion

In assessing the profession of junior college teaching and some significant ramifications, certain issues and problems rise to the surface. Specialists contributing to our survey results, supported in fact by other research, determined crucial issues and problem areas to be generally the following:

1. What teaching procedures, standards, and attitudes should be employed to best fit the needs of a variety of students in the two-year college? Once proper goals are discovered, how can they be best achieved?

2. How can personal relations, organization, and communication be improved to effect a smooth functioning operation? How can staff members cooperate and agree when issues arise, what is the best method of organizing college roles and functions, and how can clear and effective communication be established?

3. How can general working conditions (salaries, teaching schedules, administrative policies, and so on) be improved? If progress is to be made in this area, where can we find the necessary money, time, and administrative approval?

4. What type of curriculum and educational programs should we have in the two-year college? How comprehensive or narrow can we be in programs and courses, and what are the best methods in developing these?

5. How can we establish ourselves as a true partner in higher education? Can we increase status, improve identification, and create a better image for the public and other educational levels?

6. What can be done about improving staff abilities and increasing our professional growth and refreshment? How can we "weed out" poor teachers and administrators and enhance the development of those who are capable?

7. How can we eliminate problems inherent within the two-year college level and rectify or minimize certain defects in the philosophy at this level? Should we, for instance, have an open-door policy, or is there a better approach?

8. Apart from teaching and counseling, are there other ways to develop student goals, purposes, and attitudes? How can student identification with the college, participation in student government, and motivation in social relationships best be developed?

9. Can counseling and advisement personnel and procedures be improved? What changes can or should be made and what methods should be employed for these changes?

10. Where can we find qualified personnel to staff new colleges, fill new positions and vacancies? Should we continue to hire unqualified people, or are there new learning approaches which can make present faculties adequate?

The above list embraces both issues and problems and a distinction should be made between these two categories. An issue has developed when two or more people disagree on a point. We found our respondents disagreeing chiefly in these areas: curriculum goals, scope and type of programs, open-door policy, teaching procedures, status of the junior college, attitudes of students and staff, levels of instruction, and values of aspects of administrative policy and operation. While an issue is certainly a problem, there are those problems which are not issues. Our respondents found agreements on problems in chiefly these areas: maintaining standards, filling needs of all students, transient nature of student body, motivation of learning, lack of qualified teachers, professional growth and development, specific working conditions, status and identification.

A summary of faculty attitudes and opinions, of issues and problems leads clearly to what faculty want. What *do* faculty want? Our survey and studies show they want better or improved (1) salaries, (2) teaching loads, (3) free time, (4) working relations with administration and staff, (5) lines of communication, (6) standards of teaching and learning, (7) student follow-up results, (8) counseling and student placement, (9) status and prestige, (10) faculty orientation, (11) opportunities for professional growth, (12) public relations, (13) administrative leadership, (14) quality among the staff, (15) financing, (16) cooperation among staff, (17) articulation and coordination within and between levels, (18)

attitudes among students and teachers, (19) methods of teacher evaluation, (20) methods of staffing, (21) agreement on philosophy, goals, purposes, and functions, (22) continuity of learning, (23) faculty voice in
college government, (24) freedom from unnecessary pressures, (25) faculty fringe benefits.

What usually happens when a group of teachers do not get what they
want? Let's name the possibilities: they can do nothing but "gripe" to
themselves or colleagues, they can apply pressure on the administration,
they can go to the board of trustees, they can go to the public, they can
solicit the help of a professional association, they can solicit the help of
legal agencies, they can solicit the help of a labor organization, they can
refuse to follow certain rules or comply with certain duties, or they can
resign in protest, violently or unobtrusively.

Aside from resignation or failure to fulfill job obligations, perhaps
the most extreme method of fighting for professional rights and improvements is the use of the labor organization practice of strike. We make no
claims for or against this method, but, as a matter of information, we refer
you to the strike of the Chicago City College teachers. One of the rare
and most recent strikes by CJC teachers, this strike occurred twice, late
in 1966 and in January, 1967. An article by Swenson and Novar shows the
issues and events leading to the strike, the results, and the lesson learned
(351).

Called "the largest faculty strike in the history of American junior
colleges," the event included eight campuses of Chicago City College, "a
fifty year-old public junior college." The strike was called by the Cook
County College Teachers Union, Local 1600 of the American Federation
of Teachers, AFL–CIO, and involved 600 of the systems 684 instructors
in picket lines. The strike virtually closed the colleges. The teachers finally
received just about what they wanted: 12-13 hour course load, class size
limitations of 25 in English and speech and 35 in other courses, a $500
salary increase raising minimum to $6,900 and potential maximum to
$17,400, paid major health plan, sabbatical leave policy at one-half basic
salary for two semesters or full salary for one semester, indefinite accumu-
lation of sick leave at rate of one day per month, including summers, average pay amounting to 10 percent of unused sick leave at retirement or
death, assurances that the academic calendar would be reduced to no
more than 38 weeks, and a tax-sheltered annuity program.

Said the authors, ". . . CCC will be the first major two-year college
in the nation to achieve the breakthrough to a 12-hour load"; and the
major lessons were "that the faculty's demand for a major voice in the
determination of their working conditions can no longer be ignored, that
teachers are prepared to join a union and to strike if no other alternative
is available to insure improvement in their working conditions and quality education for their students, and that junior college boards and ad-

ministrations must recognize their obligation to communicate directly with elected representatives of the faculty rather than depend on outside intermediaries with no vested interest in the welfare of the junior college"; it was concluded that "The road to a peaceful resolution of differences with a faculty is to recognize the elected bargaining agent of the faculty, and to bargain in good faith with that elected representative. Crises can be avoided only if the junior college boards and administrations accord the faculty union the status, respect, and dignity reserved for an organization which has become a permanent member of the junior college community" (351:22).

In revealing an example of the success of one strike, a relatively new method of protest among teachers, we should be mindful of numerous improvements of the teacher's lot obtained by professional group negotiations with boards and administrations. Tremendous gains have been made through peaceful conferences, and future gains will continue to be made through the non-strike methods of professional associations and through local colleges striving to settle their own problems. The point is that CJC teaching is no "bed of roses" throughout a career. Crises will develop, and you, the new member of this unique society of teachers, will find yourself embroiled with the issues, problems, and solutions. Your own answers will have to be an amalgam composed of your own best interests, combined with what seem to be the best interests of the students, the community, the profession, and the college.

As a community college instructor, you will find in the coming years closer identification with higher education, greater prestige through such policies as academic rank, greater voice in government with such organizations as academic senates, clearer structures of academic freedom, combined direction of state and local control, increased federal assistance, probable increases or establishments of tuitions and fees, increased research and development, computer usage, and increased opportunities for teaching innovations.

You will find new developments or trends in the establishment of a national academy for junior colleges, a national placement agency, the development of a "teaching doctorate" for junior college teachers, the establishment of teacher assistants in every classroom (as stated in the President's education message to Congress in 1967), a national educational reearch information center (ERIC) for pooling and sharing local educational research, a regional library system for community colleges, exchange programs and personnel between industry and community colleges, diversion of lower division students almost totally to the community colleges, increasing numbers of lower-standing high school graduates entering the community colleges, establishment of more residential operations for public community colleges (particularly those in outlying areas), increase of state laws for CJC teacher benefits, and the development of national norms and tests for student performance in various subject areas. Despite all these changes there will remain some difficulties which seem to be timeless.

Alfred North Whitehead said it best: "The difficulty is just this: the apprehension of general ideas, intellectual habits of mind, and pleasurable interest in mental achievement can be evoked by no form of words, however accurately adjusted. All practical teachers know that education is a patient process of the mastery of details, minute by minute, hour by hour, day by day. There is no royal road to learning through an airy path of brilliant generalizations. There is a proverb about the difficulty of seeing the wood because of the trees. That difficulty is exactly the point which I am enforcing. The problem of education is to make the pupil see the wood by means of the trees" (390:18).

The "trees" are rather obvious: *the setting*—development and status, benefits, employment needs, instructional areas: *the assignment*—academic and professional duties and functions, philosophy and application of the art of instruction; and *the assessment*—faculty attitudes and opinions, issues and problems. The "wood" may be less obvious. Nevertheless, you have started and finished a journey in reading; the most important journey lies ahead—your career in two-year colleges. This career may not be all that this book leads you to expect, for two-year colleges, like any institution of life, have their stalemates and frustrations. We can hope only that you have gained a measure of understanding and guidance as you continue onward into the realities of teaching in the community junior college.

Appendixes

Appendix A

State Exhibits

This appendix reports the findings of our national survey of all states and major territories for the school year 1967–68. Though the facts change, the status for this time is worth recording. The respondents for the survey are identified with each exhibit. For your convenience the findings are only briefly noted. For supplemental information, peruse such publications as *American Junior Colleges* and *The Junior College Directory*. Summarized first are general findings, followed by the state entries.

1. Two-year colleges, including branches of colleges and universities, were in all 50 states, 2 territories, and the District of Columbia; there were no two-year colleges in Guam and the Virgin Islands. Nevada added its first community junior college in 1967, the last state to do so.

2. Reported were 998 two-year colleges of all types; these included 694 public and 304 private institutions. Public segments were in 48 states, the Canal Zone, and Puerto Rico, while none existed in Maine, South Dakota, District of Columbia, Guam, and the Virgin Islands. Private segments were in 42 states, Puerto Rico, and the District of Columbia, while none existed in Arizona, Colorado, Montana, Nevada, New Mexico, Utah, Washington, Wyoming, Canal Zone, Guam, and the Virgin Islands. These totals include all accredited and non-accredited colleges reported by respondents.

3. Eighty-seven schools were in planning stages, most slated for opening during the fall of 1969. About half of the states and territories opened new colleges during the previous year, and 24 planned new openings for 1969 and 1970. Planning 5 or more new colleges were Arizona, California, Connecticut, Illinois, New York, Pennsylvania, and Texas.

4. Thirty states (including Puerto Rico) had 10 or more colleges in operation; leading the group were the "big five" states having 50 or more

campuses: California (87), New York (64), Texas (60), Pennsylvania (59), and Illinois (54). (Although many campuses were joined under one district administration or board, each was counted separately in the totals in each state or territory.)

5. Ten states reported founding dates of current two-year colleges (all private) before 1900; these were Georgia, Indiana, Maryland, Michigan, Missouri, New York, North Carolina, Oklahoma, South Carolina, and Texas. Some of these schools and many others were originally college preparatory academies, but most did not convert to college status until after 1900. (Those reported in the 10 states had actually been colleges sometime prior to 1900.)

6. Control of public junior colleges was reported to be under a separate state junior college board or community college commission in 12 states, including Arizona, California, Colorado, Connecticut, Florida, Illinois, Massachusetts, Michigan, Minnesota, Mississippi, Virginia, and Washington. In most states, control at the state level was by a state board of education and a department of education headed by a superintendent of education. In some states control was exercised by a board of higher education or a board of a university or state college system.

7. State aid of some sort was given to junior colleges in virtually all states, although much of this aid was limited and in most cases restricted to the public institutions.

8. Tuition fees for students were reported in all states and territories for regular day students residing in local college districts except in the public junior colleges of Arizona and California; out-of-district tuition fees were charged in all cases. The highest reported tuition was $2600 a year for a private college, while the highest public college tuition was reportedly $600. In many cases the junior colleges, particularly the private segments, charged higher fees than those among many state colleges and universities.

9. Student enrollment figures were incomplete; the estimate, however, was approximately 1,750,000 full- and part-time students for 1967–68.

10. Faculty employment figures were incomplete; the estimate was 80,000 full- and part-time faculty for the country as a whole.

11. Virtually all states had the same general requirement for student admission—high school graduation—but many colleges opened their doors to nongraduates when they reached a certain age, usually eighteen. The open-door policy prevailed in most cases, chiefly among the public institutions.

12. States requiring teaching certificates or at least approval from some state agency were Alaska, Arizona, California, Colorado, Florida, Hawaii, Illinois, Iowa, Kansas, Missouri, Ohio, Oregon, Texas, and Washington. Certain states, such as Alaska, Colorado, and Texas, required approval of vocational-technical instructors only. A different case is Oregon, which required approval of all instructors (but not certification) by the state's department of education. In most cases the requirements from state to state varied with the subject matter field or with state or federal funding requirements.

13. The master's degree was reported to be the general requirement for employment in academic subject areas, but most states employed some academic teachers with only the bachelor's degree. Vocational-technical teachers were employed generally for their competence in the field, a criterion considered strongly in lieu of degrees. In no state was the doctorate a requirement for employment, although this degree was considered desirable for those teaching in two-year college branches of universities.

14. Reported salaries ranged from approximately $5,000 to $15,000 per school year, usually 10 months. Averages were $8,300 for public institutions and approximately $7,000 for the private colleges, but both averages covered only about one-third of the states.

15. Thirteen states reported laws guaranteeing various types of teacher benefits, and virtually all the states and territories had some form of retirement system for teachers. Tenure and certain other benefits were left generally to local policies in most states.

16. More than one-third of the states reported significant and recent statewide studies of some aspect of the junior colleges. Most of the studies dealt with status data and projections for future growth and development.

17. Reported trends dealt chiefly with sudden increases in the number of public junior college campuses. Some states had extensive reorganizations of administrative systems. Both California and Colorado reported new state boards for community colleges. Florida expanded its county area junior colleges. Georgia found sudden new growth during the decade. New colleges, curricula, and services were developing in Illinois. Iowa saw a complete change to area community colleges and vocational-technical schools. The 1965 Kansas legislature established an ultimate system for a projected 21 community colleges. Maryland developed a study projected through 1975. Michigan and Minnesota increased and improved their systems. Mississippi divided into junior college districts, with long range plans for the creation of college centers. Missouri reported a serious faculty shortage owing to its rapid development of colleges. New Jersey developed rapidly within the decade with a system of county community colleges. New York continued to expand and increase its campuses, while North Carolina improved financial support for its public segments. A master plan for state policy was prepared by Ohio in 1966. In that year Virginia established a state-controlled system of comprehensive community colleges, and increasing activity was found in Oregon, Pennsylvania, Texas, and Washington. In essence, junior college development was extensively alive in about half of the states.

18. State junior college associations of various sorts were reported existing in at least 25 states. All states and territories had agencies providing general information for teacher employment, but specific junior college placement offices existed in at least 24 states and the territories.

Alabama

RESPONDENT: Rudolph Davidson, Director, Division of Higher Education, State Department of Education, Montgomery

Alabama reported 21 junior colleges during 1967–68, 15 public and 6 private. The interesting fact is that 12 of the public junior colleges opened their doors for the first time beginning in 1965; this represented a tremendous, sudden growth. These public institutions were regulated by the Alabama State Board of Education, and they were financed both by state aid and student tuition. The tuition was $45.00 per quarter; private college tuition varied. Admission to the public institutions of higher learning was by high school graduation or its equivalent. No state credentials were required for college teaching, although for the state schools a master's degree in the subject area was indicated. No state minimum salary law existed. The range for junior college teachers was from $6,930 to $11,220. No state law existed for tenure, sick leave, sabbatical leaves, and insurance, but the State Board of Education had established policies regarding these and other benefits. Retirement was through a state plan which was in addition to Social Security. Accreditation was by the Southern Association. Studies of benefits to junior colleges included a long range plan for education in Alabama, a study of the state department of education and a study on university education. The state organization is the Alabama Association of Junior Colleges.

Alaska

RESPONDENT: Fred Koschmann, Resident Director, Juneau-Douglas Community Colleges, Juneau

Alaska had seven junior colleges in the fall of 1967–68 with no immediate plans for additional institutions. Six of the colleges were operated and controlled by the University of Alaska, and one was private. The public junior colleges were financed by tuition and allotments of money from the state legislature. Tuition ranged from $100 per semester for residents to $150 per semester for non-residents. Admission to the junior colleges was based upon high school graduation. Although teachers should have a master's degree in the subject taught, no teaching credentials were required, except for vocational and technical courses financed by the state. Salaries ranged upward from $6,300. Teachers could receive tenure after two years if advancement was made to assistant professor. Sabbatical leaves were given after 5 years. Retirement was under the state retirement system. No trends or studies were noted. Accrediting was by the Northwest Association. There was no state association for junior colleges. For information and applications for the public colleges, write to Dean of Statewide Services, University of Alaska, College, Alaska.

Arizona

RESPONDENT: John T. Condon, Executive Director, Arizona State Board of Directors for Junior Colleges, Phoenix

Six junior colleges were reported to be operating during 1967–68; all 6 were under public control. Plans included 5 others. The Arizona State Board of Directors, established in 1960, regulated and coordinated the colleges; the regional accrediting agency was the North Central Association. The state provided substantial funds for both operation and capital outlay, the remainder of cost coming from the local district. County residents were not charged tuition; out-of-state students were charged from $600 to $680 per year. Admission policies were described as "open-door." Non-high-school graduates nineteen years of age or older were admitted on a probationary status according to G.E.D. tests. Teaching credentials were issued and required by the state. A master's degree of 60 semester hours beyond the baccalaureate degree and two years of teaching experience in high school or college or directed teaching were required. Teachers had to take a course in educational psychology, sociology, or philosophy, and one covering the scope and objectives of the junior college. Forty semester hours were required for a major. A one-year occupational credential was issued to cover technical fields; applicants with a degree or five years experience were limited to teaching in the field of their recognized skills. There was no state minimum salary law for junior college teachers; the reported range was $6,000–$12,000. The state had no tenure law. Retirement was with the Arizona State Retirement system, while other benefits were determined by local colleges. The only two-year college organization was the Arizona Junior College Athletic Association. For credentials, write to the Arizona State Board of Directors for Junior Colleges, State Office Building East, Room 201, Phoenix 85007. For placement services, write to the Arizona State Employment Office, 207 East McDowell Road, Phoenix, or the Arizona Education Association, 2102 W. Indian School Road, Phoenix.

Arkansas

RESPONDENT: H. E. Williams, President, Southern Baptist College, Walnut Ridge

As of the fall of 1967, Arkansas had 7 two-year colleges, 3 public and 4 private. There was no statewide board, organization, or association for junior colleges. Colleges were free to set up their own policies and benefits affecting their junior college instructors. As an example of one operation in the state, the respondent's college required a master's degree or its equivalent for new teachers. The 1967–68 beginning salary for the degree was $5,525 and for the doctor's degree, $6,125. Among the important teacher benefits were free housing on campus, social security, a retirement plan where the college pays at least 50 percent into the teacher's account, travel allowance, $10.00 toward professional membership fees, scholarship assistance for additional training, life insurance program on which the college paid half, hospitalization on which the college paid half, sick leave and job security insurance, extra pay for extra duties, automatic pay increases and free education for dependent children of faculty members.

California

RESPONDENT: Archie L. McPherran, Acting Chief, Division of Higher Education, California State Department of Education, Sacramento

In 1967–68 California had 83 public junior colleges in operation, 8 more were in the planning stage. Four private two-year colleges were noted. The public institutions were regulated and coordinated by the Board of Governors of the California Community Colleges as of 1968. The colleges received about one third of their financial support from the state and two-thirds from local taxes. Tuition was free to local students, while those from out-of-state paid $11.00 per unit. Teaching credentials were required for junior college teachers. A bachelor's degree was sufficient for a few special areas. However, a master's degree (in an academic field) ordinarily was required. The state had a minimum salary law of $5,000. The junior college range was $5,089 to $15,000, the median being $9,745. Tenure was granted after three years in one college. There were also state laws governing sick leave and sabbaticals. Several types of insurance were available to teachers. Retirement was under the state system. Trends included new credential requirements, i.e. a person with a master's degree in an academic area could teach academic subjects in a junior college without any education course requirements. Accrediting was by the Western Association. State associations included the California Junior College Association and the California Junior College Faculty Association. For information and applications for credentials, write to Bureau of Teacher Education and Certification, California State Department of Education, 721 Capitol Mall, Sacramento, 95814. For placement services, write to the California Teachers Association, Burlingame.

Canal Zone

RESPONDENT: Division of Schools, Balboa Heights

Canal Zone College at La Boca, Canal Zone, was established as a part of the Canal Zone public school system operated by the Division of Schools. As of 1967–68 it was the only junior college in the Canal Zone. It offered a two-year program leading to an Associate of Arts degree and some courses which carried third year credit on transfer. The Division of Schools was a part of the Civil Affairs Bureau of the Canal Zone Government which was an agency of the United States Government. The Superintendent of Schools reported directly to the Civil Affairs Director who in turn reported directly to the Governor of the Canal Zone. Both officials were appointed to their offices by the Governor. There was no body of school laws nor was there a board of education. The school system, including the college, was governed by administrative regulations rather than by statutory enactments. Those interested in teaching in the college should write directly to: Dean, Canal Zone College, Box 3009, Balboa, Canal Zone.

Colorado

RESPONDENT: Dana Lefstad, Assistant Director, Community College Division, Colorado State Board for Community Colleges and Occupational Education

During 1967–68 Colorado was in the process of developing a plan for a state system of community colleges, the groundwork having been laid by the Colvert Study of 1963. It was inevitable, therefore, that the 1967 facts furnished by the Colorado respondent would undergo considerable change in the near future. In 1967–68 the state had 11 public junior college campuses. There were no private junior colleges. The Colorado State Board of Education was the state agency for these two-year colleges, its chief function being apportionment of state funds, but the colleges recently were placed in a separate board. The governor signed into law in May of 1967 the Community College and Occupational Education Act of 1967. The law formed a new state board, the Colorado Board for Community Colleges and Occupational Education. As of July 1, 1967, the board took over the supervision of the existing junior college districts and all future colleges established by the assembly. The new board, composed of 9 members appointed by the governor, had administrative responsibility for the community colleges (as distinguished from the local junior college districts). The state took over the local tax responsibility for financing these colleges. Colleges joining the state system lost their local boards. Local advisory committees (or college councils) appointed by the governor furnished liaison and made recommendations to the state board. There was also a statewide advisory committee to represent various facets of education and the economy. State assistance to the local junior college districts was given at the rate of $500 a year for each full time equivalent (45 quarter units) resident student. Some of the colleges charged no tuition for in-district students, while the largest fee was $200 per quarter for out-of-state students. To be admitted to the colleges, generally the students had to be high school graduates, to possess at least 15 high school units, and to take the American College Test. Teachers were not required to be certified by the state. A master's degree was the general requirement by local colleges. Teacher benefits, all determined by local college districts, included tenure, sick leave, sabbatical leave, various insurance and retirement programs. Teacher salaries ranged from $6,000 to $11,000 per year; administrators received up to $22,000. Recent state trends included movements toward full state support of the colleges, increased state control, emphasis on occupational program offerings, and terminal offerings. The State Department of Education was the official state accrediting agency for the junior colleges. The only statewide two-year college association noted was the Colorado Association of Junior College Presidents. For assistance in employment, write to the Colorado Education Association, 5200 South Quebec, Englewood, Colorado 80110.

Connecticut

RESPONDENTS: Theodore Powell, Executive Officer, and March H. Chiles, Secretary, Regional Community Colleges of Connecticut, Hartford

Two-year colleges operating in the fall of 1967 included 9 private colleges, 7 state community colleges, and 4 state technical colleges for a total of 20. Other colleges were offering both two-year and four-year programs. In the fall of 1968, it was planned to open an eighth state community college. Also planned was a fifth state technical college several years in the future, a total of eight being planned. All two-year colleges charged tuition, the state supported institutions charging $100 a year. Admission to the state-supported colleges was on a first-come, first-served basis to high school graduates. Faculty in the state institutions were under a state retirement system and received medical and hospital insurance coverage. Annual salaries for faculty ranged from a minimum of approximately $8,500 for an instructor to a maximum of approximately $15,000 for a professor. The public community colleges were governed by the State Board of Trustees for Regional Community Colleges. No state teaching credential was needed. Information about teaching in the state community colleges can be obtained from the board's office in Hartford, 1 Niles Street, Room 409.

Delaware

RESPONDENTS: Robert H. Parker, President, Wesley College, Dover; Paul K. Weatherly, Executive Director, Delaware Technical and Community College, Dover

In 1967 Delaware had 3 two-year colleges in operation, 2 private and 1 public. Delaware Technical and Community College, with headquarters in Dover, had one college operating at Georgetown, a second being opened in

September 1968, at Wilmington. Three branches or separate locations were being planned. The governing body for the college was a State Board of Trustees appointed by the governor and confirmed by the General Assembly. The new college board was established in 1966. The college was financed 100 percent by state funds plus any available federal funds. There was no state junior college organization and no statewide mandates relating to faculties. Wesley College, a private school, was a church-related institution which began as an academy in 1873 and became a junior college in 1922. Wesley was financing its operation by private funds and tuition. Students were admitted from approved high schools if they had the proper academic background to do college-level work. A master's degree in the field of teaching was required in most cases. Other teacher benefits included tenure after the fifth year, sick leave, and health insurance. Sabbatical leaves were being studied. Retirement was described as "half pay after thirty years of service." The third college, Brandywine, was established in 1965. No state trends or studies were reported for the state except the creation of the new state board and planned technical community colleges. Accreditation was by the Middle States Association.

District of Columbia

RESPONDENT: William A. Harper, Director of Public Relations, American Association of Junior Colleges, Washington, D.C.

Five private junior colleges were operating in the District of Columbia during 1967. Responsible only to their own individual boards, these colleges established their own policies regarding students and faculty employment. Those who may be interested in teaching in these colleges should write directly to the colleges.

Florida

RESPONDENT: James L. Wattenbarger, Assistant State Superintendent, Community Junior Colleges, State Department of Education, Tallahassee

In 1967–68 Florida had 31 junior colleges; 26 public institutions and 5 private. At least 2 other junior colleges were in the planning stage. The public junior colleges were county area schools coordinated by the State Junior College Board. Financing by the state was based upon an equalization formula. There was no tuition charge as such for local students; however, a matriculation fee of $75 to $125 per semester was charged. Out-of-state district students paid a tuition fee from $10 to $75 per semester; out-of-state students paid from $125 to $275 per semester for tuition. Admission requirements were set by each college, although high school graduation or the "profit by experience" policy prevailed. Teachers normally needed a master's degree for academic subjects or had to be "qualified" for vocational teaching. Requirements for state certification varied with the subject matter field. Salaries ranged from $4,150 to $17,000, the latter maximum prevailing during 1966 only in Miami-Dade College. The 1965–1966 median was $7,690 and the mean $7,967. In addition to sabbaticals, benefits for teachers included tenure, sick leave, insurance programs and retirement. A major statewide study was the Community College Council Report of 1957 and a Master Plan. Accrediting was set by the state and the Southern Association. An organization was the Florida Association of Junior Colleges, Tallahassee. Experiencing tremendous growth since 1960, the public junior colleges were unified under the State Junior College Board for which the Division of Community Junior Colleges, State Department of Education, Tallahassee, served as staff. For general placement information write to the Division of Community Junior Colleges in Tallahassee.

Georgia

RESPONDENT: Harry S. Downs, Director of Junior College Operations, Regents of the University System of Georgia, Atlanta

During 1967–68 Georgia had 12 established public junior colleges. Most were under the Board of Regents; 11 others operated under private control. One of the public campuses opened in 1967; others were in the planning stage, while some were in transition to four-year institutions. For the public junior colleges, the state supplied 75 percent of their funds; tuition fees accounted for the remaining 25 per cent. Tuition fees in the public segments amounted to $70 per quarter term. There was no single standard of admission, although standards were based upon students' high school averages and SAT scores. The state did not require state teaching certification. A master's degree in one's teaching field was the general requirement for employment. There was no state minimum teaching salary; the average academic year salary was $8,550. The state provided its public junior college teachers with tenure, sick leave, insurance, and retirement; sabbatical leaves were possible but not required by the state. Georgia's junior colleges were accredited by the Southern Association. A major recent state study was the 1964 report to the Board of Regents, "Regents' Study of Community Junior Colleges in Georgia." No major trends were reported. Junior college teachers could join the Georgia Education Association, although it did not maintain a placement office. The only junior college association reported was the Georgia Association of Junior Colleges.

Guam

RESPONDENT: Department of Education, Agana

This island of the Pacific, called the "Hong Kong of the Future," lies at the southernmost end of a chain of islands called the Marianas and is the largest and most populous. No two-year college existed on the island. However, the College of Guam School of Continuing Education offered programs and curricula leading toward the Associate in Arts degree. Write Department of Education, Government of Guam, Post Office Box 157, Agana, Guam 96910.

Hawaii

RESPONDENTS: Richard H. Kosaki, Vice-President for Community Colleges; and Melvin Sakaguchi, Administrative Assistant, Honolulu 96822

In 1966–67 Hawaii had 5 junior colleges, 4 state owned and 1 private: Leeward Oahu Community College, however was set to begin operations in 1968, thus setting 6 junior colleges for 1969. The public colleges were administered as a system by the Board of Regents, University of Hawaii. The Board served as a coordinating agency. Operating funds were derived from state legislative appropriations and supplemental federal funds, although tuition was charged at the rate of $50, with additional lab-shop fees varying with programs. Accrediting was by the Western Association. Admission into the schools was by high school graduation or, in certain occupational programs, by ability to meet employment requirements. Teaching credentials were required of teachers, a master's degree or occupational equivalent experience being cited. The approximmate salaries in the public junior colleges ranged from $6,171 to $11,638. The teacher benefits had not been formulated at the time of this survey, although instructors did participate in the state's retirement system plan, which called for monthly contributions by the employee and state government and allowed for clause of benefits from age 65 or upon completion of 25 years of service or upon termination of employment at the agency. A recent state study was the "Feasibility of Community Colleges in Hawaii, 1964," by Richard H. Kosaki. No specific trends were noted. Teachers can write for information or applications for teaching credentials or licenses to Community College System, 2327 Dole Street, Honolulu, 96822. The state has the Hawaii Community College Association.

Idaho

RESPONDENT: William C. Seifrit, Jr., Director of Educational Planning and Research, Boise

Idaho had 5 junior colleges in 1967, 3 public and 2 private. The state anticipated no new junior colleges in the near future. The State Board of Education exercised nominal control over the 3 public junior colleges with actual, on-site control being vested in each junior college districts' Board of Trustees; the private junior colleges had their own trustees. Chief financial support for the public junior colleges derived from district property taxes, liquor taxes, and nominal state appropriations. Tuition was required by law and ranged from $50 to $350 per semester for in-district to out-of-district state students. Admission was by accredited high school diploma or recognized equivalent. Teacher qualifications were determined by the colleges and their boards. There was no state minimum salary level; salary ranges were unavailable; there was no statutory tenure or sick leave policy; and participation in the state retirement system was optional in each district. No comprehensive studies had been completed in regard to junior college operations to date, but several were under way or contemplated for the near future. Accrediting was by the Northwest Association. There was no State Association of junior colleges; *all* higher education institutions participated in the Council of Presidents and Deans. For placement services, write directly to the office of the Dean at the respective colleges.

Illinois

RESPONDENT: Parmer Ewing, Director, Department of Higher Education, Office of Public Instruction, Springfield

Illinois had 54 recognized junior colleges operating during 1967–68; 14 were private and 40 public. Seven others were authorized to open in 1968–69. The state had a junior college board which regulated, coordinated, and supervised the colleges. The board also approved establishment and conducted various studies. Operation expenses for public units were financed as follows: 50 percent from the state, student tuition not to exceed one-third of operation cost, and balance from local taxes. The state furnished 75 percent of capital expense, while the local district provided the remainder. Admission to these colleges was by high school graduation or by qualification for post-high school ages. Some teacher credentials were required, and a master's degree with a major in the teaching field and/or competent training in some occupation field were expected. A state minimum salary law applied only to the common schools. In general, the range for junior college teachers was $6,000–$20,000. Guaranteed by state law were tenure and sick leave of 10 days per year, accumulative to 30 days. Sabbatical policies were left to the option of the colleges. Insurance programs were provided for teachers. Retirement was under the state plan for higher educational institutions. A recent statewide study was the Master Plan of 1964, which created a separate board for junior colleges and which provided for state and local districts to share the costs of education. The plan was considered an effective one. Noted trends were expanding enrollments, new colleges, and increases in curricula and services. Teachers were needed in all fields. Expansion in various areas made the demand for teachers greater than the available supply. Accreditation was by the Illinois Junior College Board, Springfield, and the North Central Association, Chicago. Junior colleges were oganized under the Illinois Junior College Association, Chicago. For information, write to the State Junior College Board or the Office of Public Instruction. For placement services, write to the Illinois Education Association, 100 E. Edwards Street, Springfield.

Indiana

RESPONDENT: Edgar B. Smith, Assistant Superintendent for Instruction Services, Indianapolis

While there were no separate public junior colleges in the state, Indiana University and Purdue University did operate essentially two-year college branches; however, these extension centers sometimes offered upper division or graduate instruction, although the bulk of offerings was in the lower division. Control of these branches rested with the parent institutions. Three other institutions were clasified as junior colleges, 2 private and 1 public. The latter, Vincennes University, was organized as Jefferson Academy in 1801. The first junior college courses were added in 1873, and the institution became a junior college in 1889. It received state aid and was subject to partial control by the governor who appointed 6 members; the others were self-perpetuating.

Iowa

RESPONDENTS: William M. Baley, Associate State Superintendent, and William F. Banaghan, Area School Consultant, Branch of Community Colleges and Area Vocational Schools, Department of Public Instruction, Des Moines 50309

Recent legislation has had an enormous impact on the development of public junior and community colleges in Iowa. Legislation passed in 1965 provided a structure for developing a statewide system of area community colleges and area vocational-technical schools. This legislation, later revised in 1967, provided for the development of not more than 17 area community colleges or area vocational-technical schools. These area schools were to be developed on a multicounty basis in such a manner as to insure an adequate base for the development of the schools. This legislation had been implemented to the extent that all but 7 of the 99 counties in the state had been included in the area school system. Fifteen area schools had been organized, 11 of these schools had been developed as area community colleges and 4 as area vocational-technical schools. In 1967–68, there were 27 public campuses, 2 of which had not yet been absorbed. The 16 junior colleges, operated by local educational agencies prior to the legislation providing for a system of area schools, largely had been incorporated into the area schools system. Fourteen of these junior colleges had either merged with the various area schools or were under contract to area schools. Two of the junior colleges operated by local educational agencies had yet to become a part of the area schools. The legislation required that the financial support for the system of area schools be provided largely by the state. The support was based on average daily enrollment in each area school. In addition, local taxes could be levied. Tuition charged by area schools to state residents could not exceed the lowest tuition charged by institutions of higher learning operated by the Board of Regents. However, tuition for out-of-state students generally was from 150 percent to 200 percent of tuition charged for residents of Iowa. In addition to the public junior colleges in operation in the state, there were 6 private junior colleges. Staff employed in the system of public area schools were required to meet the approval requirements of the Iowa State Department of Public Instruction. A master's degree was required to teach academic subjects. Fifteen area schools participated in the state retirement program, while one participated in the Teachers Insurance and Annuity Association. Teacher credentials were required. Established was the Iowa Junior College Association. For employment, contact the central offices of the area schools under the Department of Public Instruction or, in the case of non-area or private schools, the colleges themselves.

Kansas

RESPONDENT: Carl L. Heinrich, Department of Public Instruction, Kansas State Education Building, 120 East Tenth, Topeka

Twenty-one junior colleges were reported operating in Kansas during 1967; 14 were public county units, 2 each share one county, and 5 were private, church-related units. (The total does not count Haskell Institute, a federal junior college for American Indians.) Three more public units were expected to open in the near future. The 1965 legislation established a system of community colleges not to exceed 22. The State Department of Public Instruction supervised and accredited the junior colleges, the regional body being the North Central Association. In 1966–67 the operating costs of public units were financed by "local levy (40.7), student tuition (13.4), state aid (20.4) out-district tuition (16.2), and federal aid (3.2). All capital outlay expenses were borne by the local community with the exception of monies received under the Higher Education Facilities Act." In regard to tuition, the respondent noted "By law, community junior colleges cannot charge in excess of $7.00 per credit hour; in addition, the state pays the institution $2.50 tuition per credit hour." Admission policies followed a state standard, which is the registration of graduates from accredited high schools or its equivalent. Junior college teachers were required to be certified with state credentials. "The 3-year junior college certificate required a master's degree, 50 semester hours general education with distribution in 4 areas, and 8 hours of pressional education with distribution in 3 areas. A one-year certificate could be issued to an applicant with a baccalaureate degree and 8 hours of professional education. A one-year limited certificate was issued an applicant holding a baccalaureate or higher degree with recommendation of the employing agency and approval by the State Department of Public Instruction. In addition, all instructors had to meet a forty semester hour requirement in his area of specialization with at least 10 of the 40 at the graduate level." The state did not have a minimum salary law. Reported ranges were $5,200–8,200 for public junior colleges and $4,200–6,500 for private units (these appear to be minimum ranges, not maximum). Teacher benefits were determined at the local level rather than the state level, although retirement was regulated by a state retirement law covering all teachers. As to recent state studies, the respondent noted that "The Committee on Education of the Kansas Legislative Council made a comprehensive report of the role, function, organization, financing, and supervision of public junior colleges in Kansas." This report was published and released in October of 1964. A committee of the junior college association was studying the matter of eliminating the teacher certification. There was a Public Community College Association. Information about the colleges can be secured from the Kansas Public Community Junior College Association, Richard Mosier, President, c/o Colby Community Junior College, Colby, Kansas. Information about credentials can be obtained from Carl L. Heinrich, Director, College Accreditation Section, State Department of Public Instruction, 120 East 10th, Topeka. For help in placement, write to the Kansas State Teachers Association, 715 West 10th Street, Topeka.

Kentucky

RESPONDENT: Ted C. Gilbert, Executive Director, Kentucky Council on Public Higher Education, Frankfort

In 1967–68 Kentucky had 18 junior colleges, 10 controlled and managed by the University of Kentucky's Community College System, 7 private and 1 municipal school. Three new community colleges were planned. Financing of the public two-year colleges was by state appropriations and tuition, with some local support in site acquisition and original capital investment. Fees for students were the same as for the University of Kentucky: $140 a semester for resident students and $410 a semester for non-resident students. Except for one college, which was free to selected students, private junior college tuition varied from $264 to $795. Admission to schools was based generally upon high school graduation from accredited secondary schools. The state required no teaching credentials, but requirements were controlled by the regional accrediting agency, Southern Association. Generally, a master's degree was required. There was no state minimum salary law; current ranges of salaries were not reported. A retirement system prevailed for public community colleges through the University of Kentucky system. The Kentucky Junior College Association was the institutional organization. For placement services, write to the individual institution or Dean, Community College System, Lexington.

Louisiana

RESPONDENT: Norman H. Edwards, Director, Administration and Research, State Department of Education, Baton Rouge, 70804

Louisiana had 5 public and 4 private junior colleges in September, 1967. Three of the public colleges were branches of Louisiana State University. One was under the jurisdiction of the Louisiana State Board of Education and one was under a separate board. Financing was by state appropriations, tuition or fees. No credential was issued for college teaching, the boards supervising the schools themselves setting requirements. The boards adopted minimum salary only for the schools under their control. Accrediting was done by the Southern Association of Colleges and Schools. There were no junior college associations.

Maine

RESPONDENTS: Edward Y. Blewett, President, Westbrook Junior College, Portland; H. L. V. Anderson, Director, Professional Services, State Department of Education, Augusta

Maine had 2 junior colleges, Westbrook Junior College in Portland and Bliss College in Lewiston, both private. A study of higher education in the state was being made at the time of this survey. Westbrook and Bliss set their own standards and policies. The New England Junior College Council served as a regional association for most of the New England States. Maine had no legislative provisions for junior colleges, public or private. The state placement office serving all teachers in the state is the State Teacher Registration Bureau, State Department of Education, Augusta.

Maryland

RESPONDENT: Harold D. Reese, Assistant Director in Certification and Accreditation, Maryland State Department of Education, Baltimore

Counting Chesapeake College, Maryland had 19 junior colleges organized and in existence by 1967–68; 12 of these were public and 7 were private. The State Board of Education coordinated and accredited the colleges, the regional agency being the Middle States Association. The public two-year colleges were supported approximately as follows: Operation costs—one third state, one third local, and one third tuition and fees; capital costs—50–50 or state equalization fraction (whichever is larger). For regional colleges the state contributed 75 percent; the other 25 percent was from local taxes. Tuition fees approximated $200–$300 per year for each student. The "open door" policy prevailed in admission of students. The state did not require certificates from junior college teachers, although the general requirements for teaching were about the same as for four-year colleges. To teach academic subjects, the teacher should possess a master's degree with a major in the teaching field.

Fringe benefits included tenure, sick leave, and sabbatical; insurances varied with the college. Retirement was under the Teachers Retirement System and also Social Security. A recent statewide study was "Public Higher Education in Maryland 1961–1975," a report from a state commission in June, 1962. Trends included higher salaries for junior faculties to keep pace with the higher salaries in four-year colleges and universities. Although no public placement office existed among the professional associations, information and assistance could be obtained from Maryland Association of Junior Colleges, 2901 Liberty Heights Avenue, Baltimore 21215; Maryland State Teachers Association, 344 N. Charles Street, Baltimore 21201; and from the State Department of Education, 301 West Preston Street, Baltimore 21201.

Massachusetts

RESPONDENT: William G. Dwyer, President, The Massachusetts Board of Regional Community Colleges, Boston

During 1967–68 Massachusetts had 14 public and 16 private junior or community colleges offering two-year college programs. Entirely state supported were 12 of the public colleges, all of which had been established under the Regional Community College Board since 1960. Established by legislative act in 1958, the Board included 11 members appointed by the governor and had endeavored to provide regional community colleges within commuting distance of most students in the state. These colleges offered transfer and career preparation programs and evening and summer programs for both regular students and adults pursuing a part-time education. The instructional staff at the public community colleges was classified by rank, participated in the state retirement system, and was eligible for health benefits plus $2,000 life insurance. The state did not require teacher certification for the college staffs. The master's degree in the subject matter area was expected. There were no teachers' associations for exclusive two-year college faculties. Those interested in teaching in a public college should file an application with the Board of Regional Community Colleges, 74 State House, Boston 02133, or write directly to the college itself.

Michigan

RESPONDENT: Richard S. Webster, Higher Education Consultant, Department of Education, Lansing

In the fall of 1967 Michigan had 36 community colleges, 28 public and 8 private. The public segment of colleges was under the State Board for Public Community and Junior Colleges; the board recommended policy and administrative decision to the State Board of Education, to which it was advisory under the provisions of the 1963 State Constitution. The state provided assistance for operations on a full-time equated student basis $300 per FTE student during 1965–66; the legislature in 1966–67 increased the amount to $325 for "academic program" students, and $350 for "technical program" students; for 1967–68 it remained the same. The colleges received other operating expense monies from tuition and property tax funds. Capital outlay projects were aided by state legislative action up to a maximum of 50 percent of a project's cost. Tuition fees during 1967–68 ranged from $100 to $351 per year, for district residents and $250 to $523 for non-residents. Admission standards were set by each college; requirements varied for vocational-technical and terminal programs, but successful high school graduation was the normal prerequisite for associate degree programs. The state did not have a community college certification requirement, although some colleges required a secondary school teaching certificate. A master's degree in the subject area taught was a normal expectation of teachers in associate degree programs. There was no state minimum salary law for community college teachers. During 1967–68 the range of *median* salaries in 19 public community colleges was $7,500 to $9,800; the average for all schools was about $8,700. Teacher benefits (tenure, sick leave, etc.) varied with the individual institution at the discretion of the college board; benefits tended to parallel those provided for secondary school teachers. Commmunity college teachers participated in the retirement program chosen by their boards of trustees. Those holding secondary school teaching certificates could participate in the Public School Employees Retirement System. Some institutions were members of the TIAA–CREF and used the state retirement system for their non-certified teachers and administrative staffs. Two recent statewide studies in the community college area included *Study of Guidance and Counseling in Michigan Junior and Community Colleges—An Inventory and Measurement of Guidance and Counseling Services* and *Public Junior and Community Colleges Uniform Accounting Code*. The first of these was a followup to Dr. Max Raines' national study. The second study prepared a uniform accounting code which was in statewide use in 1967–68. Regarding significant trends affecting junior college teachers, the respondent wrote: "Public Act No. 379 of the Publics Acts of 1965 allows public employees including elementary, secondary, and junior college teachers to bargain collectively. Affiliates of the American Federation of Teachers and of the Michigan Education Association represent faculty members at Michigan community colleges. Regulation to bring junior and community college teachers under provisions of the state tenure act was not approved by the 1966 Legislature." The state accrediting agency for two-year colleges was the Michigan Commission on College Accreditation, Bureau of Higher Education, State Department of Education, Lansing. Two-year college associations included Michigan Council of Community College Administrators, Michigan Association of Junior Colleges, and Association of Michigan Community and Junior College Business Officials. Teachers associations and placement offices included the Michigan Education Association, 1216 Kendale, East Lansing, and the Michigan Federation of Teachers, 2011 Park Avenue, Room 815, Detroit.

Minnesota

RESPONDENT: Philip C. Helland, Chancellor, Minnesota Junior College System, St. Paul.

The respondent reported 22 junior colleges operating during 1967–68; 17 were public and 5 were private. At least two additional institutions were slated to open soon. The Minnesota Junior College Board was the controlling agency for the state's public two-year colleges. Except for the University of Minnesota Technical Institute at Crookston, these schools were financed by state appropriations and local tuition fees. The tuition charge was $5.00 per quarter hour credit for state residents and $8.00 for out-of-state residents. Admission was generally granted to high school graduates. No state teaching certificates were issued. A master's degree was the general requirement for employment. There was no state minimum salary law affecting the junior college teachers; the indicated range was $5,300 (BA only) to $12,920. Benefits included tenure after 3 years and sick leave amounting to 10 days a year, accumulative to 100 days. Retirement was with the State Teachers Retirement coordinated with Social Security. The regional accrediting agency was the North Central Association, while state accrediting was done by the Minnesota Junior College Board, Capitol Square Bldg., 500 Cedar St., St. Paul. On matters relating to teacher employment in the two-year colleges, the Minnesota Junior College Association and the Minnesota Junior College Faculty Association can be reached at the above-named board's address.

Mississippi

RESPONDENT: B. L. Hill, Supervisor of Junior Colleges, Department of Education, Jackson

Twenty-seven junior colleges were operating during 1967–68; 19 of these were public institutions. "Mississippi is now divided into districts as individual and separate juristic entities and bodies politic and corporate. Long range plans provide for centers in the districts already created. One center is planned for the immediate future." The public junior colleges were regulated by the Junior College Commission of the state. The law provided that each county in the district could levy up to 3 mills for support and 3 mills for building and improvement. The state appropriated a lump sum of money for distribution on a formula basis. Tuition and fees for the biennium beginning July 1, 1966, amounted to approximately $100 per student. Entering students were required to have 16 acceptable high school units. No state credentials were needed by teachers, but a teacher was required to have a master's degree or its equivalent and had to teach in the field of his specialization. There was no state minimum salary law. The master's degree beginning salaries for the junior colleges ranged from $5,000 to $7,000. Tenure was offered to teachers. Each institution had its own policies on such benefits as sick leave and sabbatical leave. Retirement plans were available. Recent statewide studies included surveys of (1) vocational-technical needs and (2) the role and scope of junior colleges. A major trend was the increased support from the state, appropriations having been doubled beginning in July 1966. There was an institutional organization, the Junior College Association. Accrediting of the colleges existed through the College Accrediting Commission, and the Southern Association of Colleges and Schools. For information and assistance, write to the State Department of Education, Junior College Office, Post Office Box 771, Jackson. For help in placement, write to Certification Department, State Department of Education, Post Office Box 771, Jackson, Mississippi.

Missouri

RESPONDENT: Fred E. Davis, Director, Junior College Education, State Department of Education, Jefferson City

The *Missouri Handbook for Public Junior Colleges* indicated 13 public and 8 private junior colleges for 1967–68. Two more were to be developed.

One private junior college was reported to be offering a four-year college program leading to the Bachelor of Fine Arts, and the respondent noted a total of 8 private two-year colleges. He commented that "The comprehensive community junior college is a new concept for Missouri and is developing rapidly. It is gaining the respect of all segments of education and government." All public junior colleges in the state were supervised and controlled by the State Board of Education. The board accredited, administered state aid at the rate of $320 per equated student (24 semester hours per equated student), or ½ of operating (current) whichever was less, and did some regulating and coordinating. The regional accrediting agency was the North Central Association. Besides receiving local property tax monies, each college district set its own tuition and fee rates with the approval of the state board. Admission to the public institutions was by high school diploma or its equivalent. Junior college teachers had to secure teaching certificates from the Department of Education, and these were issued upon recommendation by the chief administrators of the various colleges. A master's degree or its equivalent in the subject area taught was required. There was no state minimum salary law for the college teachers. The approximate salary range in 1967 was $5,700 to $11,000. All teacher benefits were set by the various local boards, although retirement was under the Public School Retirement System of Missouri. No major recent studies in the state were noted. Because of new junior college growth in the state, there was a trend toward a serious faculty shortage. The only statewide junior college group noted was the Missouri Junior College Association, an institutional organization, recently rejuvenated to include individual staff members and their participation. While offering no placement services, the Missouri State Teachers Association could nevertheless offer some assistance to new teachers in the state.

Montana

RESPONDENT: K. D. Smith, the Dean of Miles Community College, Miles City

In 1967–68 Montana had 3 junior colleges with 2 others expected in the near future. These colleges, regulated and supervised by the State Board of Education, were public. The colleges charged tuition of $40.00 per quarter for county residents, $70.00 per quarter for out-of-county state residents, and $120.00 per quarter for students from other states. Financial support was also given from county and state tax funds. High school graduates with good moral character were admitted to the colleges by making proper applications. Instructional staff members were not required to have state teaching certificates. The normal requirement for employment in academic areas was a master's degree with a major in the subject to be taught. The state minimum salary was $6,640 and the upper range level was $14,220, both figures for those with the master's degree. Benefits included tenure after 3 years, a health insurance plan, social security, and a state teachers retirement system. Retirement was after 35 years of teaching in the state or at age 65. Both the State Board of Education and the Northwest Association accredited the 3 colleges. There were no two-year college faculty associations, statewide. For information and/or teacher applications, write to the State Department of Education in Helena, or to the Montana Education Association in Helena.

Nebraska

RESPONDENT: Floyd A. Miller, Commissioner of Education, Nebraska State Department of Education, State Capitol, Lincoln, Nebraska 68509

In 1967–68 Nebraska had 7 junior colleges, 6 public and 1 private. While the state had no board with direct jurisdiction over the junior colleges, technically the public junior colleges were an extension of the secondary school and consequently under the State Board of Education. The State Department of Education did have the responsibility for accrediting public two-year colleges. New legislation required that private junior colleges had to have the approval of the State Board of Education before such an institution could be established. The same legislation provided for state accreditation of private colleges under the leadership of the State Department of Education working in cooperation with university officials. Public junior colleges were governed locally by each district. Legislation permitted districts to enlarge at least to the county level. Local property taxes, student tuition fees, and state aid to the extent of $7.50 for each credit hour enrolled by Nebraska resident students provided the revenue for the operation of public junior colleges, and tuition and gifts provided support for the private institutions. Tuition fees varied according to specific district charges per semester hour. Students were admitted from accredited high schools by a transcript of high school or college level credits. No teaching credentials were issued by the state. An accrediting rule indicated the requirement of a master's degree. There was no state minimum salary law for the junior colleges; the average salary was approximately $7,500. Teacher benefits were only as local districts provided for their district teachers. The state had one two-year college organization, the Nebraska Association of Junior Colleges. For information and assistance, write to Dr. LeRoy Ortgiesen, Assistant Commissioner for Instructional Services, State Department of Education, State Capitol, Lincoln, Nebraska 68509.

Nevada

RESPONDENT: Bonnie M. Smotony, Secretary to the President and the Board of Regents, University of Nevada, Reno

In 1967 Nevada established its first two-year college, Nevada Community College at Elko, the chief means for higher education prior to this development being the University of Nevada. No further information was available at the time of this publication.

New Hampshire

RESPONDENT: Everett B. Sackett, Executive Secretary, Coordinating Board of Advanced Education and Accreditation, Concord

New Hampshire had at least five two-year colleges in 1967–68, 1 public and 4 private. One other was to open in 1968–69. The respondent wrote that "New Hampshire had no system of publicly supported junior colleges . . . A commission again studied the junior college situation and made recommendations to the governor. These recommendations resulted in the introduction of a bill in the state legislature in the 1967 session to begin a statewide system of two-year publicly supported colleges. The bill was defeated because of the cost." Material sent by the respondent showed that the public institutions were controlled and supported by the state. Tuition in these schools ran from $300 to over $1,500 a year. Recommendations by the State Board of Education for the approval of junior colleges were first adopted in 1928 and later revised in 1947. In 1963 supervision of junior colleges, except those operated by the state, was transferred to the Coordinating Board of Advanced Education and Accreditation. The Coordinating Board had not prescribed detailed qualifications for junior college teachers. Write for information to the Coordinating Board of Advanced Education and Accreditation, 66 South Street, Concord, N.H., 03301.

New Jersey

RESPONDENT: Guy V. Farrell, Director of Community and Two-Year College Education, Department of Education, Trenton 08625

In 1967–68 the state had 11 private and 6 public colleges in operation. There was only 1 public campus until recently when the dramatic upsurge in public college development began. During this survey period, 14 county junior college districts had been approved by the State Board of Education; 9 of these had been established, while 7 other counties had not approved colleges. The anticipation is that every county will have a comprehensive community college along county district boundaries. The state had a junior college association. Other details for this entry were not received in time for this publication.

New Mexico

RESPONDENT: Stuart M. Pritchard, Lt. Colonel, USAF (Ret.), Public Relations Officer, New Mexico Military Institute, Roswell

During 1967–68, New Mexico reportedly had 8 two-year college campuses: 3 were branches of East New Mexico University, 3 were branches of New Mexico State University, 1 was an independent public college, and 1 was a public military institute. There were no private junior colleges. The branch colleges were, of course, subject to control and regulation by their parent universities. New Mexico Junior College, established in 1965, was the newest in the state; the oldest was New Mexico Military Institute, founded in 1891 and offering the first two years of college training as early as 1915. Accreditation was by the North Central Association, the University of New Mexico, and the New Mexico State Department of Education, depending upon the school. Junior college teachers were not required to be certified. A master's degree was required of most teachers. Benefits included insurance, sabbatical leaves, social security, and state retirement plans.

New York

RESPONDENT: Lawrence E. Gray, Chief, Two-Year College Programs, University of the State of New York, Albany

Sixty-four junior colleges were operating during 1967. Most of them listed were in the state's publication, "Going to College in New York State." The total included 36 public and 8 private institutions. All colleges in New York

State were functioning under the direction of the Board of Regents of the University of the State of New York. The board chartered (incorporated), accredited (registered), and granted degree powers. Some private junior colleges charged from $150 to $2,000 a year. Admission policies varied; some colleges had the "open door" policy and others, particularly private schools, were very selective. No teaching credentials were required, but the master's degree was normally expected except for specialized areas where experience could be substituted. There was no state salary law. Benefits varied from school to school. Retirement for public college teachers was with the New York State Teachers Retirement System and, in some cases, with T.I.A.A. Private·schools had their own retirement plans. No recent state studies or trends were noted. There was a New York State Association of Junior Colleges but no state teachers group for junior colleges.

North Carolina

RESPONDENT: John H. Blackman, Administrative Assistant, Department of Community Colleges, Raleigh

In 1967–68, North Carolina had 45 junior colleges and technical institutes: 12 were public community colleges, 15 were private junior colleges, and 18 were public technical institutes. The community colleges and technical institutes were supervised by the State Board of Education. Regarding finances, the report said, "The state finances teachers' salaries, equipment, and one half of building costs for community colleges up to $500,000; other colleges are privately supported." Tuition charges were as follows for the public two-year schools; $42 per quarter for college parallel and $32 per quarter for vocational-technical students. Admission was by high school graduation and a satisfactory score on the scholastic aptitude test. Certification of teachers was not required by community colleges and technical institutes, but a master's degree for college parallel areas and equivalent training for the technical areas were required. There was no state minimum salary law. The salary range for community colleges and technical institutes was $7,000 to $14,000 per school year. Policies were in the formative stage for community colleges insofar as teacher benefits were concerned. Retirement for public school teachers was under a state system. No statewide studies or trends were noted. Accrediting of schools was by the Southern Association. The institutional organization was the Association of Junior Colleges. For information and help in placement, write to the Director, Department of Community Colleges, Education Building, Raleigh, North Carolina 27602.

North Dakota

RESPONDENT: Kenneth E. Raschke, Commissioner, State Board of Higher Education, State Capitol, Bismarck

Five public and 2 private two-year colleges were reported to be operating in 1967–68; 2 of the public were state regulated and supported by the Board of Higher Education, and 3 were supported by local districts. Two of these 3 were controlled, as far as program is concerned, by local boards. The third, Williston Center was controlled by the University of North Dakota. For the state two-year colleges, financing came from the general fund of the state and from student fees. Local districts received money from the general fund in the amount of $450 per student. Tuition for the state institutions was $210 for residents and $534 for non-residents. Local district tuition varied according to the place of residence within and without the state. Admission was granted to all qualified high school graduates within the state. No teaching certification was required, although state junior colleges had the same requirements for employment as had the four-year colleges. Local districts set their own standards for employment of teachers. In general, a bachelor's degree was expected and a master's degree desired. There was no minimum salary law; ranges of salaries were not reported. For the state schools, regulations existed for the granting of tenure, sick leave, and sabbatical leave. A hospital and surgical plan was provided. Retirement was under T.I.A.A. on a 5 to 5 matching basis. A master plan was in progress which would include all junior colleges in some phases. Accrediting was by the North Central Association; annual evaluation of all junior colleges receiving state aid was by a State Evaluation Committee. For information and assistance, write to the State Board of Higher Education or the North Dakota Education Association, Bismarck.

Ohio

RESPONDENTS: James Furman, Executive Officer, and Jo-Ellen Brown, Secretary, Ohio Board of Regents, Columbus 43215

In 1967–68 Ohio had 12 two-year colleges, including 4 community colleges, 4 technical institutes, and 4 private junior colleges; in addition there were 15 university branches which were listed as part of the Ohio public two-year colleges. The Ohio Board of Regents planned and coordinated the public campuses, which obtained operating funds from the state, the local district, and tuition fees. The general admission standard was a high school diploma. "All teachers are required to have a state teaching certificate, which is granted by the State Department of Education." The board did not specify degree requirements, these policies being left to the discretion of the individual college. Teachers were covered by the State Teachers Retirement System and allotted sick leave. The most recent state study prepared by the Ohio Board of Regents was the Master Plan for State Policy in Higher Education, published in June 1966. Accreditation of all Ohio colleges and universities was handled through the North Central Association. No statewide junior college association was indicated.

Oklahoma

RESPONDENT: Dan S. Hobbs, Educational Programs Officer, State Capitol Station, Oklahoma City

Oklahoma had 16 junior colleges in 1967–68; 4 of these were church-related, 5 were public local school districts, and 7 were state-owned. The Oklahoma State Regents for Higher Education coordinated and accredited the junior colleges at the state level while the North Central Association served as the regional accrediting agency. The 7 state system colleges were supported from direct state appropriations and from student fees; the 5 municipal colleges were supported by local school districts and student fees. The state-supported colleges charged a general fee of $5.30 per semester credit hour, plus an activity fee; admission was granted to accredited high school graduates, who had to take the American College Test. No teaching credentials or specific degrees were required by the state, although the recommendation was a master's degree. There was no state minimum salary law for colleges. Salaries in the state junior colleges averaged between $6,550 and slightly over $7,200 per year during the 1966–67 school year; the average 9–10 month salary was $7,055. Teacher benefits varied by institution. Regarding retirement, the respondent noted, "State supported teachers are eligible under the Oklahoma Teacher Retirement Law (plus social security and supplement) to one half salary of last 5 years." Recent studies included a series of reports, "Self-Study of Higher Education in Oklahoma," continuing since 1962. No specific trends were noted, but there were several recommendations growing out of the self-study reports. An institutional association was established in 1966. For help in placement, write to Oklahoma Education Association, 323 E. Madison, Oklahoma City.

Oregon

RESPONDENT: Robert O. Hatton, Assistant Superintendent, Division of Community Colleges and Vocational Education, Salem

In 1967–68, Oregon had 12 public community colleges and three private two-year colleges. In 1968 the 1 two-year technical institute was to become a four-year college. The State Board of Education regulated some aspects and coordinated and supervised other aspects of community college operation. The state furnished financial aid to the public community colleges at the rate of $575 per FTE for the first 400, $475 FTE for the next 300, and $433 per FTE for the remaining. Vocational FTE supplementary aid was at the rate of $180 per FTE for the first 200 and $110 per FTE for all remaining. Capital support was computed on a rather involved formula which could provide up to 65 percent of the cost of capital construction. The state average had been 51 percent, however, for all projects to date. By law, the public community colleges had to admit students who were high school graduates or, in the opinion of the institution, could benefit from the educational program offered. Teaching certificates were not issued by the state for the community college instructors, although the state did require certain standards for employment of teachers. For transfer education, a master's degree in the teaching field was indicated; for vocational teachers, the requirement was the bachelor's degree in a specialty and/or adequate work experience in the specialty. There was no state minimum salary law for junior college teachers. The current range for the community college was $6,000 to $13,500. Benefits varied from college to college. There were no statewide laws for such benefits as tenure and sick leave. Retirement was in the State Public Employees Retirement System. The most recent state study was "Education Beyond the High School: A Projection for Oregon" (October 1966). Trends included an increased rate of reimbursement for vocational-technical programs and a teacher negotiation law. Accrediting was by the Northwest Association. The state had a group called the Oregon Community College Association. For information, write to the State Department of Education, Division of Community Colleges and Vocational Education, Salem, Oregon 97310. For placement services, write to Oregon Education Association, Portland.

Pennsylvania

RESPONDENT: Louis H. Bender, Director, Bureau of Community Colleges, Department of Public Instruction, Harrisburg

Fifty-nine two-year colleges were reported for Pennsylvania in 1967–68. Ten more were being planned. Seventeen of the colleges were church-related or independent, 11 were public community colleges, and 31 were campus centers operated by various four-year colleges and universities. The State Department of Public Instruction, Bureau of Community Colleges, regulated the public community colleges. These schools were financed as follows: for operating funds, one third each from state, student fees, and local districts; for capital funds, 50 percent from the state and 50 percent from local districts. Tuition fees in these same schools were approximately $300 per year. Admission was by high school graduation with selective entrance into specific curricula. The state did not issue junior college teaching credentials. For employment, a master's degree was required generally, with less than the master's for certain occupational programs. There was no state minimum salary law for these teachers. Salaries started at about $6,000 per year. There were no uniform policies for teacher benefits. Retirement could be under the Public School Employee System or any approved private plan. A recent statewide study of junior colleges was the "Ralph R. Field's Study 1965." No specific trends were indicated. Accrediting was by the Middle States Association. Information for the state's two-year colleges may be obtained from the Pennsylvania Association of Junior Colleges. Additional help may be obtained from the Bureau of Community Colleges, State Department of Public Instruction, Box 911, Harrisburg, 17126.

Puerto Rico

RESPONDENT: Roberto F. Rexach Benitez, Director, Arecibo Regional College, Arecibo, Puerto Rico 00612

Puerto Rico had 16 two-year colleges operating in 1967–68; 2 of these were private non-denominational, 11 were operated by private universities, and 3 by the University of Puerto Rico. The latter institution planned to establish 3 more two-year branches. The private schools were accredited by the Superior Educational Council, which served as the governing board of the 3 university-supported Regional Colleges at Humacao, Arecibo, and Cayey. Tuition at the last school was $68.50 a semester; for other colleges, the average was $15 per credit hour. Admission to the colleges, especially Humacao, Arecibo, and Cayey, was by high school diploma, a 2.0 average, and the college Entrance Examination Board test. No teaching credential was required. Teachers normally needed the master's degree to teach in the regular academic program of studies. There was no state minimum salary law. Junior college and university salaries averaged about $8,000 a year. Tenure was granted after 5 years of satisfactory service. Sick leave amounted to 18 days per year in the public colleges, while sabbaticals were available at full salary for 1 year. The government provided teacher insurance. Humacao, Arecibo, and Cayey teachers were under the University Retirement System and could apply for scholarship grants for further studies. A recent state study was the "Report to the Council of Education on Junior Colleges," a plan to establish a system of junior colleges in Puerto Rico. Trends thus included expansion plans for junior colleges throughout the island. Accrediting was by the Council of Higher Education, and the Middle States Association in which the Commonwealth of Puerto Rico was located. There were no two-year college associations in the Commonwealth. For information or placement, write to Office of the President, University of Puerto Rico, Rio Piedras, Puerto Rico (or) Office of the Director, Puerto Rico Junior College, Rio Piedras (or) Office of the Chancellor, Catholic University, Ponce (or) Office of the President, Inter-American University, San German.

Rhode Island

RESPONDENTS: State Department of Education, Providence; and William F. Flanagan, President, Rhode Island Junior College, Providence

In 1967–68 there were 3 two-year colleges in Rhode Island; 2 were private non-church schools and 1 was owned by the state. The latter institution, Rhode Island Junior College, was regulated, coordinated, and supervised by the Board of Trustees of State Colleges. The state appropriated about 75 percent to its junior college while student fees accounted for the remaining cost of operation. Tuition included $200 as a general fee and $20 as an activity fee. Admission was by high school diploma and a potential for success. No state teaching credential for college teachers was indicated by the respondent, but a bachelor's degree was expected and a master's degree desired. A minimum salary of $7,000 had been established by the Board of Trustees, and salaries ranged to $15,000 according to faculty rank. Faculty benefits included sick leave, life insurance, state retirement or TIAA, Blue Cross and Physicians Service, major medical coverage at group rates, and waiver of fees for full-time faculty and legal dependents at institutions (University of Rhode Island, Rhode Island College, and Rhode Island Junior College) under the jurisdiction of the Board of Trustees. Under the Board of Trustees sabbatical and tenure policies were in effect. A state commission was organized recently to study all areas of education in the state. No specific recent trends or laws were noted. Accrediting was by the New England Association. No two-year college associations existed at the state level. For information and help in placement, write to the Rhode Island Education Association, 600 Mt. Pleasant Avenue, Providence, or the Rhode Island State Department of Education, Providence.

South Carolina

RESPONDENT: T. L. Neely, President North Grenville Junior College, Tigerville

As of 1967–68, South Carolina had no framework for the public junior college. The state had 9 two-year university branches and technical schools doing the work of the junior colleges, and there were 6 private two-year colleges. The governor had set up a commission to study all of higher education problems in the state. At that point it was not known when the state would have public junior colleges. The 6 private two-year colleges were all under the control of sectarian or private boards. Since the state had no requirements or benefits established for junior colleges, except for those related to the university branches, the private institutions set their own; these factors varied from one school to the other. The colleges sought to have teachers with at least a master's degree in the field in which they taught.

South Dakota

RESPONDENT: Sister M. Alicia, President, Presentation College, Aberdeen

South Dakota had no general pattern of junior college organization; there were no state provisions for public two-year colleges. In 1967–68 there were 3 private junior colleges, 2 of which had been recently founded. These schools were church-related, charged tuition, admitted students from accredited high schools, and set their own policies for faculty employment and benefits.

Tennessee

RESPONDENTS: E. Claude Gardner, Dean-Registrar, Freed-Hardeman Co., Henderson; W. C. Westenberger, President, Martin College, Pulaski

By 1967–68, Tennessee had 7 private junior colleges and 5 public junior colleges. The public junior colleges were part of a group of state-controlled junior colleges to be launched in the next few years. (For further information write Dr. Hal Ramer, Assistant Commissioner of Education.) Six of the privately controlled junior colleges were church-related; all were coeducational and included boarding facilities. The State Board of Education approved various junior colleges for teacher preparation; accreditation was by the Southern Association. Tuition was charged by the institutions. Admission standards included high school graduation as well as certain other requirements. Teachers with a bachelor's degree could be hired, but a master's degree was expected.

Texas

RESPONDENT: David L. Norton, Junior College Director, Coordinating Board, Texas College and University System, Austin

Texas reported 60 junior colleges operating in 1967; 15 were church-related, 6 were independent private colleges, 14 were public county districts, and 25 were public local community districts. Six more districts were being planned for the immediate future. The state agency for two-year colleges was the Coordinating Board, Texas College and University System; as the name implies, its job was coordination of the public colleges. Regarding finance, the respondent noted, "Local district ad valorem tax, tuition and fees and state appropriations for instructional purposes based on full-time student equivalents based on ratio of 15 semester hours equal to one F.T.S.E. Amount appropriated would be $475 for the first 450 students and $450 on all over this number." For tuition fees, the state statute provided a maximum of $50 per semester (four half months in length) and a minimum of $15 for 3 semester hours or less. Admission to the junior colleges was by graduation from accredited high schools along with a unit requirement; by written examination for 18-year-old non-high-school graduates; by recommendation and approved abilities for those who were 21 years old; or by certain other stipulated standards and conditions. The state did not issue teaching credentials to its college teachers, except for vocational-teaching fields. A master's degree was expected for those teaching in their fields of specialization; terminal program instructors had to have satisfactory technical training, experience, and personal qualifications for their specific work. There was no state minimum salary law. Junior college salaries ranged from $4,000 to $11,000 per year. There was no state policy for benefits such as tenure. Retirement was under the Texas Teachers Retirement System. The "teacher contributed 6 percent of his salary up to a maximum salary of $8,400." A statewide study was the Governor's Committee on Education Beyond the High School, which culminated in the establishment of the Coordinating Board and placed the public junior colleges under its jurisdiction rather than under the Texas Education Agency. The Coordinating Board was charged with developing and recommending certain basic changes and improvements in instruction and other areas. Accrediting was by the State Accrediting Agency of the Association of Texas Colleges and Universities and by the regional agency Southern Association. Two-year college associations were the Texas Junior College Teachers Association, the Texas Junior College Association, The Association of Texas Junior College Board Members and Administrators, the Texas Council of Junior College Presidents, and the Texas Private Junior College Foundation. For information and assistance, write to the Coordinating Board, Texas College and University System, Dr. David L. Norton, Junior College Director, Sam Houston State Office Building, 201 East 14th Street, Austin, Texas 78701. Although they have no placement office, you may secure further assistance from the Texas Junior College Teachers Association.

Utah

RESPONDENT: Merle E. Allen, Director, Utah Coordinating Council of Higher Education

In 1967–68 Utah possessed 3 two-year colleges, all of which were publicly controlled at the state level; 2 were directed by university boards and 1 by the State Board of Education. Accreditation of these schools was by the Northwest Association of Secondary and Higher Schools. Those who aspire to teach in one of these institutions should write directly to the colleges.

Vermont

RESPONDENT: Max W. Barrows, Deputy Commissioner of Education, State Department of Education, Montpelier

Vermont had 5 junior colleges in 1967; there were no plans for additional campuses: 4 of these were private and 1 was public. The Board of Trustees of the Vermont State Colleges controlled the public junior college, while the State Board of Education regulated the private junior colleges. The state made annual appropriations to the public institution. Tuition was charged by both the public and private colleges. The admission standards were determined by each college. There were no teaching credentials required for college teaching; each college set its own standards for qualification. No salary data were given. Benefits and retirement information were not given. No trends or statewide studies were noted. Accrediting was done by the New England Association of Colleges and Secondary Schools, Boston. No junior college association existed, statewide. For placement services, write to Vermont Education Association, 5 Baldwin Street, Montpelier.

Virginia

RESPONDENTS: Prince B. Woodard, Director, State Council of Higher Education, Richmond 23219; and James Bradley, Coordinator for Information and Publications, Department of Community Colleges, Richmond 23219

In 1966–67 Virginia had 26 two-year colleges, 15 public and 11 private. "The 1966 General Assembly of Virginia enacted an entirely new status which established a state-controlled system of comprehensive community colleges. In essence, this legislation provided for a network of community colleges throughout the state with the initial locations being those of existing two-year branches of four-year institutions, existing vocational-technical schools, and technical colleges. In other words, all of these will be under one umbrella, the State Board for Community Colleges. In the years ahead, additional sites and institutions will be created so that a community college will be in commuting distance for every citizen of the Commonwealth. The State Council of Higher Education for Virginia is the coordinating agency for all higher education and the Community College Board [comes] under its general coordinating role as the other state institutions of higher education do." The respondent added that "we did not become the Department of Community Colleges until July 1, 1966. We have been in the process of formulating our basic standards for operation." A re-survey for 1968 had not been received for this publication.

Virgin Islands

RESPONDENT: Carol M. Hay, Secretary to the President, College of the Virgin Islands, St. Thomas

College of the Virgin Islands, previously a two-year college, was converted to a four-year college status.

Washington

RESPONDENT: N. C. Richardson, Acting Director, State Board for Community College Education, Olympia

In 1967–68, the Washington Community College System consisted of 22 comprehensive colleges operating under an open-door policy. Local control in 22 community college districts resided in boards of trustees appointed by the governor. State level control was exercised by the State Board for Community College Education, also appointed by the governor. Funds for maintenance, operation, and capital support, except for tuition and fee charges, were provided by state appropriation. Tuition for Washington residents was $50 per quarter and for non-residents, $150 per quarter. A maximum of $20 in fees could be charged additionally. Certification, either academic or vocational, was required. While a master's degree was desired, certification could be on the basis of secondary credentials. The faculty salaries for 1967 ranged from $6,500 to $12,500 and averaged $9,350. Tenure was by continuing contract; retirement was under the State Teachers Retirement System; other benefits were determined by individual district boards. Community colleges were accredited by the Northwest Association of Secondary and Higher Schools. The Washington Association of Community Colleges provided an institutional organization. Appropriate certification, on the basis of established standards, was recommended by the community college president after employing an instructor.

West Virginia

RESPONDENTS: John F. Montgomery, President, Greenbrier College, Lewisburg; and Harry G. Straley, Coordinator, State Department of Education, Charleston

In 1967–68 West Virginia had 5 two-year colleges, 2 of which were public institutions under the Board of Governors of West Virginia University. The official state accrediting agency for West Virginia colleges was the West Virginia Board of Education. Regional accreditation was by the North Central Association. The colleges charged tuition, the lowest being $212 at the two-year state college. Faculty at this school followed the same requirements and received the same general benefits of West Virginia University. Details of these requirements and benefits were not secured at the time of this publication. The private colleges established their own individual requirements and benefits, none of which was submitted by the respondents.

Wisconsin

RESPONDENT: Earl S. Beard, Dean, Sheboygan County Center of the University of Wisconsin, Sheboygan

Of Wisconsin's 22 two-year colleges, most are part of the University of Wisconsin Center System. With 13 centers, there were 2 private and 7 other public segments. The lower-division programs were essentially the same in the centers and in the university. Underlying the work of the university is the famous "Wisconsin Idea, that a university is not just one place but rather a public instrument for the widespread production, dissemination, and application of knowledge." As the respondent noted in his letter, "The Center System as a whole is regarded as one of the four principal administrative units of the University, the other three being the Madison Campus, the Milwaukee Campus, and University Extension (combining general and agricultural extension services of the University). These three units are also headed by chancellors who report to the president." The latter reports to the Regents of the University. The respondent stated that teacher requirements and benefits coincide with those prevailing throughout the university. "Each academic department of the Center System has its own chairman, usually resident on the Madison Campus. The chairmen have initial responsibility for the recruitment of faculty and their assignment to the various two-year branch campuses."

Wyoming

RESPONDENT: John W. Gates, Executive Secretary, Wyoming Community College Commission, Laramie

In 1967–68 Wyoming had 6 public junior colleges, all functioning under the Wyoming Community College Commission. The colleges were financed as follows: one fourth by state, one fourth by tuition, and one half by local property taxes. Tuition and admission standards varied with each college. Teaching credentials were not issued by the state, although a master's degree was expected. There were no state standards in the law relating to minimum salaries or teaching schedules. Benefits varied with the college. Retirement was under the state retirement system. Accrediting was done by the University of Wyoming for 4 schools and by the North Central Association for 2 schools. The institutions were under the Community College Commission. Formation of a professional organization for community college professional personnel was being attempted. For information and help on placement, write to the University of Wyoming, Laramie.

Appendix B

Respondents for College-Faculty Survey

A survey conducted during the fall of 1967 secured additional information for various chapters of this book. Twenty-three two-year colleges participated, 1 of which was not received in time for inclusion within findings. The colleges, randomly selected, represent all major geographical areas and types of institutions. A total of 131 teachers returned questionnaires, 118 being received in time for analysis. The questionnaire included two parts, one dealing with the status and evaluation of the college and another with facts related specifically to the instructional area in which the teacher worked. Although the supplied information was useful through the book, chief areas utilizing findings were Chapter Four dealing with selected instructional areas and Chapters Nine and Ten dealing with faculty attitudes, opinions, problems, issues and solutions. Owing to the great amount of data and the restricted size of this book, original tables of data and verification had to be eliminated. Interested readers are advised to correspond with the authors if they wish further information.

Participants reported a variety of previous employment experience. Fifty-six specialists (46%) had been employed previously in high school teaching, 21 people (18%) in four-year college teaching, 19 (16%) in CJC teaching, 12 (10%) in university teaching, and 3 (−1.0%) in elementary school teaching. Thirty-five specialists (29%) had experience in other occupations, chiefly vocational-technical fields, while 5 persons had come directly to CJC teaching after university graduation. Eighty-seven people had had only one previous type of occupational position, 20 had held two previous types of positions, 5 had held three, and 1 had held four. These were not previous jobs but previous levels of teaching or types of occupational labor. Twenty-two of our sample were women, but answers seemed to reflect little differences among sex, religion, politics, or other profile characteristics. The names of participating colleges and teachers follow:

1. *Black Hawk College, Moline, Illinois. Alban E. Reid, President.*
   Aitchison, Lillian; Anderson, Donald L.; Barber, Garnet; Batell, Thomas; Fiedler, Leigh; Fox, Gary L.; Havener, Ralph; Johnson, Erwin R.; Kienle, Thomas William; Moon, Ronald F.; O'Leary, Vincent C.; Stover, Marshall.

2. *Bradford Junior College, Bradford, Massachusetts. Dorothea L. Smart, Dean.*
   Hinkle, Vernon.

3. *Broome Technical Community College, Binghamton, New York. Herbert L. Hurst, Dean.*
   Beers, Robert B.; Ferrari, George P.; Kalbaugh, A. J.; Kapral, Jr., Michael, J.; Kushner, John; Roach, Lois S.; Schum, Mary E.

4. *Calhoun (John C.) Junior College and Technical School, Decatur, Alabama. Jack E. Campbell, Dean.*
   Barton, Hugo; Bishop, Sr., Jim B.; Mitchell, William L.; Stephens, Robert E.

5. *College of Eastern Utah, Price, Utah. Charles S. Peterson, Acting Director.*
   Allred, Edith; Postma, Frank; Salvatore, Joseph.

6. *Community College of Baltimore, Maryland. Leonard S. Bowlsrey, Dean of Instruction.*
   Bowlsbey, Blanche F.; Davies, Malcolm; DeHaven, Clarence T.; Forster, Louis; Hokuf, Steve M. P.; Perlman, Bennard B.

7. *Community College of Philadelphia, Pennsylvania, James A. Richards, Dean of Instruction.*
   Anderson, Edward A.; Goldwater, Daniel L.; Minnis, Jack H.; Namelak, Joseph S.; Robertson, R. D.; Weiss, Eleanor.

8. *Glendale Community College, Glendale, Arizona. C. B. Smith, President.*
   Braasch, Vernon; Gentry, Warren; Holt, Hal; Kitts, F.; Lorenzini, August P.; Mikus, Andres; Squires, Carl E.

9. *Hinds Junior College, Raymond, Mississippi. Robert M. Mayo, President.*
   Brooks, Jr., Frederick Lee; Denton, Katherine A.; Dyer, Reuben J.; Griffin, William W.; Reeves, James L.; Stewart, Lurline; Williams, Claude.

10. *Martin College, Pulaski, Tennessee. W. C. Westenberger, President.*
    Bass, Harold; Burks, William; Keys, Lois; Rayburn, Willie Ray; Wilkerson, J. Kenneth.

11. *Maui Community College, Kahului, Hawaii. Donald C. Bridgman, Provost.*
    Brunish, R.; Cherednik, John Ross; Rippey, Clayton.

12. *Missouri Baptist College, Hannibal-La Grange, Missouri. Larry L. Howard, Dean.*
    Ayer, Ronald F.; Bates, Edwin; Dierker, William W.; Doerr, Beulah; Groves, Florence; McClellan, V. Eugene; Mitchell, Mary M.; Pope, Kenneth H.; Schoonover, Charlotte; Woods, Noel A.

13. *Oakland Community College, Bloomfield Hills, Michigan. John E. Tirrell, President.*
    Anderson, Roland A.; Bradner, James; Davenport, John A.; Dotseth, James H.; Ellert, Ernest E.; Greenberg, Dan; Shuert, Keith; Woughter, G. L.

14. *Ricks College, Rexburg, Idaho*
    Biddulph, Lowell G.; Davenport, Lynn H.; Dixon, Gordon A.; Forsyth, Marion G.; Partridge, Alden; Pearson, L. C.; Ricks, Norman E.

15. *Roger Williams College, Providence, Rhode Island. J. Harold Way, Dean.*
    Finger, Mary; Hathaway, Carol Joyce; Jungwirth, Charles; Williams, Sue K.

16. *Roswell Branch, East New Mexico University* (formerly Roswell Community College), *Roswell, New Mexico. Dale T. Traylor, Dean.*
    Leonard, Charles; Reeves, Larry T.; Smith, John E.

17. *Shanandoah College, Wincheter, Virginia. Kenneth Kyre, Dean.*
    Barbour, Robert S.; Brown, Rector S.; Clarke, P. W.; Pugh, Walter L.; Shrader, Charles W.; Souders, Bruce C.; Stein, Maurice H.

18. *Southern Technical Institute, Marietta, Georgia. Hoyt L. McClure, Director.*
    Arntson, C. A.; Holladay, C. T.; Lawson, George; Orvold, C. R.

19. *Southwestern Oregon Community College, Coos Bay, Oregon. John Rulifson, Dean of Instruction.*
    Hall. H. A.; Leuck, Frank; Piencey, James P.; Sorensen, Hagbarth; Swearingen, Jack.

20. *St. Mary's Junior College, Minneapolis, Minnesota. Sister Anne Joachim, C.S.J., President.*
    Claesgens, Roger F.; Kennedy, Margaret Mary; McCann, Lester J.; Minton, John; Wyman, Eva.

21. *Union College, Cranford, New Jersey. Kenneth C. MacKay, President.*
    Boly, R.; Keen, Arnold J.; Swackhamer, Farris S.; Zirnite, George P.

22. *University College, Raymond Walters Branch, University of Cincinnati, Ohio. Hilmar C. Krueger, Dean.*
    Baughin, William A.; Bright, Don; Gomes, Audrey S.; Osborne, Helen B.; Pathe, Amy; Siegrist, Albert R.

Note: Not received in time for the survey: Gaston College, Dallas, North Carolina; Ball, Jr., George A.; Brooks, Peter D.; Hartung, A. Bruce; Eckard, Miles L.; McCartney, Thomas C.; Merritt, John C.

Appendix C

Questions and Projects for
Study and Discussion

For your convenience, the following sample questions and problems are listed
in relationship to specific chapters. Items may be used as starting points or as
supplements to those developed by professors and students. The lists are designed particularly for those who are in training for entrance into the field of
CJC teaching.

Chapter One: Junior College Development in The United States

Discussion Questions

1. What forces seem to have fostered the unique development of the
   two-year college? Is any one force more important than another?
2. Why did private junior colleges develop before their public counterparts? What delayed the public segments?
3. How do CJC purposes differ among communities? What purposes
   seem to be standard nationwide?
4. What are some common criteria for the establishment of a CJC?
   How might criteria vary from state to state?
5. What are the advantages and disadvantages to a state board of control rather than a local board? How do articulation and accreditation
   activities relate to this control?

Research Problems

1. Develop a case study of the founding of two-year colleges in a particular geographical area or state.
2. Determine the role of a person or organization in contributing to the
   establishment of a particular two-year college.
3. Design a survey to find public and educational attitudes toward

junior colleges or some phase of their programs; show significant differences between attitudes.

4. Compare and contrast CJC purposes and programs to find likenesses and differences in regard to various degrees of value and success.

5. Prepare what you consider to be an ideal plan for a new CJC. Describe the type of college, the community, the college philosophy, the programs, the faculty, and the facilities.

Chapter Two: Benefits for Junior College Teachers

Discussion Questions

1. Should two-year college teachers have a salary based upon academic rank (the merit system), upon a single schedule, or upon a combination of both? Why?

2. What should be desirable features of a retirement plan? Should the plan be the same for all levels?

3. How and why did tenure develop? In what ways are teachers protected by tenure? How are the colleges protected from tenured teachers who fail to perform acceptably?

4. Which professional membership do you think is best for CJC teachers? Compare the value of the various memberships open to you.

5. What is sabbatical leave? Why is it given, and what are the qualifications? Name a few types of other leaves. Are any unique to the CJC?

Research Problems

1. Participate in a salary study of junior colleges in one geographical area. Determine ranges, means, and medians. Show contributing factors and make comparisons and contrasts.

2. Try to determine through research whether states having certification, employment, and tenure laws differ in teacher mobility from states without such laws.

3. Design a survey questionnaire for selected faculties to discover how institutional benefits relate to morale.

4. Prepare surveys or reports on such areas as academic freedom, teaching load, professional relationships, and retirement or insurance plans.

5. Interview several non-teaching members of the community. Determine their perceptions of the benefits for CJC teachers.

Chapter Three: Employment Requirements and Techniques

Discussion Questions

1. What, to you, would be valid requirements for teacher certification? How do states differ in their requirements?

2. What qualities should CJC officers seek in a teacher applicant? How do you think you measure up to these qualities?

3. Should letters of recommendation include both strong and weak points, or should only positive items be used? What information is

usually included in letters of application? What are some things to avoid?

4. What are your feelings about personal interviews? What are the most crucial points in good interview situations? If you were the employing officer, what would you want to observe or learn about the applicant?

5. What are some areas of adjustment that new teachers are apt to face after employment?

Research Problems

1. Study and report upon CJC training programs as they exist in colleges and universities in various parts of the nation. Look for common standards and significant differences. Estimate the success of these programs.

2. Write to several CJC employing officers and ask them what criteria they employ in selecting their instructors. From collected data, recommend criteria that seem to be most valid.

3. Study placement office procedures and services and establish the ideal situation most helpful to teacher applicants.

4. Request permission to observe a CJC teacher employment interview; make written observations and follow up an interview case to determine reasons why applicants were selected or turned down for positions.

5. Study faculty problems that arise after new employment; check the nature of these problems, how long they exist for the new teacher, and methods of resolution; establish a list of recommendations useful to new CJC teachers.

Chapter Four: Selected Instructional Areas

Discussion Questions

1. Of the areas discussed in this chapter, which ones seem to be most inviting to you as a potential teacher? Why? If you are now in a CJC, discuss with the class why you selected the field you are now in.

2. To what degree do you think these separate areas contribute to general education? To transfer education? To terminal or vocational education? Why?

3. If you were setting graduation requirements for the A.A. degree, what courses from these areas would you list? How would you justify your selections to a faculty or administrative group?

4. Go through each area one by one and suggest a teaching method that might be most appropriate in each case. Why would it help a CJC teacher to know that such methods are used in these areas?

5. Which of the areas is most likely to demand outside time, i.e.— evening and weekend activity?

Research Problems

1. Select various CJC catalogs and compare the instructional areas as noted in course group headings. Make a listing and note the number

of times each area appears. Try to discover reasons behind the choice of some areas rather than others.

2. Prepare a list of statements or checklist items in respect to one or more of the areas discussed in this chapter and mail these to appropriate teachers in selected colleges. For instance, ask art instructors about problems or benefits in their fields. Findings might be useful to administrators as well as art teachers themselves.

3. Basing your analysis on college bulletins, compare and contrast the offerings in your field as they are described in a CJC and a senior institution. What courses are you unlikely to teach in lower division?

Chapter Five: Academic Duties and Functions

Discussion Questions

1. How do you think a course outline should be developed? What should it contain? How does it aid the teacher? Should outlines be different from one level to another?

2. What are some important criteria for textbook selection? Who should be responsible for the final selection? Why?

3. What effects can the adoption of a controversial text have on the instructor and the college? What does the instructor do when faced with community reaction to one of his book selections? (See guidelines provided by the A.A.U.P. and the American Library Association.)

4. Can attendance accounting be justified at the CJC level? How can the job be handled to save time?

5. What system of grading would you like to use as a teacher? Justify your system in respect to other systems.

Research Problems

1. Study the course descriptions and outlines of a particular course in at least a dozen junior colleges; check for conformity and uniqueness. An extension of this study might be to determine how well instructors follow the outline.

2. Survey attitudes and opinions regarding criteria for textbook selection. Discover whether selection can be improved.

3. Study the use of television or some other aid as a value to teaching. Report experiments and findings as to advantages derived from the use of various aids.

4. Conduct a statistical study of dropouts and grades in (a) courses where there is an established class policy and elaborate student orientation and (b) courses without such established policy and orientation in the instructor's initial class meetings. You are seeking to learn how early class policy orientation or lack of it contributes to dropouts or determines grading curves.

5. Using Bloom's suggestions in *Taxonomy of Educational Objectives* and other aids, prepare an original outline for a course you expect to teach in the CJC.

Chapter Six: Professional Duties and Functions

Discussion Questions

1. What is the possible difference between so-called *mandatory* and *obligatory* duties? Which duties might be placed in each area of concern?

2. How must a teacher prepare for a college committee meeting? What role should he take during the meeting? What factors seem to diminish the effectiveness of a committee meeting? What are the advantages and disadvantages to committee rather than individual decisions and recommendations?

3. Do you think in-service institutes or workshops can be beneficial to the teacher? In what ways? What subjects should be considered in these meetings?

4. What should be the relationship of a club adviser to the campus club and its members? What problems could develop from poor advising? How should club advisers be selected? For how long a term should they serve?

5. Discuss possible problems in night teaching and outside employment.

Research Problems

1. Research several existing CJC policies for professional duties and functions. Discover how they are alike and how they differ. Make some recommendations.

2. Study some of the more notable in-service training programs that exist among publicized junior colleges. Determine how combined findings might be useful to new colleges setting up their own programs.

3. Conduct a survey of at least 100 club members in at least ten different junior colleges to find what they perceive the role of the faculty adviser to be; ask them if their present advisers measure up to this role and to what degree. You might also ask the advisers to evaluate themselves and the club members. Knowing the college policies on club sponsorship would help.

4. Interview teachers engaged in outside employment; describe the problems they face and how they resolve them. Show what colleges might do to eliminate the need for outside work.

5. Determine the institutional support for professional activities. Should support include travel, room, board, provision of a substitute? How far away, for how long, and for what purposes are also elements to consider.

Chapters Seven and Eight: The Art of Junior College Instruction: Philosophy and Application

Discussion Questions

1. How do the art and science of CJC teaching differ? In what ways does the art of teaching differ from level to level?

2. What are the essentials in the communication process employed in the classroom? Which is most important—content, organization, or delivery? Or are they of equal value?
3. Describe your philosophy of teaching at this time. Do you think your beliefs will change with added experience? Why?
4. Show how a teacher can benefit from having knowledge and insight into the psychology of learning. Which psychological approaches are best for a variety of CJC students?
5. What are some potential strengths and weaknesses in lecture method? In innovation of method? In student evaluation of teachers and courses? In administrative evaluation?

Research Problems
1. Conduct a statistical study of the improvement rates of students following various methods of teaching. Use control groups and their test reports. Analyze to determine success with each method studied.
2. Secure from various junior colleges copies of evaluative instruments used to gauge effective teachers and teaching. By comparison, determine the degree of values placed upon the various criteria.
3. Study the lives of several "great" teachers of the past in order to find similarities and uniquenesses. Provide some general conclusions that might help new teachers solve their own teaching problems.
4. Provide a summary report on how various authors define the art of teaching. Or you might give a report on one book, such as Gilbert Highet's *Art of Teaching*.
5. Analyze the strengths and weaknesses of the department head, the dean of instruction, and the president as evaluators of teaching effectiveness.

Chapter Nine: Faculty Opinions and Attitudes

Discussion Questions
1. According to the college-faculty survey reported in this chapter, how well do faculty like CJC teaching? Do you think the same results might be found in a similar survey of teaching at other levels?
2. Discuss what the faculty like best and what they like least about the two-year college. To what extent do you feel these opinions are representative of all two-year college faculty opinions?
3. Which institutional aspects are rated high by the faculty in this survey? Which are rated low? Discuss the possible reasons for differences among faculty ratings of this sort.
4. Determine your own opinions and attitudes about the CJC. Do your feelings differ much from the experienced respondents in this survey?
5. What are some administrative and supervisory views and policies? How much supervision should there be in the CJC?

Research Problems
1. Select a CJC in your immediate area and design your own survey to determine faculty feelings. See if findings correlate with our survey or others.

2. Make a study of administrative opinions and attitudes and compare with other surveys.
3. Find out what influences opinions about the CJC. Show how opinions might be controlled to best advantage.
4. Study various institutional changes in policies, programs, or procedures, and discover the effect of these changes upon CJC personnel. Did faculty have a voice in these changes?
5. Compare different definitions of academic freedom as found in the literature. Establish an "ideal" definition and then see how a sample of educators regard it.

Chapter Ten: Issues, Problems, and Solutions

Discussion Questions

1. What is significant in the fact that "teaching procedures, standards, and attitudes" rank highest as a problem area in this chapter? If the CJC specializes in the art of teaching, why should the greatest problems exist in this area?
2. As a beginning CJC teacher, how would you rank the ten problem areas? Why?
3. Comment on the solutions offered by the respondents. Can you thing of more valid solutions?
4. Discuss the relative value of money and time as solutions to all problems listed. Is it not possible that a simple meeting of minds might solve almost any problem in the CJC?
5. Is there any difference between an issue and a problem? If so, which of the described items tend to be issues and which tend to be problems?

Research Problems

1. List and describe the ten issue or problem areas for a group of CJC faculty or administrators and have them rank the items according to degree of significance. Provide conclusions.
2. Prepare an in-depth study of morale in one or several colleges. Look for causes and effects and provide a condition ideal for all.
3. Study the sources of finance for a college. Offer suggestions or possible solutions to the money problem.
4. Find examples of trends among the colleges. Show how trends affect issues, problems, and solutions. Suggest what new trends would be helpful.
5. Study the influences of professional associations, such as the American Association of Junior Colleges. Describe how these associations help in solving CJC problems and in improving the image and status of these institutions.

Bibliography

Bibliography

1. Abbott, Frank C., ed., *Faculty-Administration Relationships* (Washington, D.C., American Council on Education, 1958).

2. "Academic Freedom and Tenure, 1940 Statement of Principles," *AAUP Bulletin*, Vol. 49 (June, 1963), pp. 192-193.

3. *Administrative Procedures for the Approval and Accreditation of Community Colleges and Junior Colleges in Maryland* (Baltimore, Maryland State Department of Education) n.d., m.

4. *Admission and Retention Policies for the Oklahoma State System of Higher Education* (Oklahoma City, Oklahoma State Regents for Higher Education, January, 1963).

5. "American River Junior College Faculty Profile," a paper (Sacramento, California, American River Junior College, 1966).

6. *The American Teacher*, California edition (American Federation of Teachers, AFL–CIO, March, 1967).

7. Anderson, Oscar A., "Who Shall Supervise College Teaching?" *School and Society*, Vol. 30 (November 9, 1929), pp. 645-647.

8. Angers, William P., "The Psychology of the Teacher," *Improving College and University Teaching*, Vol. 11 (Spring, 1963), pp. 115-117.

9. *Annual Report of Services, 1961–62* (Tallahassee, Division of Commmunity Junior Colleges, State Department of Education, 1962) m.

10. *Arizona Junior Colleges*, a brochure, n.d.

11. Armstrong, W. Earl and Stinnet, T. M., *A Manual on Certification Requirements for School Personnel in the United States* (Washington, D.C., National Education Association, revised periodically).

12. Ashmore, Henry L., "The Committee in Administration," *Junior College Journal*, Vol. 29 (September, 1958). pp. 40-42.

13. Astin, Alexander, W., and Lee, Calvin, B. T. "Current Teachers," *Educational Record*, Vol. 47 (Summer, 1966) pp. 361-375.

14. *Attending a College or University in West Virginia, 1965-66* (Charleston, The West Virginia Association of College and University Presidents, 1965).

15. Bard, Harry; Lerner, Leon; and Morris, Leona, S., "Operation: Collegiate Horizons in Baltimore," *Junior College Journal*, Vol. 39 (September, 1967), pp. 16-21.

16. Barrett, Mary B., "In Defense of the Modern Drama Course," *Junior College Journal*, Vol. 35 (March, 1965), pp. 20-22.

17. Bartky, John, "The Nature of Junior College Administration," *Junior College Journal*, Vol. 28 (September, 1957), pp. 3-7.

18. Bashaw, W. L., "The Effect of Community Junior Colleges on the Portion of the Local Population Who Seek Higher Education," *Journal of Educational Research*, Vol. 58 (March, 1965), pp. 327-329.

19. *Basic Standards and Operational Provisions for Texas Public Junior Colleges* (Austin, Coordinating Board, Texas College and University System, 1966).

20. Baur, E. Jackson, "A Student Guide for Interpreting Case Material," *Improving College and University Teaching*, Vol. 8 (Summer, 1960), pp. 104-108.

21. Beach, Leslie, "The Use of Instructorless Student Groups in College Learning," *College and University*, Vol. 36 (Winter, 1961), pp. 190-200.

22. Beckes, Issac, "The Case for Community Junior Colleges," *Junior College Journal*, Vol. 34 (April, 1964), pp. 25-28.

23. Bell, R. Dermont, "The Role of the College Teacher," *Improving College and University Teaching*, Vol. 8 (Autumn, 1960), pp. 141-142.

24. Bladen, V. W., "The Lecture," *Improving College and University Teaching*, Vol. 10 (Spring, 1962), pp. 118-120.

25. Blauch, Lloyd E., ed., *Accreditation in Higher Education* (Washington, D.C., U.S. Department of Health, Education, and Welfare, Office of Education, U.S. Government Printing Office, 1959).

26. Blocker, Clyde E., "Are Our Faculties Competent?" *Junior College Journal*, Vol. 36 (December, 1965), pp. 12-17.

27. Blocker, Clyde E., and Richardson, Jr., Richard C., "Human Relations Are Important," *Junior College Journal*, Vol. 35 (April, 1964), pp. 19-22.

28. Blocker, Clyde E., and Wolfe, Wendell, "Academic Rank in Two-year Colleges," *Junior College Journal*, Vol. 35 (December, 1964), pp. 21-25.

29. Blocker, Clyde E., Plummer, Robert M., and Richardson, Jr., Richard C., *The Two-Year College: A Social Synthesis* (Englewood Cliffs, New Jersey, Prentice-Hall, 1965).

30. Bloland, Paul A., "The Role of the Student Organization Advisor," *Personnel and Guidance Journal*, Vol. 41 (September, 1962), pp. 44-49.

31. Bloom, Benjamin S., ed., *Taxonomy of Educational Objectives*, The Classification of Educational Goals, Handbook I: Cognitive Domain (New York, David McKay, 1956).

32. Bogdan, James A., "Honors in History: A Junior College Experiment," *Junior College Journal*, Vol. 33 (December, 1962), pp. 185-189.

33. Bogue, Jesse P., *The Community College* (New York, McGraw-Hill Book Co., 1950).

34. Bogue, Jesse P., *The Development of Community Colleges* (Washington, D.C., American Association of Junior Colleges, 1957).

35. Boozer, Howard, "North Carolina Is Counting on Community Colleges," *Junior College Journal,* Vol. 34 (December, 1963), pp. 8-11.

36. Boren, Claude B., "Why a Junior College Movement?" *Junior College Journal,* Vol. 24 (February, 1954), pp. 345-357.

37. Bossone, Richard, "Understanding Junior-College Students," *Journal of Higher Education,* Vol. 36 (May, 1965), pp. 279-283.

38. Brick, Michael, *Form and Focus for the Junior College Movement* (New York, Teachers College, Columbia University, Bureau of Publication, 1964).

39. Brick, Michael, "Staff Development: Faculty Orientation and In-Service Programs," in *Selected Papers, 47th Annual Convention American Association of Junior Colleges, February 27–March 3, 1967, San Francisco, California* (Washington, D.C., American Association of Junior Colleges, 1967), pp. 44-46.

40. Brown, Wimberly, and Adams, O. Burton, "A Design for Independent Study," *Junior College Journal,* Vol. 36 (May, 1966), pp. 29-31.

41. Brown, Wimberly, and Adams, O. Burton, "Seminars in a Junior College," *Improving College and University Teaching,* Vol. 13 (Autumn, 1964), pp. 251-252.

42. Brubacher, John S., and Rudy, Willis, *Higher Education in Transition* (New York, Harper and Brothers, 1958).

43. Brumbaugh, A. J., *Guidelines for the Establishment of Community Junior Colleges* (Atlanta, Southern Regional Education Board, n.d.).

44. Buswell III, James O., "Perspective by Participation," *Improving College and University Teaching,* Vol. 38 (Spring, 1960), pp. 57-59.

45. Butler, Nathaniel, "The Six-Year High School," *School Review,* Vol. 12 (January, 1904), pp. 22-25.

46. *California Junior College Association News,* Vol. 2 (October, 1965).

47. *The California Professor,* Vol. 1 (Burlingame, California, California Teachers Association, March, 1967).

48. Campbell, Doak S., "Graduation Titles and Academic Costume," *Junior College Journal,* Vol. 4 (April, 1934) pp. 362-365.

49. Canavan, P. Joseph, "Compensations and Problems of Junior College Teaching," *Junior College Journal,* Vol. 32 (May, 1962), pp. 509-516.

50. Carlyon, Donald J., "Innovation Is a Way of Life," *Junior College Journal,* Vol. 37 (March, 1967), pp. 34-38.

51. Carpenter, W. W., "Early Interest of the University of Missouri in the Junior College," *Junior College Journal,* Vol. 32 (April, 1962), pp. 476-484.

52. Carpenter, W. W., *The Organization and Administration of the Junior College* (Columbia, Missouri, Lucas Brothers, 1939).

53. Carter, Barbara, "Junior Colleges Are Blooming in the Sunshine State," *NEA Journal,* Vol. 56 (May, 1967), pp. 22-24.

54. *Catalog of the University of Wisconsin Center System,* 1966–67.

55. Chambers, M. M., "Six Rules for Economizing in Higher Education," *Journal of Higher Education,* Vol. 33 (January, 1962), p. 83.

56. Chapman, Charles E., "Resharpening the Tools of Instruction," *Junior College Journal,* Vol. 37 (October, 1966), pp. 34-37.

57. Charles, Searle F., and Summerer, Kenneth H., "Building a Junior College Faculty," *Junior College Journal*, Vol. 29 (March, 1959), pp. 421-423.

58. Christian, Floyd T., and Wattenbarger, James L., "Ten Years—A Plan Evolves in Florida," *Junior College Journal*, Vol. 38 (September, 1967), pp. 44-47.

59. *The Chronicle of Higher Education* (Baltimore, Editorial Projects for Education, Inc., March 8, 1967).

60. Clark, Burton R., *The Open-Door College: A Case Study* (New York, Mc-Graw-Hill, 1960).

61. Clark, Glynn E., "Staff Development: Faculty Orientation and In-Service Programs," in *Selected Papers, 47th Annual Convention American Association of Junior Colleges, February 27–March 3, 1967, San Francisco, California* (Washington, D.C., American Association of Junior Colleges, 1967), pp. 41-42.

62. Coffelt, John J., ed., *Organization and Plan, Report One, Self Study of Higher Education in Oklahoma* (Oklahoma City, Oklahoma State Regents for Higher Education, January, 1962).

63. Collins, Charles C., "Grading Standards in the Community Colleges: A Proposal," *Junior College Journal*, Vol. 36 (December, 1965), pp. 33-36.

64. Collins, Charles C., *Junior College Student Personnel Programs* (Washington D.C., American Association of Junior Colleges, 1967).

65. Collins, Charles C., "A Point of View on Grading Standards," *Junior College Journal*, Vol. 35 (April, 1965), pp. 21-23.

66. Collins, John J., "An Experiment in the Use of Teaching Machines," *Junior College Journal*, Vol. 33 (October, 1962), pp. 73-77.

67. Colvert, C. C., "A Half Century of Junior Colleges," *Junior College Journal*, Vol. 17 (February, 1947), pp. 244-247.

68. Colvert, C. C., "Professional Development of Junior College Instructors," *Junior College Journal*, Vol. 25 (April, 1955), pp. 474-478.

69. Colvert, C. C., *A State Program for Public Junior Colleges in Colorado* (May, 1963).

70. Colvert, C. C., and Baker, M. L., *The Status of College and University Offerings and Services in the Area of Junior College Education and Professional Upgrading of Junior College Faculty Members* (Austin, Research Office, American Association of Junior Colleges, University of Texas, 1955).

71. Colvert, C. C., and Littlefield, Henry, "Brief History of the American Association of Junior Colleges." *Junior College Journal*, Vol. 31 (February, 1961), pp. 36-40.

72. *Community Junior Colleges, 1963–64 through 1965–66* (Denver, Colorado State Department of Education, 1966).

73. *Community Junior Colleges*, Report of the Advisory Committee on Junior Colleges (Topeka, Kansas Legislative Council, 1964).

74. Conley, William H., "The Junior College Instructor," *Junior College Journal*, Vol. 9 (May, 1939), pp. 507-512.

75. Connolly, John J., "International Students and the Two-Year College," *Junior College Journal*, Vol. 37 (February, 1967), pp. 20-21.

76. Cooper, Russell M., ed., *The Two Ends of the Log* (Minneapolis, University of Minnesota Press, 1958).

77. Cope, Robert G., "Should You Consider Year-Round Operation?" *Junior College Journal*, Vol. 35 (September, 1964), pp. 20-23.

78. Cosand, Joseph, "Three Years of Progress in St. Louis," *Junior College Journal*, Vol. 36 (February, 1966), pp. 9-12.

79. Coulter, E. M., *College Life in the Old South* (New York, Macmillian, 1928).

80. Cowan, Gregory; Hawkins, Richard; McPherson, Elizabeth; "Incompetence in Comp: A Realistic Solution," *Junior College Journal*, Vol. 35 (September, 1964), pp. 24-27.

81. Cowley, W. H., "College and University Teaching, 1858-1958," *Educational Record*, Vol. 39 (October, 1958), pp. 311-326.

82. Coyle, Edward J., ed., *Faculty Salaries in the Oklahoma State System of Higher Education 1965–66* (Oklahoma City, Oklahoma State Regents for Higher Education, April, 1966).

83. D'Amico, Louisa, and Bokelman, W. Robert, "Tuition and Fee Charges by Public Junior Colleges," *Junior College Journal*, Vol. 33 (September, 1962), pp. 36-39.

84. Daniels, Roy P., "The Case for the College Faculty Counselor," a paper (New York, Fashion Institute of Technology, n.d.).

85. Dannick, Lionel, and Carson, Robert B., "The Seminar Method and the Junior College: A Proposal," *Junior College Journal*, Vol. 33 (December, 1962), pp. 204-209.

86. Davis, Robert J., "Secrets of Master Lecturers," *Improving College and University Teaching*, Vol. 13 (Summer, 1965), pp. 150-151.

87. Dawson, Merle C., "Sophomore Honors English in the Junior College," *Junior College Journal*, Vol. 33 (December, 1962), pp. 236-240.

88. DeCora, Paul J., "Two-Year College Transfers: Graduates of Organized Occupational Curriculums," *College and University*, Vol. 40 (Fall, 1964), pp. 68-73.

89. Dobrovolny, Jerry S., "Preparation of Junior College Teachers of Technical Subjects," *Junior College Journal*, Vol. 35 (December, 1964), pp. 9-13.

90. Doyle, William T., "Teaching with Buzz Groups," *Junior College Journal*, Vol. 35 (February, 1965), pp. 12-14.

91. Dressel, Paul L., "Teaching, Learning, and Evaluation," *Improving College and University Teaching*, Vol. 8 (Winter, 1960), pp. 11-15.

92. Eckert, Ruth E., and Stecklein, John E., "Career Motivation and Satisfactions of Junior College Teachers," *Junior College Journal*, Vol. 30 (October, 1959), pp. 83-89.

93. *Education Beyond High School Age: The Community College*, Submitted to the Sixtieth Iowa General Assembly, December, 1962 (Des Moines, The Iowa State Department of Public Instruction, 1962).

94. Eells, Walter Crosby, ed., *American Junior Colleges, 1940* (Washington, D.C., American Council on Education, 1940).

95. Eells, Walter Crosby, "Dissertations on the Improvement of College Teaching —1960," *Improving College and University Teaching*, Vol. 11 (Winter, 1963), pp. 51-54.

96. Eells, Walter Crosby, *The Junior College* (Boston, Houghton Mifflin Co., 1931).

97. Eells, Walter Crosby, "Junior College Terminal Education," *Junior College Journal*, Vol 10 (January, 1940), pp. 244-250.

98. Eells, Walter Crosby, *Present Status of Junior College Terminal Education* (Washington, D.C., American Association of Junior Colleges, 1941).

99. Eells, Walter Crosby, *Why Junior College Terminal Education?* (Washington, D.C., American Association of Junior Colleges, 1941).

100. Eldrige, Donald A., "New Dimensions for the Two-Year College," *Junior College Journal*, Vol. 38 (September, 1967), pp. 10-12.

101. Endicott, Frank S., "Guidelines for the Recruitment of Teachers," in *Teaching Opportunities for You*, Association for School, College, and University Staffing, 1967 Annual, pp. 17-19.

102. Engleman, Lois E., and Eells, Walter Crosby, *The Literature of Junior College Terminal Education* (Washington, D.C., American Association of Junior Colleges, 1941).

103. Epstein, Harold, "Where Do Junior Colleges Fit In?" *Junior College Journal*, Vol. 37 (February, 1967), pp. 17-19.

104. Erickson, Clifford, "Multi-Campus Operation in the Big City," *Junior College Journal*, Vol. 35 (October, 1964), pp. 17-21.

105. Erickson, Clifford, "Rebirth in Illinois," *Junior College Journal*, Vol. 36 (September, 1965), pp. 28-29.

106. *Establishing Junior Colleges, A Report of a National Conference* (Los Angeles, Occasional Report No. 5, Junior College Leadership Program, University of California at Los Angeles, 1964).

107. Eurich, Alvin C., "Staffing Junior Colleges," *Junior College Journal*, Vol. 33 (March, 1963), pp. 8-12.

108. *Faculty Salary Schedules in Public Community-Junior Colleges, 1965–66*, Research Report 1967–69 (Washington, D.C., Research Division, National Education Association, 1967).

109. Fawcett, Claude W. "Professional Practice in Educational Placement," in *Teaching Opportunities for You*, Associates for School, College, and University Staffing, 1967 Annual.

110. Felder, Dell, "Independent-Study Practices in Colleges and Universities," *Journal of Higher Education*, Vol. 35 (June, 1964), pp. 335-338.

111. Fields, Ralph R., *The Community College Movement* (New York, McGraw-Hill, 1962).

112. Fields, Ralph R., "The Program Defined and Implemented," Ch. 9 in Nelson B. Henry, ed., *The Public Junior College*, 55th Yearbook of the National Society for the Study of Education, Part 1 (Chicago, University of Chicago Press, 1956).

113. Fields, Ralph R.; Mastin, John W.; and Walsh, James P., "Educational Programs: Community College Programs," *Review of Education Research*, Vol. 35 (October, 1965), pp. 294-297.

114. Fincher, Cameron, *Impact of the Presence of a Junior College upon College Attendance* (memorandum, November 18, 1964).

115. Findley, Robert A., "A Study of Fringe Benefits of Full-Time Faculty Members in Private Junior Colleges in the United States," unpublished doctoral dissertation (Tallahassee, Florida State University, 1967).

116. Fletcher, Leon, "Take to the Road, Teacher!" *Junior College Journal,* Vol. 37 (October, 1966), pp. 19-21.

117. *Florida Annual Report of Services,* 1961-62 (Tallahassee, Division of Community Junior Colleges, Florida State Department of Education, 1962).

118. *Florida's Public Junior Colleges* (Tallahassee, State Department of Education, March, 1966).

119. Fredenburgh, Franz A., "Innovating Instruction Through Team Teaching," *Junior College Journal,* Vol. 37 (October, 1966), pp. 12-18.

120. Frederick, Lee M., *Teaching Opportunities* (Washington, D.C., U.S. Department of Health, Education, and Welfare, Office of Education, U.S. Government Printing Office, 1964).

121. Frederick, Jr., Robert W., Consultant, Texas 2-year College Programs, a *letter* dated May 16, 1966.

122. Freiberger, Helenes T., and Crawford, W. H., "Junior College Academic Rank and Title," *Junior College Journal,* Vol. 33 (October, 1962), pp. 89-92.

123. Fretwell, Jr., Elbert K., "Establishing a Junior College," Ch. 14 in Nelson B. Henry, ed., *The Public College,* 55th Yearbook of the National Society for the Study of Education, Part I (Chicago, The University of Chicago Press, 1956).

124. Fretwell, Jr., E. K., "New York: The Next Five Years," *Junior College Journal,* Vol. 33 (March, 1963), pp. 22-25.

125. Garrison, Roger, "Effective Administration for Superior Teaching," *Junior College Journal,* Vol. 32 (May, 1962), pp. 517-525.

126. Garrison, Roger, *Junior College Faculty: Issues and Problems* (Washington, D.C., American Association of Junior Colleges, 1967).

127. Garrison, Roger, "Leading the Collegiate Horse to Water," *Junior College Journal,* Vol. 36 (November, 1965), pp. 26-28.

128. Garrison, Roger, "Reality and Illusion in Teaching," *Junior College Journal,* Vol. 34 (February, 1964), pp. 15-19.

129. Garrison, Roger, "The Teacher in the Two-year College," *Improving College and University Teaching,* Vol. 8 (Autumn, 1960), pp. 138-140.

130. Garrison, Roger, "The Teacher's Professional Situation," *Junior College Journal,* Vol. 37 (March, 1967), pp. 15-18.

131. Garrison, Roger, "Teaching as Counseling," *Junior College Journal,* Vol. 34 (October, 1963), pp. 12-15.

132. Giffin, Kim, and Bowers, John Waite, "An Experimental Study of the Use of Lectures to Large Groups of Students in Teaching the Fundamentals of Speech," *Journal of Educational Research,* Vol. 55 (May, 1962), pp. 383-385.

133. Giles, Fred, "Washington: New Life at Forty," *Junior College Journal,* Vol. 34 (May, 1964), pp. 28-31.

134. Gleazer, Jr., Edmund J., "AAJC Approach," *Junior College Journal,* Vol. 35 (March, 1965), pp. 2-3.

135. Gleazer, Jr., Edmund J., "AAJC Approach," *Junior College Journal,* Vol. 37 (April, 1967), p. 7.

136. Gleazer, Jr., Edmund J., "AAJC Approach: Preparation of Junior College Instructors," *Junior College Journal,* Vol. 35 (September, 1964), pp. 3-4.

137. Gleazer, Jr., Edmund J., ed., *American Junior Colleges 6th ed.* (Washington, D.C., American Council on Education, 1963).

138. Gleazer, Jr., Edmund J., ed., *Junior College Directory, 1960* (Washington, D.C., American Association of Junior Colleges, 1960).

139. Gnagey, William, "The Comparative Effects of Small-Group vs. Teacher-Led Discussion Sessions upon Student Achievement and Perception in Educational Psychology," *Journal of Educational Research*, Vol. 56 (September, 1962), pp. 28-32.

140. *Going to College in New York State* (Albany, The University of the State of New York, The State Education Department, Division of Higher Education, 1965).

141. Goode, Delmer, "The Centrality of Evaluation," *Improving College and University Teaching*, Vol. 8 (Winter, 1960), pp. 16-18.

142. Gordon, Shirley B., and Whitfield, Raymond P., "Teacher Preparation: Rationale and Practice," *Junior College Journal*, Vol. 37 (May, 1967), pp. 26-28.

143. Graybeal, William S., "Salaries in Junior Colleges—1965-1966," *Junior College Journal*, Vol. 36 (May, 1966), pp. 12-15.

144. Green, Charles, "An Investigation of the Problems of the Probationary Teachers of the Public Junior Colleges of California," unpublished dissertation (Los Angeles, University of California at Los Angeles, 1961).

145. Greene, E. B., "The Relative Effectiveness of Lecture and Individual Reading as Methods of College Teaching," *Genetic Psychology Monograph*, Vol. 4 (1928), pp. 457-463.

146. Greenman, Robert, "The Effective Faculty Member: Some Administrators' Views," in *Selected Papers, 47th Annual Convention American Association of Junior Colleges, February 27–March 3, 1967, San Francisco, California* (Washington, D.C., American Association of Junior Colleges, 1967), pp. 54-56.

147. Greenshields, Myrel J., Lindsay, Frank B., and Crawford, William H., "Junior College Teachers as Guidance Workers," *Junior College Journal*, Vol. 29 (March, 1959), pp. 366-373.

148. *Guidelines for Improving Articulation Between Junior and Senior Colleges* (Washington, D.C., American Council on Education, 1965).

149. Guilford, J. P., "Factors That Aid Creativity," *Teachers College Record*, Vol. 63 (February, 1962), pp. 380-392.

150. Gustad, John W., ed., *Faculty Personnel for the Two-Year Colleges*, Proceedings of a Regional Conference, Sponsored by the New England Board of Higher Education, May 26, 1960 (Winchester, Massachusetts, 1960).

151. Hannelly, Robert J., "The Explosion in Arizona," *Junior College Journal*, Vol. 34 (September, 1963), pp. 16-18.

152. Hardee, Melvene D., and Powell, Orrin B., *The Faculty in College Counseling* (New York, McGraw-Hill, 1959).

153. Harper, William A., "How Community Colleges Are Organized, Started, and Controlled," *Nation's Schools*, Vol. 77 (February, 1966), pp. 53-56.

154. Harper, William, ed., *Junior College Directory, 1967* (Washington, D.C., American Association of Junior Colleges, 1967).

155. Harrington, John C., "Academic Rank in the Community College," *Junior College Journal*, Vol. 35 (March, 1965), pp. 24-27.

156. Harris, Norman, "Major Issues in Junior College Technical Education," *Educational Record*, Vol. 45 (Spring, 1964), pp. 128-138.

157. Harris, Norman C., "On Being a Consultant," *Junior College Journal*, Vol. 37 (April, 1967), pp. 9-13.

158. Harris, Norman C., *Technical Education in the Junior College: New Programs for New Jobs* (Washington, D.C., American Association of Junior Colleges, 1964).

159. Hartnett, James, "Oral Examinations," *Improving College and University Teaching*, Vol. 13 (Autumn, 1965), pp. 208-209.

160. Hatch, Winslow R., and Bennett, Ann, *Independent Study, New Dimensions in Higher Education*, No. 1 (Washington, D.C., Department of Health, Education, and Welfare, U.S. Government Printing Office, 1960).

161. Hayden, Shelden, "The Junior College as a Community Institution," *Junior College Journal*, Vol. 10 (October, 1939), pp. 70-73.

162. Helland, Philip C., "Minnesota Turns to State Junior Colleges," *Junior College Journal*, Vol. 36 (December, 1965) pp. 40-41.

163. Hendrix, Vernon, "Academic Rank: Mostly Peril?" *Junior College Journal*, Vol. 34 (December, 1963), pp. 28-31.

164. Hendrix, Vernon, "Academic Rank Revisited," *Junior College Journal*, Vol. 35 (February, 1965), pp. 24-28.

165. Hengst, Herbert, "The Quiet Revolution," *Michigan Education Journal*, Vol. 40 (February, 1963), pp. 414-416.

166. Henninger, C. Ross, *The Technical Institute in America* (New York, McGraw-Hill, 1959).

167. *Higher Education Coordinating Act of 1965*, Texas House Bill No. 1, a copy by Wilson Cory.

168. "Higher Education Enrollment and Costs Data," CJCA *News*, Vol. 11 (April, 1965), p. 1.

169. *Higher Education for American Democracy*, The Report of the President's Commission on Higher Education (New York, Harper and Row, 1948).

170. Highet, Gilbert, *The Art of Teaching* (New York, Alfred A. Knopf, 1950).

171. Hill, Merton E., "History of Terminal Courses in California," *Junior College Journal*, Vol. 12 (February, 1942), pp. 311-313.

172. Hillway, Tyrus, *The American Two-Year College* (New York, Harper and Brothers, 1958).

173. Hobbs, Dan S., ed., *Higher Education Opportunities and Needs in Oklahoma, Report Seven, Self Study of Higher Education in Oklahoma* (Oklahoma City, Oklahoma State Regents for Higher Education, September, 1965).

174. Hoffmann, Randall W., "Students Portray the Excellent Teacher," *Improving College and University Teaching*, Vol. 11 (Winter, 1963), pp. 21-24.

175. Hoffmann, Randall W., and Plutchik, Robert, *Small-Group Discussion in Orientation and Teaching* (New York, G. P. Putnam's Sons, 1959).

176. Holderman, Kenneth, "The Case for University Branch Campuses," *Junior College Journal*, Vol. 34 (April, 1964) pp. 25-30.

177. Honer, Stanley M., "Faculty Power and Participation," *Junior College Journal*, Vol. 36 (February, 1966), pp. 28-32.

178. Horton, Robert, "Improving Scholastic Standards at a Community College," *Junior College Journal*, Vol. 31 (December, 1960), pp. 214-220.

179. Howe, Ray A., "Faculty-Administration Relations in Extremis," *Junior College Journal,* Vol. 37 (November, 1966), pp. 14-15.

180. Hunt, Mary R., "A Remarkable Instrument for Learning," *Junior College Journal,* Vol. 36 (December, 1965), pp. 9-11.

181. Hurst, John G., "The Relationship Between Teaching Methods and Course Objectives in Educational Psychology," *Journal of Educational Research,* Vol. 57 (November, 1963), pp. 147-151.

182. Ingles, E. T., "Criteria for Adding New Courses to the Junior College Curriculum," *California Journal of Secondary Education,* Vol. 31 (March, 1956), pp. 218-221.

183. *Internship in Junior College Administration,* a brochure (Berkeley School of Education, University of California). n.d.

184. James, Craig W., "Honors Seminar in Social Science," *Junior College Journal,* Vol. 36 (December, 1965), p. 44.

185. Jarvie, L. L., "Making Teaching More Effective," in Nelson B. Henry, ed., *The Public Junior College,* 55th Yearbook, Part I, National Society for the Study of Education (Chicago, University of Chicago Press, 1956).

186. Jensen, Arthur, "The Placement Coordinator of a Junior College," *Junior College Journal,* Vol. 31 (March, 1961), pp. 391-395.

187. Jersild, A., *When Teachers Face Themselves* (New York, Columbia University, Teachers College, 1955).

188. Johnson, B. Lamar, "Experimental Junior Colleges: Some Stirrings," *Junior College Journal,* Vol. 37 (October, 1966), pp. 6-9.

189. Johnson, B. Lamar, *General Education in Action* (Washington, D.C., American Council on Education, 1952).

190. Johnson, B. Lamar, "Islands of Innovation," *Junior College Journal,* Vol. 34 (February, 1964), pp. 9-14.

191. Johnson, B. Lamar, "Needed: Experimental Junior Colleges," *Junior College Journal,* Vol. 6 (October, 1965), pp. 17-20.

192. Johnson, B. Lamar, "Problems of Preparing Junior College Teachers," *Report of the State-Wide Conference on the Preparation of Junior College Teachers,* (Sacramento, California State Department of Education, 1958). m.

193. Johnson, B. Lamar, *Starting a Community Junior College* (Washington, D.C., American Association of Junior Colleges, 1964).

194. *Junior Colleges: 20 States* (Washington, D.C., American Association of Junior Colleges, 1966).

195. Kamrath, W. A., "Julius Sumner Miller—Telly-Guru," *Junior College Journal,* Vol. 36 (February, 1966), pp. 13-15.

196. *Kansas House Bill No. 893,* as enacted by the Kansas Legislature.

197. Kastner, Harold, "The Economic Value of Community Junior Colleges," *Junior College Journal,* Vol. 36 (November, 1965), pp. 29-34.

198. Kegel, Charles E., "The Distinguished Teacher," *Improving College and University Teaching,* Vol. 12 (Spring, 1964), pp. 102-104.

199. Kelley, Win, *The Art of Public Address* (Dubuque, Iowa, William C. Brown, 1965).

200. Kelley, Win D., "Credos for the College Instructor," *Improving College and University Teaching,* Vol. 15 (Spring, 1967), pp. 125-127.

201. Kelley, Win D., "Criteria for Directing Junior College Instruction," unpublished doctoral dissertation (Los Angeles, The University of Southern California, 1962).

202. Kennedy, Gerald, "Preparation, Orientation, Utilization, and Acceptance of Part-Time Instructors," *Junior College Journal*, Vol. 37 (April, 1967), pp. 14-15.

203. *Kentucky College and University Enrollments, 1965* (Frankfort, Kentucky Council on Public Higher Education, December, 1965).

204. Kimball, John R., "Analysis of Institutional Objectives in Michigan Community Colleges," unpublished doctoral dissertation (East Lansing, Michigan, Michigan State University, 1960).

205. Kintzer, Frederick C., *Faculty Handbook in California Junior Colleges* (Los Angeles, University of California at Los Angeles, School of Education, 1961).

206. Knoell, Dorothy, "Focus on the Transfer Program," *Junior College Journal*, Vol. 35 (May, 1965), pp. 5-9.

207. Knoell, Dorothy, "New York Challenges Its Urban Colleges," *Junior College Journal*, Vol. 37 (March, 1967), pp. 9-11.

208. Knoell, Dorothy, and Medsker, Leland L., *From Junior to Senior College: A National Study of the Transfer Student* (Washington, D.C., American Council on Education, 1965).

209. Koile, Earl A., and Tatem, Diane Wolf, "The Student-Oriented Teacher," *Junior College Journal*, Vol. 36 (February, 1966), pp. 24-26.

210. Koos, Leonard V., *The Junior College* (Minneapolis, University of Minnesota Press, 1924).

211. Kosaki, Richard, "Hawaii Plans for Community Colleges," *Junior College Journal*, Vol. 36 (November, 1965), pp. 5-7.

212. Kosaki, Richard, "The Master Plan for Hawaii's New Community College," *Junior College Journal*, Vol. 38 (September, 1967), pp. 13-15.

213. Kuhns, Eileen P., "Part-Time Faculty," *Junior College Journal*, Vol. 33 (January, 1963), pp. 8-12.

214. Lahti, Robert E., "Junior College Education in Wyoming," *Junior College Journal*, Vol. 33 (October, 1962), pp. 93-95.

215. Lange, Alexis F., "The Junior College as an Integral Part of the Public School System," *School Review*, Vol. 25 (September, 1917), pp. 465-479.

216. Lee, Calvin B. T., "Open-Door Classrooms for Open-Door Colleges," *Junior College Journal*, Vol. 37 (February, 1967), pp. 11-13.

217. Lewis, Lanora G., *Placement Services for Personnel in Higher Education* (Washington, D.C., U.S. Department of Health, Education, and Welfare, Office of Education, U.S. Government Printing Office, 1961).

218. Littlefield, Henry W. "Critical Issues Facing America's Junior Colleges," *Junior College Journal*, Vol. 31 (March, 1961), pp. 361-364.

219. Litton, Maurice L., and Rogers, James T., "Retired Military Personnel: A Source of Additional Instructors," *Junior College Journal*, Vol. 35 (May, 1965), pp. 17-18.

220. Lombardi, John, "Faculty in the Administrative Process," *Junior College Journal*, Vol. 37 (November, 1966), pp. 9-16.

221. Lombardi, John, "Occupational Education in California Junior Colleges," *Educational Record*, Vol. 45 (Spring, 1964), pp. 142-147.

222. Lorenzoni, Larry N., "The Use of Special Faculty Competences for Community and Students at Cabrillo College," seminar paper (Los Angeles, University of California at Los Angeles, School of Education, 1967).

223. Lynes, Russell, "The Teacher Is an Iceberg," *Junior College Journal*, Vol. 36 (April, 1966), pp. 8-12.

224. Majella, Mother M., "Enriched Program for Liberal Arts Students," *Junior College Journal*, Vol. 33 (October, 1962), pp. 100-108.

225. Margulies, Stuart, and Eigen, Lewis D., eds., *Applied Programmed Instruction* (New York, John Wiley and Sons, 1962).

226. Marsee, Stuart, "Political Activity of Teachers," *Junior College Journal*, Vol. 31 (October, 1960), pp. 82-84.

227. Marsee, Stuart, "A President's View of Institutional Research," *Junior College Journal*, Vol. 35 (May, 1965), pp. 24-25.

228. Martorana, S. V., "The Legal Status of American Public Junior Colleges," in Edmund J. Gleazer, Jr., ed., *American Junior Colleges* (Washington, D.C., American Council on Education, 1963), pp. 31-47.

229. Martorana, S. V., and McHugh, Robert, "State Legislation: 1962-64," *Junior College Journal*, Vol. 36 (March, 1966), pp. 27-36.

230. *Maryland Standards for Community and Junior Colleges*, Maryland School Bulletin, Vol. 37 (Baltimore, Maryland State Department of Education, June, 1961).

231. Maul, Ray O., "Are Junior College Salaries Competitive?" *Junior College Journal*, Vol. 34 (March, 1964), pp. 20-23.

232. Maul, Ray O., "The Biggest Problem: Finding Good Teachers," *Junior College Journal*, Vol. 36 (December, 1965), pp. 5-8.

233. Maul, Ray O., "Can We Get Enough Good Teachers?" *Junior College Journal*, Vol. 34 (December, 1963), pp. 3-7.

234. Mayer, Frederick, "Creative Teaching," *Improving College and University Teaching*, Vol. 8 (Spring, 1960), pp. 40-42.

235. Mayer, Frederick, "A Program of Action," *Improving College and University Teaching*, Vol. 8 (Autumn, 1960), pp. 134-135.

236. McClosky, Herbert, "Implanting the Democratic Idea," CTA *Journal*, Vol. 61 (January, 1965), pp. 11-12.

237. McDowell, F. M., *The Junior College* (Washington, D.C., U.S. Bureau of Education Bulletin No. 35, U.S. Government Printing Office, 1919).

238. MacKay, Kenneth, "Something New in New Jersey," *Junior College Journal*, Vol. 34 (April, 1964), pp. 4-7.

239. McKay, Robert E., "A Major New Commitment to Quality and Equality," CTA *Journal*, Vol. 61 (May, 1965), pp. 15-17.

240. McKeachie, Wilbert J., "Current Research in Teaching Effectiveness," *Improving College and University Teaching*, Vol. 10 (Winter, 1962), pp. 15-19.

241. McKeachie, Wilbert J., "The Instructor Faces Automation," *Improving College and University Teaching*, Vol. 8 (Summer, 1960), pp. 91-95.

242. McKeachie, Wilbert, *Teaching Tips* (Ann Arbor, Michigan, The George Wahr Publishing Co., 1960).

243. McKeefery, William, "Some Observations on Effective Teaching," *Collegiate News and Views* (March, 1959), pp. 2-4.

244. McKenna, Charles D., "You and Your Future in Teaching," in *Teaching Opportunities for You*, Association for School, College, and University Staffing, 1967 Annual, pp. 24-25.

245. McKenney, J. Wilson, "We Teach Freedom," *CTA Journal*, Vol. 61 (January, 1965), pp. 6-9.

246. McKowen, Clark, "Teachers Should Be Unprepared," *Junior College Journal*, Vol. 36 (May, 1966), pp. 36-39.

247. Medsker, Leland L., *The Junior College: Progress and Prospect* (New York, McGraw-Hill Book Co., 1960).

248. Medsker, Leland L., "Patterns for the Control of Community Colleges," *Establishing Legal Bases for Community Colleges* (Washington, D.C., American Association of Junior Colleges, 1962).

249. Medsker, Leland L., "The Two-Year College," *Teachers College Record*, Vol. 63 (October, 1961), pp. 40-52.

250. Mikalson, Ray J., "Reader-Aids: A Means to Many Ends," *Junior College Journal*, Vol. 33 (December, 1962), pp. 216-220.

251. Miller, Calvin Charles, "Instructors of Non-Academic Subjects in Publicly Supported Junior Colleges: A Study of Certification and Employment Practices and Proposals for Certification," an unpublished doctoral dissertation (Tallahassee, Florida State University, 1959).

252. *Missouri Handbook for Public Junior Colleges* (State Department of Education, Publication No. 24H, 1964 edition).

253. Monroe, Walter S., ed., *Encyclopedia of Educational Research*, Revised Edition (New York, The Macmillan Company, 1952).

254. Moore, Carlos, "The Image of the Junior College," *Junior College Journal*, Vol. 33 (December, 1962), pp. 195-197.

255. Moore, Everett, "Merit Pay: Bane or Blessing?" *Junior College Journal*, Vol. 36 (October, 1965), pp. 32-37.

256. Moore, James W., and Rioux, Jay William, "Two Challenges of the Economic Opportunity Act," *Junior College Journal*, Vol. 35 (March, 1965), pp. 17-18.

257. Morrison, D. G., Martorana, S. V., *Criteria for the Establishment of Two-Year Colleges* (Washington, D.C., U.S. Government Printing Office, 1960).

258. Morrison, D. G., and Martorana, S. V., *State Formulas for the Support of Public 2-Year Colleges*, Bulletin 1962, No. 14 (Washington, D.C., U.S. Department of Health, Education, and Welfare, Office of Education, U.S. Government Printing Office, 1962).

259. Morrison, D. G., and Novak, Robert, "How Your District Can Start a Community College," *School Management*, Vol. 5 (March, 1961), pp. 56-60, 112, 114, 116, 118.

260. Morrison, D. G.; Brunner, Ken August; and Martorana, S. V., *The 2-Year Community College*, An annotated List of Unpublished Studies and Surveys, 1957-61 (Washington, D.C., U.S. Department of Health, Education, and Welfare, Office of Education, U.S. Government Printing Office, 1963).

261. Morrissey, Kermit C., "An Alternative: State Control," *Junior College Journal*, Vol. 36 (May, 1966), pp. 16-19.

262. Morton, John R., *University Extension in the United States* (Birmingham, University of Alabama Press, 1953).

263. Morton, Richard K., "The Junior College and the New Student," *Junior College Journal*, Vol. 31 (April, 1961), pp. 434-436.

264. Morton, Richard K., "Personal Backgrounds of Effective Teaching," *Improving College and University Teaching*, Vol. 8 (Autumn, 1960), pp. 136-137.

265. Morton, Richard K., "The Use of the Voice in Teaching," *Improving College and University Teaching*, Vol. 10 (Summer, 1962), pp. 121-122.

266. Moustakas, Clark E., *The Alive and Growing Teacher* (New York, Philosophical Library, 1959).

267. Muck, Steven J., "A Survey of Views of Teachers, Counselors, and Administrators on Selected Issues in the Open-Door College," a seminar paper (Los Angeles, School of Education, 1966).

268. Murphy, Gardner, *Freeing Intelligence Through Teaching* (New York, Harper and Brothers, 1961).

269. "Need for College Teachers Grows," *NEA Research Bulletin*, Vol. 41 (December, 1963), pp. 108-115.

270. Nelson, Helge, "Overcoming Reading Deficiencies at the Community College Level," *Junior College Journal*, Vol. 33 (December, 1962) pp. 221-224.

271. *New Jersey Two-Year Colleges Are on the Move*, Report of New Jersey's Two-Year College Program (July, 1966).

272. Newsham, Louis R., "Iowa Sets Its Course," *Junior College Journal*, Vol. 36 (October, 1965), pp. 14-16.

273. *Notes and Announcements* from Southeastern Junior College Leadership Program, Vol. 5 (May, 1965).

274. Nunis, Jr., Doyce B., and Bossone, Richard M., "The Junior College's Search for an Educational Identity," *Junior College Journal*, Vol. 33 (November, 1962), pp. 121-124.

275. *Occupational Educational Bulletin*, Vol. 2 (Washington, D.C., American Association of Junior Colleges, September, 1967).

276. *The Oklahoma State System of Higher Education* (Oklahoma City, Oklahoma State Regents for Higher Education, February, 1966).

277. *One Hundred and Seventh Report of the Superintendent of Public Instruction, for the Biennium 1962-64* (Lansing, Michigan, Department of Public Instruction, 1965).

278. O'Neill, Daniel J., "You Have to Have Heart," *College and University*, Vol. 37 (Winter, 1962), pp. 135-144.

279. Oosting, Kenneth W., "Equating Faculty Loads," *Junior College Journal*, Vol. 36 (May, 1966), pp. 10-11.

280. Orvis, Paul, *Design for Opportunity: A Plan for a State System of Community Colleges in Connecticut* (Hartford, State Board of Trustees for Regional Community Colleges, December, 1965).

281. Parker, Franklin, "Community Junior College—Enfant Terrible of American Education: A Bibliography of 226 Doctoral Dissertations," *Junior College Journal*, Vol. 32 (December, 1961), pp. 193-204.

282. Parnes, Sidney J., "Education and Creativity," *Teachers College Record*, Vol. 64 (January, 1963), pp. 331-339.

283. Payne, Raymond, "Teaching Techniques for Larger Classes," *Improving College and University Teaching*, Vol. 13 (Autumn, 1965), pp. 243-245.

284. Pence, Don, "The Oregon Story," *Junior College Journal*, Vol. 34 (November, 1963), pp. 4-8.

285. Pessen, Edward, "How Does the Professor Spend His Time?" *Junior College Journal*, Vol. 32 (January, 1962) pp. 280-283.

286. Peterson, Houston, *Great Teachers* (New Brunswick, N. J., Rutgers University Press, 1946).

287. Pfiffner, John M., *An Outline of the Supervisor's Job* (New York, American Management Association, 1946).

288. "Plans for a Junior College Academic Senate," Draft Recommendation of Committee for Faculty Participation in Policy Making (California State Federation of Teachers, The Federation, 1963).

289. President's Committee on Education Beyond the High School, *Second Report to the President* (Washington, D.C., U.S. Government Printing Office, 1957).

290. Price, Hugh G., *California Public Junior Colleges*, Vol. 27 (Sacramento, Bulletin of the California State Department of Education, February, 1958).

291. Price, Hugh G., "The Role of Administration in Excellent Teaching," *Junior College Journal*, Vol. 24 (September, 1953), pp. 37-42.

292. Priest, Bill J., "Faculty-Administrator Relationships," *Junior College Journal*, Vol. 34 (March, 1964), pp. 4-8.

293. *Principles of Legislative Action for Community Junior Colleges* (Washington, D.C., American Association of Junior Colleges, 1962).

294. *The Privately Supported Junior College—A Place and Purpose in Higher Education* (Washington, D.C., American Association of Junior Colleges, 1963).

295. *Proceedings* of the 46th Annual Meeting of the National University Extension Association, 1960-61.

296. *Public Higher Education in Maryland 1961-1975*, The Report of the Commission for the Expansion of Public Higher Education in Maryland (Baltimore, June, 1962).

297. Pullias, Earl V., "A Professional Reading Shelf for College Faculties," *Improving College and University Teaching*, Vol. 9 (Autumn, 1961), pp. 181–183.

298. Pullias, Earl V.; Lockhart, Aileene; and others, *Toward Excellence in College Teaching* (Dubuque, Iowa, Wm. C. Brown, 1963).

299. Pyle, Gordon B., "Strengthening the Junior College Teaching Profession," *Junior College Journal*, Vol. 32 (May, 1962), pp. 526-533.

300. Quick, Alan, and Wolfe, Arnold, "The Ideal Professor," *Improving College and University Teaching*, Vol. 13 (Summer, 1965), pp. 133-134.

301. Raines, Max R., "The Student Personnel Situation," *Junior College Journal*, Vol. 36 (February, 1966), pp. 6-8.

302. Rainey, William G., "Analysis of Criticisms of Junior College Teachers by University and Senior College Staff," *Junior College Journal*, Vol. 30 (December, 1959), pp. 208-212.

303. Rainey, William G., "Philosophies Related to Research and Publication by Faculty Members," *Junior College Journal*, Vol. 32 (October, 1961), pp. 86-90.

304. Rapp, Marvin, "Making Teaching More Effective," *Improving College and University Teaching*, Vol. 9 (Autumn, 1961), pp. 163-165.

305. Rawlinson, Howard E., "Evaluating Community Service in Public Junior Colleges," an unpublished doctoral dissertation (Carbondale, Southern Illinois University, 1963).

306. *The Regents' Statewide Plan for the Expansion and Development of Higher Education, 1964* (Albany, The University of the State of New York, The State Education Department, April, 1965).

307. *Regents' Study on Community Junior Colleges in Georgia*, A Staff Report to the Board of Regents (Atlanta, University System of Georgia, June, 1965).

308. *Report to the Governor and the General Assembly by the Study Commission on Higher Education* (Hartford, Connecticut, February, 1965).

309. Reyes, Raul, "Otero Experiments with English Composition," *Junior College Journal*, Vol. 38 (September, 1967), pp. 34-36.

310. Reynolds, James W., "Administrative and Supervisory Practices for Improving Instruction," *Junior College Journal*, Vol. 18 (December, 1947), pp. 181-190.

311. Rice, James G., ed., *General Education: Current Ideas and Concerns* (Washington, D.C., Association for Higher Education, 1964).

312. Rice, Joseph P., Jr., "Differing Views of Institutional Aims Among College Students, Teachers, and Administrators," *California Journal of Educational Research*, Vol. 12 (September, 1961), pp. 165-172.

313. Richardson, Jr., Richard C., and Elsner, Paul A., "General Education for the Disadvantaged," *Junior College Journal*, Vol. 36 (December, 1965), pp. 18-24.

314. Riggs, Roderick D., "Nuclear Reactor Technology at Jackson Junior College," *Junior College Journal*, Vol. 33 (November, 1962), pp. 177-179.

315. Roberts, Clarence W., "A Study of Fringe Benefits of Full-time Faculty Members in Public Junior Colleges in the United States," an unpublished doctoral dissertation (Tallahassee, Florida State University, 1967).

316. Roberts, Clarence W., letter sent August 8, 1967, to Win Kelley.

317. Roberts, John L., "A Plan to Abandon Teaching Facts," *Junior College Journal*, Vol. 35 (March, 1965), p. 23.

318. Robinson, Donald W., "The Role of the Faculty in the Development of Student-Personnel Services," *Junior College Journal*, Vol. 31 (September, 1960), pp. 15-21.

319. Rogers, James F., "A Philosophy for the Junior College with Implications for Curriculum," *Junior College Journal*, Vol. 30 (November, 1959), pp. 13-15.

320. Runkel, P. J., "Cognitive Facilitation of Communication Effects—An Empirical Study," unpublished doctoral dissertation (Ann Arbor, Michigan, University of Michigan, 1956).

321. Sack, Saul, "The First Junior College," *Junior College Journal*, Vol. 30 (September, 1959), pp. 13-15.

322. *Salaries in Higher Education*, 1965-66, Research Report 1962-R2 (Washington, D.C., Research Division, National Education Association, February, 1966).

323. Sarko, Laura, "The Problem of Teaching in Community Colleges," *Journal of Higher Education*, Vol. 35 (October, 1964), pp. 384-386.

324. Schenz, Robert Frank, "An Investigation of Junior College Courses and Curricula for Students with Low Ability," an unpublished doctoral dissertation (Los Angeles, University of California at Los Angeles, 1963).

325. Seager, Daniel A., "Professor, Let's Get That Book," *Improving College and University Teaching*, Vol. 8 (Spring, 1960), p. 62.

326. Seashore, Carl E., *The Junior College Movement* (New York, Holt, Rinehart, and Winston, 1940).

327. Seashore, Harold, "Academic Abilities of Junior College Students," *Junior College Journal*, Vol. 29 (October, 1958), pp. 74-80.

328. Selden, William K., *Accreditation: A Struggle over Standards in Higher Education* (New York, Harper and Brothers, 1960).

329. Sessions, Virgil D., "Video Tape: The Greatest Innovation for Junior College

Speech Courses Since Chalk," a paper (Los Angeles, University of California, 1967).

330. Sexson, John A., and Harbeson, John W., *The New American College* (New York, Harper and Row, 1946).

331. Siehr, Hugo E., "Problems of New Faculty Members in Community Colleges," an unpublished doctoral dissertation (East Lansing, Michigan State University, 1962).

332. Siehr, Hugo E.; Jamrich, John; and Hereford, Karl T., *Problems of New Faculty Members in Community Colleges* (East Lansing, Michigan, Michigan State University, 1963).

333. Skaggs, Kenneth G., "Shattering Shibboleths in Junior Colleges," in *Selected Papers, 47th Annual Convention American Association of Junior Colleges February 27–March 3, 1967, San Francisco, California* (Washington, D.C., American Association of Junior Colleges, 1967), p. 17.

334. Skaggs, Kenneth G., Burris, Douglas W., and Fibel, Lewis R., "Report and Forecast: AAJC's Occupational Education Project," *Junior College Journal,* Vol. 37 (March, 1967), pp. 23-25.

335. Skidmore, H. M., "Supervision of Junior College Instruction," *Junior College Journal,* Vol. 2 (June, 1932), pp. 542-546.

336. Smart, Dorothea L., Dean, Bradford Junior College, a letter to Win Kelley, dated September 20, 1967.

337. Smith, Perle E., "A Study of Certain Characteristics of 'Good' Teachers in a Junior College as Compared with a Control Group," an unpublished doctoral dissertation (Austin, University of Texas, 1955).

338. *South Dakota Colleges* (South Dakota College Public Relations Association, n.d.).

339. *Southeastern Junior College Messenger,* Vol. 4, Published in conjunction with the Kellogg Southeastern Leadership Program (May, 1964).

340. *Southeastern Regional Junior College Leadership Program,* Fifth Annual Report, 1964-65, September 24, 1965, m.

341. Staerkel, William S., "Where and When Public Schools Can Help Start a Community College," *Nation's Schools,* Vol. 77 (February, 1966), pp. 60-62, 92.

342. Starrak, James A., and Hughes, Raymond M., *The Community College in the United States* (Ames, Iowa, Iowa State University Press, 1954).

343. Stevens, Nancy D., "Placement Readiness and Placement Success," *Personnel and Guidance Journal* (April, 1963), pp. 700-704.

344. Stevens, Nancy D., "Preparation for Interview Readiness," in *Teaching Opportunities for You,* Association for School, College, and University Staffing, 1967 Annual.

345. Stolurow, Lawrence, "Implications of Current Research and Future Trends," *Journal of Educational Research,* Vol. 55 (June-July, 1962), pp. 519-527.

346. Storer, Donald E., "Emphasis on Vocational Counseling," *Junior College Journal,* Vol. 36 (May, 1966), pp. 40-42.

347. Strawbridge, James R., and Wattenbarger, James L., "Articulation—Florida Style," *Junior College Journal,* Vol. 37 (May, 1967), pp. 50-52.

348. Strayer, George D., *A Report of a Survey of the Needs of California in Higher Education* (Sacramento, California, California State Department of Education, 1948).

349. A *Study of Oregon Community Colleges, 1962–1965* (Prepared for the Post-High School Study Committee of the Education Coordinating Council, Division of Community Colleges and Vocational Education, State Department of Education, February, 1966).

350. Sullens, Zay Rusk, "Personal Reading in the Curriculum," *Junior College Journal,* Vol. 36 (December, 1965), pp. 37-39.

351. Swenson, Norman G., and Novar, Leon, "Chicago City College Teachers Strike," *Junior College Journal,* Vol. 37 (March, 1967), pp. 19-22.

352. Swets, Marinus, "Honors in the Junior College: A Second Look," *Junior College Journal,* Vol. 36 (December, 1965), pp. 72-74.

353. A *System of Higher Education for Oklahoma,* The Report of the State Coordinating Board (Oklahoma City, Oklahoma State Regents for Higher Education, June 1, 1942).

354. Taylor, Walter, "Bold Plans for the Bay State," *Junior College Journal,* Vol. 34 (March, 1964), pp. 24-27.

355. *Teacher Supply and Demand in Universities, Colleges, and Junior Colleges,* 1963-64 and 1964-65, Research Report, 1965-R4 (Washington, D. C., Research Division, National Education Association, April, 1965).

356. *Teaching Opportunities for You,* Association for School, College, and University Staffing, 1967 Annual.

357. Tead, Ordway, "Character and the College Teacher," *Journal of Higher Education,* Vol. 35 (May, 1964), pp. 269-272.

358. Tead, Ordway, *The Climate of Learning* (New York, Harper and Brothers, 1958).

359. Tead, Ordway, "Why the Independent Two-Year College?" *Junior College Journal,* Vol. 30 (January, 1960), pp. 249-253.

360. Tewkesbury, Donald G., *The Founding of American Colleges and Universities Before the Civil War* (New York, Teachers College, Columbia University, 1932).

361. Thornton, Jr., James W., *The Community Junior College,* 2nd ed. (New York, John Wiley & Sons, 1966).

362. Thornton, Jr., James W., "Who Are the Students in the Junior College?" *Junior College Journal,* Vol. 29 (October, 1958), pp. 89-96.

363. Throckmorton, Adel F., *Kansas State Plan for Community Junior Colleges* (State Superintendent of Public Instruction, n.d.)

364. Thurston, Alice, "Now That We Are Nine Feet Tall: A Look at Junior College Students," *Junior College Journal,* Vol. 32 (February, 1962), pp. 334-339.

365. Tickton, Sidney, "What's Ahead for the Public Junior Colleges," *Junior College Journal,* Vol. 34 (November, 1963) pp. 9-11.

366. Tillery, Dale, "Academic Rank: Promise or Peril," *Junior College Journal,* Vol. 33 (February, 1963), pp. 6-9.

367. Timmons, Richard H., "Fund Raising in Junior Colleges," *Junior College Journal,* Vol. 33 (September, 1962), pp. 3-6.

368. Tirrell, John, "(Total!!) Independent Study at Oakland," *Junior College Journal,* Vol. 36 (April, 1966), pp. 21-23.

369. Tirrell, John E., and Cosand, Joseph P., "Flying a College on the Computer," *Junior College Journal,* Vol. 35 (September, 1964), pp. 5-8.

370. *To Work in a Junior College* (Washington, D.C., American Association of Junior Colleges, 1966).

371. Trabue, Ann McDowell, "Fifteen Basic Assumptions Regarding College Teaching," *Improving College and University Teaching*, Vol. 10 (Summer, 1962), pp. 110-117.

372. Tunnell, James Wesley, "Faculty Involvement in Policy Formulation in the Public Junior College," an unpublished doctoral dissertation (Lubbock, Texas Technological College, 1963).

373. Twitchell, Theodore, "Overcoming Obstacles to Effective Teaching," a paper (Blythe, California, Palo Verdes College, 1966).

374. Tyler, Henry T., "Full Partners in California's Higher Education," *Junior College Journal*, Vol. 35 (March, 1965), pp. 4-7.

375. Tyler, Ralph W., "The Teaching Obligation," *Junior College Journal*, Vol. 30 (May, 1960), pp. 525-533.

376. Underwood, David L., "College Organization and Administration: Some Faculty Views," in *Selected Papers, 47th Annual Convention American Association of Junior Colleges, February 27–March 3, 1967, San Francisco, California* (Washington, D.C., American Association of Junior Colleges, 1967), pp. 19-20.

377. Underwood, Kenneth E., "An Analysis of Letters of Recommendation," in *Teaching Opportunities for You*, Association for School, College, and University Staffing, 1967 Annual, pp. 34-35.

378. Unikel, Graham, "Training Technical Communicators," *Junior College Journal*, Vol. 35 (March, 1965), pp. 28-32.

379. U.S. President's Commission, *Higher Education for American Democracy: A Report*, Vol. 1 (New York, Harper and Brothers, 1948).

380. Vaccaro, Louis C., "A Survey and Evaluation of the Practices Used by Michigan Community Colleges in the Recruitment and Selection of Faculty," an unpublished doctoral dissertation (East Lansing, Michigan State University, 1963).

381. Vavoulis, Alexander, "A Faculty Role in Policy Making," *Junior College Journal*, Vol. 34 (April, 1964), pp. 32-34.

382. *The Vermont Colleges* (Vermont Higher Education Council, 1963).

383. Walker, Carl Eugene, "Provisions for Teacher Welfare Other Than Salary in Selected Non-Public Junior Colleges," an unpublished doctoral dissertation (Denver, University of Denver, 1959).

384. *Wanted: 30,000 Instructors for Community Colleges* (Washington, American Council on Education, 1949).

385. Ward, Phebe, *Terminal Education in the Junior College* (New York, Harper and Brothers, 1947).

386. Warfield, Jack W., "ETV: Boom or Bust?" *Improving College and University Teaching*, Vol. 8 (Autumn, 1960), pp. 149-150.

387. Watanabe, Akira, "Junior Colleges Blossom in Japan," *Junior College Journal*, Vol. 37 (February, 1967), pp. 28-30, 34.

388. Wattenbarger, James, "Five Years of Progress in Florida," *Junior College Journal*, Vol. 34 (October, 1963), pp. 16-18.

389. Wetzler, Wilson, "Team Teaching," *Improving College and University Teaching*, Vol. 12 (Winter, 1964), pp. 40-41.

390. Whitehead, Alfred N., *The Aims of Education* (New York, Macmillan Co., Mentor Books, 1929).

391. Wilbur, Leslie, "Open Door–Color TV," *Junior College Journal*, Vol. 38 (February, 1968), pp. 20-22.

392. Wilbur, Leslie, and Dabbs, Lowell, *Improving College English Skills* (Chicago, Scott Foresman, 1962).

393. Wilking, S. Vincent, "Merit Pay and Better Teaching," *Teachers College Record*, Vol. 63 (January, 1962), pp. 297-304.

394. Wilson, J. Bruce, and Vandusen, C. Raymond, "Democratic Course Planning for the Junior College," *Junior College Journal*, Vol. 33 (November, 1962), pp. 159-160.

395. Wilson, Robert E., "The Role of the Junior College in International Education in America," *Junior College Journal*, Vol. 33 (December, 1962), pp. 225-235.

396. Wise, W. Max, *They Come for the Best of Reasons* (Washington, D.C., American Council on Education, 1958).

397. Woellner, R. C., and Wood, M. Aurilla, *Requirements for Certification of Teachers and Administrators for Elementary Schools, Secondary Schools, and Junior Colleges,* Thirtieth Edition, 1965-66 (Chicago, The University of Chicago Press, 1965).

398. Wood, William R., "Professional Personnel for Community Colleges," *Junior College Journal*, Vol. 20 (May, 1950), pp. 513-522.

399. Woodworth, James R., "Large Versus Small Classes," *Improving College and University Teaching*, Vol. 8 (Summer, 1960), pp. 96-98.

400. Wotherspoon, James R., "Building Rapport Through Recordings," *Junior College Journal*, Vol. 37 (March, 1967), pp. 61-62.

401. Yoder, Marlen, and Beals, Lester, "Student Personnel Services in the West," *Junior College Journal*, Vol. 37 (October, 1966), pp. 38-41.

402. Young, James D., "Team Teaching," *Improving College and University Teaching*, Vol. 8 (Summer, 1960), pp. 109-110.

403. Zook, George F., ed., *National Conference of Junior Colleges*, 1920 (Washington, D.C., U.S. Department of the Interior, Bureau of Education Bulletin No. 19, U.S. Government Printing Office, 1922).

Index

285